John S. C. Abbott

Prussia and the Franco-Prussian War

Containing a brief narrative of the origin of the kingdom, its past history, and a detailed account of the causes and results of the late war with Austria

John S. C. Abbott

Prussia and the Franco-Prussian War

Containing a brief narrative of the origin of the kingdom, its past history, and a detailed account of the causes and results of the late war with Austria

ISBN/EAN: 9783337299002

Printed in Europe, USA, Canada, Australia, Japan

Cover: Foto ©ninafisch / pixelio.de

More available books at **www.hansebooks.com**

PRUSSIA

AND THE

Franco-Prussian War.

CONTAINING

A BRIEF NARRATIVE OF THE ORIGIN OF THE KINGDOM,
ITS PAST HISTORY, AND A DETAILED ACCOUNT
OF THE CAUSES AND RESULTS OF THE
LATE WAR WITH AUSTRIA;

WITH

AN ACCOUNT OF THE ORIGIN OF THE PRESENT WAR WITH
FRANCE, AND OF THE EXTRAORDINARY CAMPAIGN
INTO THE HEART OF THE EMPIRE.

INCLUDING

Biographical Sketches of King William and Count von Bismarck.

By JOHN S. C. ABBOTT,

AUTHOR OF "LIFE OF NAPOLEON I.," "LIFE OF NAPOLEON III.," "LIFE OF FREDERICK
THE GREAT," "PRESIDENTS OF THE UNITED STATES," ETC.

BOSTON:
PUBLISHED BY B. B. RUSSELL, 55 CORNHILL.
PHILADELPHIA: QUAKER-CITY PUBLISHING-HOUSE.
CHICAGO: JAMES P. SNELL.
SAN FRANCISCO: A. L. BANCROFT & CO.
PORT HOPE, ONT.: P. R. RANDALL & CO.
1871.

TO

THE GERMANS WHO FROM "VATERLAND,"

AND

THE FRENCH WHO FROM "LA BELLE FRANCE,"

HAVE MET

BENEATH THE STARS AND STRIPES OF THE UNITED STATES OF AMERICA,

AS FELLOW-CITIZENS, COMRADES, AND BROTHERS,

This Book is Dedicated,

WITH THE HOPE THAT GERMANY AND FRANCE MAY SOON CLASP HANDS
FRATERNALLY ACROSS THE RHINE.

JOHN S. C. ABBOTT.

PREFACE.

IT is less than two hundred years since the petty Marquisate of Brandenburg and the little Duchy of Prussia were united in a kingdom. Prussia, as thus constituted, was so insignificant a realm in territory and population as quite to excite the contempt of the proud monarchs of Europe. England, France, Austria, and Russia were by no means disposed to admit the newly-created king of so paltry a domain on social equality with them.

Prussia is now recognized not only as one of the great powers, but as, probably, the first military power in Europe. The steps by which this greatness has been attained constitute one of the most interesting chapters in the history of modern times. Prussia is the representative, not of liberalism, but of absolutism. It has been under the banner of despotic sway that most of its victories have been achieved.

Prussia now presents to the world the somewhat appalling spectacle of a nation of forty millions, in which every able-bodied man is a trained soldier. It has been able, at a moment's warning, to send into the field armies so overwhelming in numbers, and so admirably organized and disciplined, as to crush the military power of France, to batter down her strongest fortresses, and even to penetrate the heart of the empire, and invest her proud metropolis with beleaguering hosts. The object of this volume is to give a narrative of the origin, growth, and present condition, of this gigantic power. It would be difficult to find anywhere a theme more full of instructive and exciting incidents.

The mad pranks of the half-crazed Frederick William; the wild and wonderful career of Frederick the Great; the awful reverses which overwhelmed Prussia in the wars of the French Revolution; the astounding victories and conquests achieved in the late war with Austria, which culminated in the great battle of Sadowa, where Austria, a helpless victim, lay prostrate at the feet of the conqueror; and the recent campaign in France, which has excited the wonder of the world, as the French armies have melted away before the Prussian legions, as fortress after fortress has fallen before their batteries, and as Paris itself has surrendered to hosts such as Attila could scarcely have brought into the field, — these are events which are to be chronicled among the most momentous which have transpired upon our globe.

The narrative here given of the Franco-Prussian War is an impartial recital of facts known by all intelligent men. If this record be not substantially true, then is it impossible to obtain any truth of history. Never did events take place under a broader blaze of day. Wherever our sympathies may rest, the facts here given are indisputable; and it is a weakness for one to shrink from impartial truth because it is not, in all respects, flattering to national pride.

It cannot be gratifying to any Frenchman to read this record of the utter humiliation and the ruin of his country, and of that lamentable want of stability on the part of his countrymen which has caused this humiliation and ruin.

And, in the creation of the new Germanic Empire, there have been some distinctly-avowed motives which have inspired the actors, and some measures which have been adopted before the eyes of all the world, which many Germans will not reflect upon with pleasure.

But both French and Germans will find in these pages as honest and impartial a record of facts as it is possible to give. The intelligent American community, who month after month have watched with the utmost interest the development of these transactions, will be able to testify from its own personal observation to the accuracy of this account of the Franco-Prussian War. But we must remember that it is a pardonable weakness for men, when in a foreign country, to be even unduly zealous in reference to the good name of their native land.

The accuracy of the portraits, we think, may be relied upon. They have been obtained from the most authentic sources. The beautiful group of the Imperial Family of France has been taken, by express permission, from the private collection of the Emperor, and has been engraved by the most skilful of French artists. The writer can testify to the remarkable fidelity of the likenesses.

JOHN S. C. ABBOTT.

NEW HAVEN, CONN.

CONTENTS.

CHAP.		PAGE.
I.	Origin of the Monarchy	9
II.	Fritz, and the Commencement of his Reign	25
III.	The Seven-Years' War	40
IV.	The Partition of Poland, and the Invasion of France	53
V.	Prussia and the French Revolution	68
VI.	Prussia Overwhelmed	83
VII.	Frederick William III. and the New Coalition	97
VIII.	Struggles for Liberty	113
IX.	King William I.	125
X.	The Chief Supporters of the Crown	137
XI.	Schleswig and Holstein	152
XII.	The Liberation of Italy	166
XIII.	The German War	174
XIV.	France demands her Ancient Boundary	183
XV.	The Policy of Count Bismarck	192
XVI.	The Declaration of War	200
XVII.	The Eastern Question	208
XVIII.	France Invaded	217
XIX.	Prussian Victories and French Defeats	223
XX.	The Capture of Sedan	234
XXI.	The Overthrow of the Empire	247
XXII.	The Prisoner and the Exile	260
XXIII.	War and its Woes	271

CHAP.		PAGE.
XXIV. THE GERMANIC EMPIRE	. . . .	287
XXV. THE SIEGE OF PARIS	. . . .	312
XXVI. THE POLITICAL EMBARRASSMENTS	. . . . . .	327
XXVII. PEACE	. . . .	341

ILLUSTRATIONS.

FREDERICK THE GREAT	*Frontispiece.*
PRUSSIAN GROUP. — Containing Portraits of King William, the Crown Prince, Prince Frederick Charles, Count Bismarck, and Gen. Von Moltke	137
IMPERIAL GROUP. — Viz., Napoleon III., the Empress Eugénie, and the Prince Imperial.	247

MAPS.

Prussia, 1740	31
Prussia, 1786	61
Prussia, 1815	107
Prussia, 1866	181
March of the Germans to Paris	221
The German Empire	247

HISTORY OF PRUSSIA.

CHAPTER I.

ORIGIN OF THE MONARCHY.

ABOUT the year of our Lord 997, Adelbert, Bishop of Prague, with two companions, set out on a missionary tour to the shores of the Baltic. The savage inhabitants killed him. Still Christianity gradually gained ground. As the ages rolled on, idolatry disappeared, and nominal Christianity took its place. The people were poor, ignorant, widely dispersed, and but partially civilized. During weary centuries, as generations came and went, nothing in that region occurred of interest to the world at large.

When, in the sixteenth century, Protestantism was rejected by Southern Europe, it was accepted by the inhabitants of this wild region. At the commencement of the eighteenth century, there was found upon the southern shores of the Baltic a small territory, about as large as the State of Massachusetts, called the Marquisate of Brandenburg. The marquis belonged to a very renowned family, known as the House of Hohenzollern. At the distance of some miles east of this marquisate, there was a small duchy called Prussia. The Marquis of Brandenburg, who had come into possession of the duchy, being a very ambitious man, by skilful diplomacy succeeded in having the united provinces of Prussia and Brandenburg recognized by the Emperor of Germany as the kingdom of Prussia. The sovereigns of Southern Europe looked quite contemptuously upon this new-born and petty realm, and were not at all disposed to receive the *parvenu* king into their society as an equal.

Berlin was the capital of the Marquisate of Brandenburg: Königsberg was the capital of the Duchy of Prussia. Though the marquis, Frederick, was crowned at Königsberg, he chose Berlin as the capital of his new kingdom. He took the title of Frederick I. The king had a son, Frederick William, then ten years of age. As heir to the throne, he was called the Crown Prince. When eighteen years of age, he married Sophie Dorothee, his cousin, a daughter of George, Elector of Hanover, who subsequently became George I. of England. On the 24th of January, 1712, a son was born to the Crown Prince, who received the name of Frederick, and subsequently became renowned in history as Frederick the Great. The babe, whose advent was hailed throughout the kingdom with so much joy as heir to the crown, had at that time a sister, Wilhelmina, three years older than himself. At the time of the birth of Frederick, the monarchy was but twelve years old. His grandfather, Frederick I., was still living; and his father was Crown Prince.

When Frederick was fourteen months old, his grandfather, Frederick I., died, and his father, Frederick William, ascended the throne. He was one of the strangest men of whom history makes mention. It is difficult to account for his conduct upon any other supposition than that he was partially insane. His father had been fond of the pageantry of courts. Frederick William despised such pageantry thoroughly. Immediately upon assuming the crown, to the utter consternation of the court he dismissed nearly every honorary official of the palace, from the highest dignitary to the humblest page. His household was reduced to the lowest footing of economy. Eight servants were retained, at six shillings a week. His father had thirty pages. All were dismissed but three. There were one thousand saddle-horses in the royal stables. Frederick retained thirty. Three-fourths of the names were struck from the pension-list.

The energy of the new sovereign inspired the whole kingdom. Everybody was compelled to be industrious. Even the apple-women were forced, by a royal decree, to knit at their stalls. The king farmed out the crownlands, drained bogs, planted colonies, established manufactures, and encouraged every branch of industry by all the energies of absolute power.

Frederick William, a thick-set, burly man, ever carried with him, as he walked the streets of Berlin, a stout ratan-cane. Upon the slightest provocation, he would soundly thrash any one whom he encountered. He especially hated the refinement and polish of the French nation. If he met a lady in rich attire, she was sure to be rudely assailed: he would often even give her a kick, and tell her to go home and take care of her brats. No young man fashionably dressed could cross the king's path without receiving a sound caning if the royal arm could reach him. If he met any one who seemed to be lounging in the streets, he would hit him a blow over the head, exclaiming, "Home, you rascal, and go to work!"

Frederick was scrupulously clean. He washed five times a day. He would allow in the palace no carpets or stuffed furniture. They caught the dust. He ate rapidly and voraciously of the most substantial food, despising all luxuries. His dress usually consisted of a blue military coat with red cuffs and collar, buff waistcoat and breeches, and white linen gaiters to the knee. A well-worn triangular hat covered his head.

By severe economy, small as were his realms, and limited as were his revenues, he raised an army of nearly a hundred thousand men. An imposing army seemed to be the great object of his ambition. He drilled his troops, personally, as troops were never drilled before. Possessing an iron constitution, and regardless of comfort himself, he had no mercy upon his soldiers. Thus he created the most powerful military engine, for its size, ever known upon earth.

The French minister at Berlin, Count Rothenburg, was a very accomplished man. He wore the dress, and had the manners, of the French gentlemen of that day. He and his associates in the embassy excited the ire of the king as they appeared at Berlin in the gorgeous court-dresses of the Tuileries and Versailles. The king, in his homespun garb, resolved that the example should not spread.

There was to be a grand review at Berlin. The French embassy would be present in their accustomed costume of cocked hats, flowing wigs, and laced coats.

The king caused a party of the lowest of the populace of Berlin, equal in number, to be dressed in the most grotesque caricature of the French costume. As soon as the French appeared upon the field, there was a great sound of trumpets; and these harlequins were brought forward to confront them. Military discipline reigned. There was no derisive laughter. There was perfect silence. The king sat upon his horse as immovable as a marble statue. With French politeness, the ministers of Louis submitted to the discourtesy, and ever after appeared in the homespun garb of Berlin.

Frederick was very desirous that his son, whom he called by the diminutive Fritz, should develop warlike tastes; but, to his bitter disappointment, the child seemed to be of an effeminate nature. He was gentle, affectionate, fond of music and books, and clung to his sister Wilhelmina with almost feminine love. The king deemed these qualities unmanly, and soon began to despise, and then to hate, the child. Still the energetic king resolved to leave no efforts untried to make a soldier of his boy.

When Fritz was six years old, his father organized a company of a hundred high-born lads, to be placed under his command. The number was gradually increased to a regiment, of which Fritz was colonel. When seven years of age, he was placed under the care of tutors, who were directed to press forward his education, intellectual and military, with the most merciless vigor. In the orders given to the distinguished military men to whom the education of the child was intrusted, the king said, —

"You have in the highest measure to make it your care to infuse into my son a true love for the soldier-business, and to impress on him, that as there is nothing in the world which can bring a prince renown and honor like the sword, so he would be a despised creature before all men if he did not love it and seek his sole glory therein."

The poor little fellow was exposed to almost incredible hardships. His father took him on his journeys to review his garrisons. Their carriage was what was called a sausage-car. It consisted merely of a stuffed pole, about ten feet long, upon which one sat astride, as if riding a rail. This pole rested upon wheels before and behind, without springs. Thus they rattled over the mountains and through the mud. The delicate, sensitive child was robbed of his sleep as his cast-iron father pressed him along on these wild adventures, regardless of fatigue or storms. "Too much sleep," said the king, "stupefies a fellow."

Every fibre in the soul of Fritz recoiled from this rude discipline. He hated hunting boars, and riding on the sausage-car, and being drenched with rain, and spattered with mud.

Instinctive tastes are developed very early in childhood. When Frederick William was a boy, some one presented him with a very beautiful French dressing-gown embroidered with gold. He thrust the robe into the fire, declaring that he would never wear such finery.

Fritz, on the contrary, could not endure homespun. He loved clothes of fine texture, and tastefully ornamented. Most of the early years of the prince were spent at Wusterhausen. This was a plain, rectangular palace, surrounded by a ditch, in a very unattractive region. Though there were some picturesque drives, yet, to Frederick's eye, the gloomy forests and pathless morasses had no charms. The palaces of Berlin and Potsdam, which the pleasure-loving monarch, Frederick I., had embellished, still retained much splendor; but the king furnished the apartments which he occupied in stoical simplicity.

The health of Fritz was frail. He was very fond of study, particularly of the Latin language. His illiterate father, who could scarcely write legibly, and whose spelling was ludicrous, took a special dislike to Latin. One day he caught his son with a Latin book in his hand, under the guidance of a teacher. The king was infuriated. The preceptor escaped a caning only by flight. Still more vehemently was he enraged in detecting his son playing the flute, and with some verses which he had written by his side. With inexpressible scorn he exclaimed, "My son is a flute-player and a poet!"

There was no point at which the father and the son met in harmony. Every month, they became more estranged from each other. The mother of Fritz, Sophie Dorothee, and his sister Wilhelmina, loved him tenderly. This exasperated the king. He extended his hatred for the boy to his mother and sister.

At length, another son was born,—Augustus William,—ten years younger than Frederick. The father now evidently wished that Frederick would die, that Augustus William might become heir to the throne. He hoped that he would develop a different character from that of Fritz. Still the king persevered in his endeavors to inspire Fritz with his own rugged nature and tastes.

George of Hanover having become George I. of England, his daughter, the mother of Fritz, became very desirous of marrying her two children, Wilhelmina and

Fritz, to Frederick and Amelia, the two children of her brother George, who was then Prince of Wales. But Frederick William, and George, Prince of Wales, had met as boys, and quarrelled; and they hated each other thoroughly. The other powers of Europe were opposed to this double marriage, as thus the kingdoms of Prussia and England would virtually be united.

The young English Frederick bore the title of the Duke of Gloucester. It was at length agreed by the English court that Frederick should marry Wilhelmina; but there were still obstacles in the way of the marriage of Fritz with Amelia. The Duke of Gloucester sent an envoy with some presents to Wilhelmina. In the following graphic terms, the Prussian princess describes the interview: —

"There came, in those days, one of the Duke of Gloucester's gentlemen to Berlin. The queen had a *soirée*. He was presented to her as well as to me. He made a very obliging compliment on his master's part. I blushed, and answered only by a courtesy. The queen, who had her eye on me, was very angry that I had answered the duke's compliments in mere silence, and rated me sharply for it, and ordered me, under pain of her indignation, to repair that fault to-morrow. I retired, all in tears, to my room, exasperated against the queen and against the duke. I vowed I would never marry him."

Wilhelmina was a very remarkable girl, endowed with a very affectionate, intellectual, and noble nature. Frederick of England was eighteen years of age, a very dissolute fellow, and exceedingly unattractive in personal appearance. Wilhelmina says that her grandfather, George I., after he became King of England, was intolerably puffed up with pride. He was disposed to look quite contemptuously upon her father, who was king of so feeble a realm as that of Prussia. Though George had given a verbal assent to the marriage of his grandson with Wilhelmina, he declined, upon various frivolous excuses, signing a marriage-treaty. Wilhelmina was quite indifferent to the matter. She declared that she cared nothing for her cousin Fred, whom she had never seen; and that she had no wish to marry him.

When Fritz had attained his fourteenth year, his father appointed him captain of one of the companies in the Potsdam Grenadier Guard. This was a giant regiment created by the caprice of Frederick William, and which had obtained world-wide renown. Such a regiment never existed before, and never will again. It was composed of giants, the shortest of whom were nearly seven feet high: the tallest were almost nine feet in height. Frederick William had ransacked Europe in search of gigantic men. No expense of money, intrigues, or fraud, were spared to obtain such men wherever found. The Guard consisted of three battalions, — eight hundred in each.

Frederick William swayed a sceptre of absolute power never surpassed in Turkey. It was a personal government. The property, the liberty, and the lives of his subjects were entirely at his disposal. He was anxious to perpetuate a race of giants. If he found in his domains any young woman of remarkable stature, he would compel her to marry one of his military Goliaths. It does not, however, appear that he thus succeeded in accomplishing his purpose.

One only thought seemed to engross the mind of Sophie Dorothee, — the double marriage. Her maternal ambition would be gratified in seeing Wilhelmina Queen of England, and her beloved son Fritz married to an English princess. Frederick William, with his wonderfully determined character, his military predilections, and his army of extraordinary compactness and discipline, began to be regarded by the other powers as a very formidable sovereign, and one whose alliance was greatly to be desired. Notwithstanding he had an army of sixty thousand men, — which army he was rapidly increasing, and subjecting to discipline hitherto unheard of in Europe, — he practised such rigid economy, that he was rapidly filling his treasury with silver and gold. In the cellar of his palace a large number of casks were stowed away, filled with coin. A vast amount of silver was also wrought into massive plate, and even into furniture and the balustrades of his stairs. These, in case of emergency, could be melted and coined.

This strange king organized a peculiar institution, which was called "The Tobacco Parliament." It consisted of a meeting of about a dozen of his confidential friends, who were assembled almost daily in some room in the palace to drink beer, smoke their pipes, and talk over matters. Distinguished strangers were sometimes admitted. Fritz was occasionally present, though always reluctantly on his part. His sensitive physical system recoiled from the beer and the smoke. Though he was under the necessity of putting the pipe in his mouth, he placed no tobacco in the bowl. His father despised the fragile boy, whom he deemed so effeminate.

The double marriage was still the topic of conversation in all the courts of Europe. In the year 1726, the Emperor of Germany, who was invested with extraordinary power over all the German princes, issued a decree, declaring that he could not consent to the double nuptial alliance with England. This decision did not trouble Frederick William; for he so thoroughly hated his English relatives, that he was not desirous of any very intimate alliance with them. He was willing that Wilhelmina should marry the Duke of Gloucester, because she would thus become eventually Queen of England.

On the other side, the King of England earnestly desired that his grand-daughter Amelia should marry Fritz; for she would thus become Queen of Prussia. He therefore declared that he would not allow the Duke of Gloucester to marry Wilhelmina unless Amelia also married Fritz.

But Frederick William was opposed to the marriage of Fritz and Amelia for three reasons: First, He was, by nature, an intensely obstinate man; and the fact that the King of England was in favor of any project was sufficient to make him opposed to it. Secondly, He hated Fritz, and did not wish him to enjoy the good fortune of marrying a rich and beautiful English princess. And, thirdly, He knew that Amelia, as the bride of Fritz, would bring to Berlin wealth of her own, and the refinements of the British court, and that thus Fritz might be able to organize a party against his father.

Frederick William therefore said, "Frederick of England may marry Wilhelmina; but Fritz shall not marry Amelia." George I. replied, "Both marriages, or none." Thus matters were brought to a dead lock.

While these intrigues were agitating both courts, Fritz was residing, most of the time, at Potsdam, — a favorite royal residence, about seventeen miles west from Berlin. In the year 1729 he was seventeen years of age, a very handsome boy, attracting much attention by his vivacity and his engaging manners. He was occasionally dragged by his father into the Tobacco Parliament, where, sickened by the fumes of tobacco and beer, he sat in mock gravity, puffing from his empty white clay pipe.

In June, 1729, a courier brought the intelligence to Berlin that George I. had suddenly died of apoplexy. He was sixty-seven years of age when Death's fatal shaft struck him, while on a journey in his carriage. As he sank before the blow, he exclaimed, "All is over with me!" and his spirit passed away to the judgment.

Much as the half-insane King of Prussia hated George I., his sudden death deeply affected him. He became very religious in all pharisaic forms of self-denial, and in spreading almost sepulchral gloom over the palace by the interdict of all enjoyment. Wilhelmina writes of her father at this time, —

"He condemned all pleasures. 'Damnable all of them,' he said. You were to speak of nothing but the word of God only. All other conversation was forbidden. It was always he who carried on the improving talk at table, where he did the office of reader, as if it had been a refectory of monks. The king treated us to a sermon every afternoon. His *valet-de-chambre* gave out a psalm, which we all sang. You had to listen to this sermon with as much devout attention as if it had been an apostle's. My brother and I had all the mind in the world to laugh. We tried hard to keep from laughing; but often we burst out. Thereupon reprimand, with all the anathemas of the Church hurled on us, which we had to take with a contrite, penitent air, — a thing not easy to bring your face to at the moment."

Fritz, about this time, was taken by his father on a visit to Augustus, King of Poland, at Dresden. The court was exceedingly dissolute, filled with every temptation which could endanger an ardent young man. Fritz, who had hitherto encountered only the severity and gloom of his father's palace, was bewildered by scenes of voluptuousness and sin which could have hardly been surpassed at Belshazzar's feast.

He was very handsome, full of vivacity, and remarkably qualified to shine in society; and, being direct heir to the throne of Prussia, he was the object of incessant attentions and caressings. Child as he was, he fell before these great temptations. It was a fall from which he never recovered. His moral nature received a wound which poisoned all his days.

Upon his return to Potsdam, after a month of reckless abandonment to sin, he was seized with a severe fit of sickness. It was many years before his constitution recovered its vigor. His dissipated habits clung to him. He chose for his companions those who were in sympathy with his newly-acquired tastes and character. His vigorous father, keeping an eagle-eye upon his son, often assailed him with the most insane ebullitions of rage.

Still, Sophie Dorothee, notwithstanding all obstacles, clung with a mother's pertinacity to the idea of the double marriage. Her brother, George II., was now King of England; and Frederick was Prince of Wales, direct heir to the crown. He was then twenty-one years of age, living an idle and dissolute life in Hanover. Wilhelmina was nineteen years old.

Fritz, though he had never seen Amelia, had received her miniature. She was pretty; would bring with her a large dowry; and the alliance, in point of rank, would be as distinguished as Europe could furnish. He was, therefore, quite desirous of securing Amelia for his bride. By the advice of his mother, he wrote to Queen Caroline, the mother of Amelia, expressing his ardent affection for her daughter, and his unalterable resolve never to lead any one but her to the altar.

Frederick William knew nothing of these intrigues; but his dislike for his son had now become so intense, that often he would not speak to him, or recognize him in the slightest degree. He treated him at the table with studied contempt. Sometimes he would give him nothing whatever to eat: he even boxed his ears, and smote him with his cane. Fritz was induced to write a very suppliant letter to his father, endeavoring to win back at least his civil treatment. The answer which Frederick William returned, incoherent, confused, and wretchedly spelled, was as follows. Contemptuously he spoke of his son in the third person, writing *he* and *his* instead of *you* and *yours*.

"His obstinate, perverse disposition, which does not love his father; for when one does every thing, and really loves one's father, one does what the father requires, not while he is there to see it, but when his back is turned too. For the rest, he knows very well that I can endure no effeminate fellow who has no human inclination in him; who puts himself to shame; cannot ride or shoot; and withal is dirty in his person; frizzles his hair like a fool, and does not cut it off. And all this I have a thousand times reprimanded, but all in vain, and no improvement in nothing. For the rest haughty, proud as a churl; speaks to nobody but some few; and is not popular and affable; and cuts grimaces with his face as if he were a fool; and does my will in nothing but following his own whims; no use to him in any thing else. This is the answer.

"FREDERICK WILLIAM."

The king was a hard drinker; very intemperate. In January, 1729, he was seized with a severe attack of the gout. His boorish, savage nature was terribly developed by the pangs of the disease. He vented his spleen upon all who came within hearing of his tongue, or reach of his crutch; and yet this most incomprehensible of men, while assailing his wife with the most vituperative terms which the vocabulary of abuse could afford, would never allow a profane expression or an indelicate allusion in his presence! His sickness lasted five weeks. Wilhelmina writes, "The pains of purgatory could not equal those which we endured."

The unhappy royal family at this time consisted of the following children: Wilhelmina, Fritz, Frederica, Charlotte, Sophie Dorothee, Ulrique, August Wilhelm, Amelia, and Henry, who was a babe in arms.

Frederica, who is described as beautiful as an angel, and a spoiled child of fifteen, became engaged to the Marquis of Anspach. She was the only one of the family who ventured to speak to her father with any freedom. One day, at the table, just before her approaching nuptials, the king, who was then suffering from the gout, asked her how she intended to regulate her housekeeping. She replied, —

"I shall have a good table, delicately served, — better than yours; and, if I have children, I will not maltreat them as you do, nor force them to eat what they have an aversion to."

"This," writes Wilhelmina, "put the king quite in a fury; but all his anger fell on my brother and me. He first threw a plate at my brother's head, who ducked out of the way. He then let fly another at me, which I avoided in like manner. He then rose into a passion against the queen, reproaching her with the bad training which she gave her children.

"We rose from the table. As we had to pass near him in going out, he aimed a great blow at me with his crutch, which, if I had not jerked away from it, would have ended me. He chased me for a while in his wheelchair; but the people drawing it gave me time to escape to the queen's chamber."

While the king's peculiarly irascible nature was thus stimulated by the pangs of the gout, he was incessantly venting his rage upon his wife and children.

"We were obliged," writes Wilhelmina, "to appear at nine o'clock in the morning in his room. We dined there, and did not dare to leave it, even for a moment. Every day was passed by the king in invectives against my brother and myself. He no longer called me any thing but the *English blackguard:* my brother was named the *rascal Fritz*. He obliged us to eat and drink the things for which we had an aversion. Every day was marked by some sinister event. It was impossible to raise one's eyes without seeing some unhappy people tormented in one way or another. The king's restlessness did not allow him to remain in bed: he had placed himself in a chair on rollers, and was thus dragged all over the place. His two arms rested upon crutches which supported them. We always followed this triumphal car, like unhappy captives who are about to undergo their sentence."

CHAPTER II.

FRITZ, AND THE COMMENCEMENT OF HIS REIGN.

AS we have mentioned, Fritz was very fond of music. A teacher from Dresden, by the name of Quantz, was secretly instructing him on the flute. His mother, in sympathy with her child, aided him in this gratification. They both knew full well, that, should the king detect him with a flute in his hand, the instrument would instantly be broken over the poor boy's head. Fritz resided with his regiment at Potsdam. He never knew when his father would make his appearance.

Whenever Fritz was with his music-teacher, an intimate friend, Lieut. Katte, was placed on the lookout. His mother also, at Berlin, kept a vigilant watch, ready to despatch a courier to her son whenever she suspected that the king was about to visit Potsdam.

One day, the prince, luxuriating in a rich French dressing-gown, was in the height of his clandestine enjoyment with his flute, when he was terrified by Katte's bursting into the room with the announcement that his wily and ever-suspicious father was already at the door. Katte and Quantz seized flute and music-books, and rushed into a wood-closet. Fritz threw off his dressing-gown, and, hurrying on his military coat, sat down at the table as if engaged in some abstruse mathematical problem. The father burst into the room, frowning like a thunder-cloud. A French barber had dressed Fritz's hair in the most approved Parisian style. The sight of his frizzled curls called down upon the head of the prince the most astonishing storms of vituperative epithets.

Just then, the king caught sight of the dressing-gown. With a new outburst of rage, he crammed it into the fire. Hating every thing that was French, he searched the room, and collected every book he could find in that language, of which Fritz had quite a library. Sending for a neighboring bookseller, he ordered him to take them away, and sell them for what they would bring. Had he chanced to open the door of the wood-closet, Katte and Quantz would have been terribly beaten, even had they escaped the headsman's block.

"The king," writes Wilhelmina, "almost caused my brother and myself to die of hunger. He always acted as carver, and served everybody except us. When, by chance, there remained any thing in the dish, he spit into it to prevent our eating of it. I was abused with insults and invectives all day long, in every possible manner, and before everybody.

"The queen contrived in her bedroom a labyrinth of screens, so that I could escape without being seen, should the king suddenly enter. One day, he surprised us. In attempting to escape, several of the screens fell. The king was at my heels, and tried to catch hold of me and beat me. He overwhelmed me with abuse, and endeavored to seize me by the hair. I fell upon the floor, near the fire. The scene would have had a tragical end had it continued, as my clothes were actually beginning to take fire. The king, fatigued with crying out and with his passion, at length put an end to it, and went his way."

Again Wilhelmina writes, "This dear brother passed his afternoons with me. We read and wrote together, and occupied ourselves in cultivating our minds. The king now never saw my brother without threatening him with the cane."

The following occurrence is recorded by Wilhelmina, as related to her by Fritz: "As I entered the king's room this morning, he first seized me by the hair, and then threw me on the floor; along which, after having exercised the vigor of his arm upon my person, he dragged me, in spite of all my resistance, to a neighboring window. His object, apparently, was to perform the office of the mutes of the seraglio; for, seizing the cord belonging to the curtain, he placed it around my neck. I seized both of his hands, and began to cry out. A servant came to my assistance, and delivered me from his hands."

In view of this event, Fritz wrote to his mother, "I am in despair. The king has forgotten that I am his son. This morning, at first sight of me, he seized me by the collar, and struck me a shower of cruel blows with his ratan. He was almost beside himself with rage. I am driven to extremity. I have too much honor to endure such treatment, and I am resolved to put an end to it one way or another."

In June, 1730, the King of Poland held a magnificent review at Mühlberg. Frederick William attended, taking his son with him. Fritz was exposed to every mortification which his unnatural parent could inflict upon him. In the presence of the monarch, the lords and ladies, he was treated by his father with the grossest insults. The king even openly flogged him with a ratan. Adding mockery to his cruelty, he said, —

"Had I been so treated by my father, I would have blown my brains out. But this fellow has no honor: he takes all that comes."

Fritz, goaded to madness, attempted, with the aid of a friend (Lieut. Katte), to escape to England. He was arrested. The king, in his rage, seized him by the collar, hustled him about, tore out handfuls of his hair, and smote him on the face with his cane, causing the blood to gush from his nose.

"Never before," exclaimed the unhappy prince, "did a Brandenburg face suffer the like of this. I cannot endure the treatment which I receive from my father, — his abuse and blows. I am so miserable, that I care but little for my own life."

The king assumed that his son, being an officer in the army, was a deserter, and merited death. He imprisoned him in a strong fortress to await his trial as a deserter. He assailed Wilhelmina with the utmost ferocity because she was in sympathy with her brother.

"He no sooner noticed me," writes Wilhelmina, "than rage and fury took possession of him. He became black in the face, his eyes sparkling fire, his mouth foaming. 'Infamous wretch,' said he, 'go keep your scoundrel brother company!'

"So saying, he seized me with one hand, striking me several blows in the face with the other fist. One of the blows struck me on the temple. I lay on the floor without consciousness. The king, in his frenzy, proceeded to kick me out of the window, which opened to the floor. The queen and my sisters ran between, preventing him. My head was swollen with the blows which I had received. They threw water upon my face to bring me to life; which care I lamentably reproached them with, death being a thousand times better in the pass things had come to. The king's face was so disfigured with rage, that it was frightful to look upon.

"'I hope,' said he, 'to have evidence to convict the rascal Fritz and the wretch Wilhelmina, and to cut their heads off. As for Fritz, he will always, if he lives, be a worthless fellow. I have three other sons, who will all turn out better than he has done.'"

Wilhelmina was imprisoned in her room. Two sentinels were placed at the door. She was fed upon the coarsest prison-fare. A court-martial was convened. By order of the king, Fritz was condemned to die. Lieut. Katte, the friend of Fritz, was accused of being privy of the attempt of Fritz to escape, and of not making it known. He was condemned to two years', some say to life-long, imprisonment. The king was exasperated by the leniency of the verdict.

"Katte," he exclaimed, "is guilty of high treason! He shall die by the sword of the headsman!"

A scaffold was erected in the yard of the castle where Fritz, then a slender, fragile boy of eighteen, was imprisoned. Katte was taken to the scaffold on the death-cart. Four grenadiers held Fritz at the window to compel him to see his friend beheaded. Fritz fainted as Katte's head rolled upon the scaffold. The Emperor of Germany interfered in behalf of the prince, whom his father intended to have also beheaded. The kings of Poland and Sweden also interfered. Thus the life of Fritz was saved.

Such were the influences under which the character of Frederick the Great was formed. On the 20th of

November, 1731, Wilhelmina was, by moral compulsion, married to the Marquis of Baireuth. The king gradually became so far reconciled to his son as to treat him with ordinary courtesy. By a similar compulsion, on the 8th of January, 1733, Fritz was married to Elizabeth, daughter of the Duke of Brunswick. Elizabeth was beautiful, amiable, and accomplished, and of irreproachable integrity of character.

But the Crown Prince of Prussia was cold, severe, unloving. With undisguised reluctance, he took the hand of his innocent bride; while, then and ever after, he treated her with the most cruel neglect. Soon after the ceremony of marriage was performed, he caused, by previous arrangement, a false alarm of fire to be raised. Frederick rushed from the apartment of his bride, and did not return. He had often declared that he never would receive the princess as his wife.

Frederick ever recognized the legal tie of their marriage. On state occasions, he gave Elizabeth the position of queen, and treated her with that stately courtesy with which he addressed other ladies of the court who were entitled to his respect. Such was the only recognition Elizabeth ever received as his wife.

On the 31st of May, 1740, Frederick William, after a long and painful sickness, found himself dying. That dread hour had come to him, which, sooner or later, comes to all. He sent for a clergyman, M. Cochius, and, as he entered, exclaimed, —

"Pray for me! — pray for me! My trust is in the Saviour."

He called for a mirror, and carefully examined his emaciated features. "Not so worn out as I thought," he said: "an ugly face, — as good as dead already."

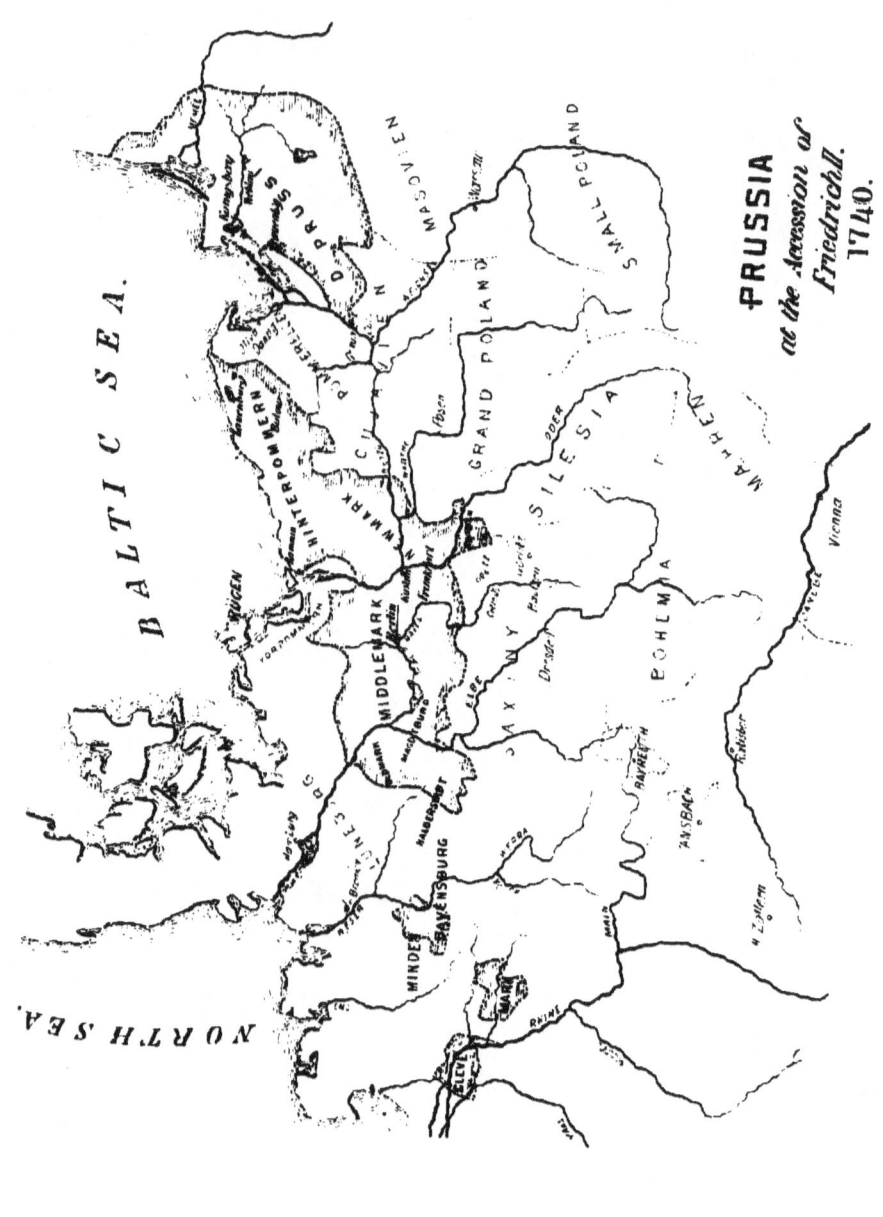

As he was thus faintly and almost inarticulately talking, he seemed to experience some monition that death was immediately at hand. "Lord Jesus," he exclaimed, "to thee I live; Lord Jesus, to thee I die. In life and in death, thou art my gain."

These were his last words on earth. Thus the soul of Frederick passed to the judgment-seat of Christ.

Fritz was now King of Prussia, — King Frederick II. He was just completing his twenty-eighth year. His realms comprised an area of about fifty-nine thousand square miles; being about the size of the State of Michigan. It contained a population of 2,240,000 souls. Frederick was absolute monarch, restrained by no parliament, no constitution, no custom, or laws superior to his own resolves. He commenced his reign by declaring that there should be entire freedom of conscience in religion, that the press should be free, and that it was his wish to make every one of his subjects contented and happy.

Speedily he taught all about him that he was to be undisputed monarch. "I hope," said a veteran officer, speaking in behalf of himself and his sons, "that we shall retain the same posts and authority as in the last reign."

"The same *posts*," replied the king, "certainly. Authority — there is none but that which resides in the sovereign."

One of his boon-companions advanced, as had been his wont, to meet him jovially. The young monarch, fixing a stern eye upon him, almost floored him with the rebuff, "I am now king!"

Those who had been his friends in the days of his adversity were not rewarded; those who had been his foes were not punished. The Giant Guard was disbanded; and, instead of them, four regiments of men of ordinary stature were organized. The king unexpectedly developed a very decided military taste. He immediately raised his standing army to over ninety thousand men. Very systematically, every hour was assigned to some specific duty. He rose at four o'clock in the morning: a single servant lighted his fire, shaved him, and dressed his hair. He allowed but fifteen minutes for his morning toilet. The day was devoted untiringly to the immense cares which devolved upon him.

His nominal wife he recognized in public as queen, and ever treated her, when it was necessary that they should meet, with cold civility. Gradually these meetings grew rare, until, after three or four years, they ceased almost entirely. Frederick was anxious to embellish his reign with men of literary and scientific celebrity. He established an academy of sciences, corresponded with distinguished scholars in other parts of Europe, and commenced correspondence and intimate friendship with Voltaire.

On the River Maas, a few miles from Liege, there was a renowned castle, which, with some thousand surrounded acres of land, had long been considered a dependency of the lords of Herstal. Frederick demanded this property upon a claim too intricate to be here fully explained. Voltaire, who drew up the manifesto, declares the claim to have been a mere pretext. Two thousand men, horse and foot, were sent to take possession of the surrounding territory, and to quarter themselves upon the inhabitants until the property, or its equivalent, was surrendered.

The Bishop of Liege, who was in possession, was a

feeble old man of eighty-two years. Resistance was impossible. The sum of a hundred and eighty thousand dollars was paid as a ransom. "This," writes Voltaire, "the king exacted in good hard ducats, which served to pay the expenses of his pleasure-tour to Strasburg."

On the 20th of October, 1740, the Emperor Charles VI. died. He left no son. That he might secure the crown to his daughter, Maria Theresa, and thus save Europe from a war of succession, which otherwise appeared inevitable, he issued a decree called "The Pragmatic Sanction." This law had been accepted and ratified by the several estates of the Austrian monarchy. Prussia, all the leading powers of Europe, — England, France, Spain, Russia, Poland, Sweden, Denmark, — and the Germanic body, had solemnly pledged themselves to maintain the Pragmatic Sanction.

Thus, by the death of the emperor, his daughter Maria Theresa, a very beautiful young wife, twenty-four years of age, whose husband was Francis, Duke of Lorraine, and who was just about to become a mother, inherited the crown of Austria. She was inexperienced; had scarcely the shadow of an army; and her treasury was deplorably empty.

On the south-eastern frontier of Prussia, between that kingdom and Poland, Maria Theresa had a province called Silesia. It was about twice as large as the State of Vermont, and contained a population of two millions. For more than a century, Silesia had belonged to Austria. The assent of Europe had sanctioned the title.

Frederick was ambitious of enlarging his dominions: it was not pleasant to be king of a realm so small, that other sovereigns looked upon it with contempt. With his powerful standing army, it was easy to take military possession of Silesia: it had no strong fortresses: there were not two thousand Austrian soldiers in the province. Frederick could present no claim to the territory which was deserving the slightest respect. In conversation with his friends, he frankly admitted, that "ambition, interest, the desire of making people talk about me, carried the day; and I decided for war."

With the utmost secrecy he matured his plans, gathered his army near the frontier, and then, after some slight diplomatic manœuvring, but without any declaration of war, rushed his troops across the border, and commenced taking military possession of all the important posts. It was proposed that he should place upon the banners the words, "For God and our Country." "Strike out the words, '*For God*,'" said the king: "I am marching to gain a province, not for religion."

That Austria might not send troops to the rescue of her invaded province, Frederick commenced his campaign in mid-winter. The roads were miry: storms of sleet swept the bleak plains: there was scarcely any enemy to be encountered. In the course of a few weeks, the whole country seemed subjugated. Frederick left Berlin for this campaign on the 12th of December, 1740. The latter part of January, he returned to receive the congratulations of his subjects upon the conquest of Silesia. In six weeks he had overrun the province, and virtually annexed it to his realms.

But Maria Theresa developed character which alike surprised Frederick and all Europe. The chivalric spirit of the surrounding monarchies was enlisted in behalf of a young queen thus unjustly assailed, and despoiled of an important province of her realms. The preparations which Maria Theresa made to regain her lost possessions induced Frederick to send an army of sixty thousand men into Silesia to hold firmly his conquest. A terrible war was the consequence, — a war in which nearly all the nations of Europe became involved, and which extended even to the distant colonial possessions of England and France. Millions of money were expended, hundreds of thousands of lives sacrificed, cities sacked, and villages burned; while an amount of misery was spread through countless homes which no imagination can gauge.

Year after year rolled on, while the strife was continuing in ever-increasing fury. France, wishing to weaken Austria, joined Frederick; England, jealous of France, joined Maria Theresa; Prussia, Sweden, and Poland were drawn into the maelstrom of fire and blood. The energy displayed by Frederick was such as the world had never before witnessed: he was alike regardless of his own comfort and that of his soldiers. His troops were goaded forward, alike over the burning plains, beneath the blaze of a summer's sun, and through winter's storms and drifts and freezing gales.

"On the head of Frederick," writes Macaulay, "is all the blood which was shed in a war which raged during many years and in every quarter of the globe, — the blood of the column of Fontenoy, the blood of the brave mountaineers who were slaughtered at Culloden. The evils produced by this wickedness were felt in lands where the name of Frederick was unknown. In order that he might rob a neighbor whom he had promised to defend, black men fought on the coast of Coromandel, and red men scalped each other by the Great Lakes of North America."

Frederick was equally versed in diplomacy and in war. He did not hesitate to resort to any measures of intrigue, or of what would usually be called treachery, to accomplish his ends. Several of the victories which he gained gave him world-wide renown. By a secret treaty, in which he perfidiously abandoned his French allies, he obtained possession of the Fortress of Neisse, and thus became, for a time, undisputed master of Silesia.

On the 11th of November, 1741, Frederick returned to Berlin, congratulating himself and his subjects with the delusion, that his conquest was established, and that there would be no further efforts on the part of Austria to regain the province. He was thus secure, as he supposed, in the possession of Silesia.

There seems to have been no sense of honor or of honesty in any of these regal courts. The province of Moravia was a part of the Austrian kingdom: it was governed by a marquis, and was about one-third larger than the State of Massachusetts. Frederick entered into an alliance with Saxony, Bavaria, and France, to wrest that territory from Maria Theresa. Moravia, which bounded Silesia on the south, was to be annexed, in general, to Saxony; but Frederick, in consideration of his services, was to receive a strip five miles in width along the whole southern frontier of Silesia. This strip contained the important military posts of Troppau, Friedenthal, and Olmutz. Again the storms of war burst forth with renewed fury; again Frederick displayed that extraordinary energy which has filled the world with his renown.

In the midst of winter, on the 26th of January, 1742, Frederick set out upon this campaign. Speaking of the first day's movement from Glatz to Landscrona, Gen. Stille says, —

"It was such a march as I never before witnessed. Through the ice and through the snow which covered that dreadful chain of mountains, we did not arrive till very late: many of our carriages were broken down, and others were overturned more than once."

By the skilful diplomacy of Frederick, aided by France, Maria Theresa was thwarted in her efforts to place her husband, Duke Francis, on the throne of the empire; and Charles Albert, King of Bavaria, was chosen emperor. This was regarded as a great triumph on the part of Frederick. Charles Albert, whose life from the cradle to the grave was a constant tragedy, took the title of the Emperor Charles VII.

Frederick, in the intensity of his earnestness, was greatly annoyed by the lukewarmness of his allies. He was not disposed to allow any considerations of humanity to stand in the way of his plans. Regardless of his own comfort, he was equally regardless of that of his troops. But the allies, whom he had with some difficulty drawn into the war, and who were not goaded on by his ambition, had no taste for campaigning through blinding, smothering snow-storms, and bivouacking on frozen plains swept by wintry gales.

At last, Frederick, in disgust, withdrew from his allies, and with marvellous sagacity and determination, though at an awful expense of suffering and death on the part of his troops, conducted the campaign to suit his own purposes, and in accordance with his own views. An incessant series of bloody battles ensued. Cities were bombarded, villages laid in ashes, and whole provinces devastated and almost depopulated. Frederick was again triumphant.

On the 11th of June, 1742, a treaty of peace was signed at Breslau. Again his conquest was assured to him: Silesia was ceded to Frederick and his heirs forevermore. Elate with victory, the young conqueror cantoned his troops in Silesia, and, with a magnificent suite, galloped to Berlin, greeted all along the road by the enthusiastic acclaim of the people.

In the following terms, Frederick, in his " Histoire de mon Temps," narrates the results of these two campaigns: —

" Thus was Silesia re-united to the dominions of Prussia. Two years of war sufficed for the conquest of this important province. The treasure which the late king had left was nearly exhausted. But it is a cheap purchase where whole provinces are bought for seven or eight millions of crowns. The union of circumstances at the moment peculiarly favored this enterprise. It was necessary for it that France should allow itself to be drawn into the war; that Russia should be attacked by Sweden; that from timidity the Hanoverians and Saxons should remain inactive; that the successes of the Prussians should be uninterrupted; and that the King of England should become, in spite of himself, the instrument of its aggrandizement.

" What, however, contributed most to this conquest was an army, which had been formed for twenty-two years by means of a discipline admirable in itself, and superior to the troops of the rest of Europe; generals who were true patriots; wise and incorruptible ministers; and, finally, a certain good fortune which often accompanies youth, and often deserts a more advanced age."

Maria Theresa regarded the loss of Silesia as the act of a highway robber. She never ceased to deplore the calamity. If the word " Silesia " were spoken in her presence, her eyes would be immediately flooded with tears.

CHAPTER III.

THE SEVEN-YEARS' WAR.

FREDERICK, having obtained Silesia, felt now disposed to cultivate the arts of peace. He had withdrawn from his allies, and entered into externally friendly relations with Austria. But still the storms of war were raging over nearly the whole of Europe. Though Frederick had dexterously escaped from the tempest with the spoil he had seized, other nations were still involved in the turmoil.

Maria Theresa became signally victorious over France. Austrian generals had arisen who were developing great military ability. Bohemia and Bavaria were reconquered by Austria; and the emperor, Charles VI., desolate, sad, and pain-stricken, was driven from his realms. Encouraged by these successes, Maria Theresa was quietly preparing to win back Silesia.

Thus influenced, Frederick, in the spring of 1744, entered into a new alliance with France and the emperor. With characteristic foresight, he had kept his army in the highest state of discipline; and his magazines were abundantly stored with all the materials of war. Having arranged with his allies that he was to receive, as his share of the spoils of the anticipated victory, the three important Bohemian principalities of Königgratz,

Buntzlau, and Leitmeritz, he issued a manifesto, saying, with unblushing falsehood, —

"His Prussian majesty requires nothing for himself: he has taken up arms simply to restore to the emperor his imperial crown, and to Europe peace."

In three strong military columns the king entered Bohemia, and on the 4th of September, having thus far encountered no opposition, invested Prague. The campaign proved to be the most sanguinary and woful he had yet experienced. The sweep of maddened armies spread desolation and misery over all Bohemia. Starving soldiers snatched the bread from the mouths of starving women and children. Houseless families froze in the fields. In the dead of winter, Frederick was compelled to retire to Silesia in one of the most disastrous retreats recorded in the annals of war.

Cantoning his shattered army in the Silesian villages, he returned to Berlin to prepare for a new campaign. His pecuniary resources were exhausted, his army dreadfully weakened, and his *matériel* of war impaired or consumed.

It was in such hours of difficulty that the genius of Frederick was developed. The victorious Austrians had pursued his troops into Silesia. The unhappy emperor died in poverty and pain. France alone remained an ally to Frederick. His situation seemed almost hopeless. On the 29th of March, 1745, he wrote from Neisse to his minister, Podewils, at Berlin.—

"We find ourselves in a great crisis. If we do not, by mediation of England, get peace, our enemies from different sides will come plunging in against me. Peace I cannot force them to; but, if we must have war, we will either beat them, or none of us will ever see Berlin again."

On the 20th of April he again wrote, "If we needs must fight, we will do it like men driven desperate. Never was there a greater peril than that I am now in. The game I play is so high, one cannot contemplate the issue in cold blood."

Another desolating campaign, with its series of sanguinary battles, ensued. At Hohen-Friedberg and at Sohr, Frederic gained great victories, though at the expense of the terrible slaughter of his own and of the Austrian troops. Dreadful as were the blows he inflicted upon others, he received blows almost equally terrible himself. At length, once more a victor, having captured Dresden, the capital of Saxony, he again sheathed his dripping sword, and concluded a peace. In his comments upon this war, Frederick writes, —

" Considering, therefore, things at their true value, we are obliged to acknowledge that this contest was in every respect only useless effusion of blood, and that the continued victories of the Prussians only helped to confirm to them the possession of Silesia. Indeed, if consideration and reputation in arms meant that efforts should be made to obtain them, undoubtedly Prussia, by gaining them, was recompensed for having undertaken the war. But this was all she gained for it; and even this imaginary advantage excited feelings of envy against her."[1]

Frederick returned to his capital on the 1st of January, 1746. Prussia now enjoyed a few years of repose. The king, with energies which never tired, devoted himself to the development of the resources of his realms, and,

[1] Histoire de mon Temps

like Cæsar, to writing the history of his own great achievements. In a letter to Voltaire upon this subject, he writes modestly, —

"'The History of my Own Time,' which at present occupies me, is not in the way of memoirs or commentaries. My own history hardly enters into my plan; for I consider it a folly in any one to think himself sufficiently remarkable to render it necessary that the whole universe should be informed of the details relating to him. I describe generally the disturbed state of Europe; and I have particularly endeavored to expose the folly and the contradictions which may be remarked in those who govern it."[1]

The impulse which Frederick gave to industry was very great; and the reforms which were introduced into the laws by the *Code Frederick* were worthy of all praise, when compared with the semi-barbaric and confused system which had before existed. During this time, Frederick became involved in a bitter quarrel with Voltaire, into the details of which we have no space here to enter. But again the clouds of war began to gather, and darken the horizon.

Maria Theresa, ever anxious to regain Silesia, entered, with that object in view, into a secret alliance with Elizabeth, Empress of Russia, and with Augustus III. of Poland. Both Elizabeth and Maria Theresa entertained a very strong personal dislike for Frederick. The Marchioness of Pompadour, who ruled France, had considered herself insulted by the sarcasms of his Prussian majesty. Anxious for revenge, she also joined the alliance. It so chanced, at that time, that three women

[1] Letter to Voltaire of the 24th of April, 1747.

ruled Continental Europe. These three women were arrayed against Frederick. Thus, in addition to the important diplomatic issues which were involved, personal pique envenomed the conflict. There were also many rumors that Frederick was contemplating additional conquests. Frederick, by bribery, became acquainted with the plan of the coalition. It was nothing less than taking possession of Prussia, and essentially dividing it between them; leaving to their vanquished foe, perhaps, a small duchy or marquisate. The king resolved to anticipate his foes, and to strike them before they had begun to move. France was at that time at war with England, and hoped to take Hanover. This led the British court, trembling for its Continental possession, to enter into a reluctant and inefficient alliance with Prussia. Thus commenced the Seven-Years' War.

France had already assembled an immense force on the Rhine to march upon Prussia from the west. The Swedes, who had been drawn into the alliance, and the Russians, were marshalling their forces in Pomerania and Livonia for an attack from the north. Austria had gathered a hundred and fifty thousand men on the frontiers of Silesia to invade Prussia from the south. Prussia seemed now doomed to destruction.

Frederick, having demanded, as a matter of form, the object of these military demonstrations, and receiving an evasive answer, informed the court of Vienna that he considered their answer a declaration of war. Immediately, three divisions of the Prussian army, amounting in all to over a hundred thousand men, entered Saxony, and were soon united near Dresden. Dresden was easily captured; and its archives fell into the hands of the victor. Immense sums of money were levied from the people.

Austria rushed to the aid of Saxony. The utmost human energy was expended in the mortal struggle. The reader would weary at the recital of the names even of the battle-fields. Dispersing his foes, though at a vast expense of misery and blood on the part of his own troops, the Prussian monarch rushed into Bohemia, and fell fiercely upon the Austrian troops intrenched outside of the walls of Prague. The renowned battle of Prague, which, says Carlyle, " sounded through all the world, and used to deafen us in drawing-rooms within man's memory," was fought on the 5th of May, 1757.

"This battle," writes Frederick, " which began towards nine in the morning, and lasted till eight at night, was one of the bloodiest of the age. The enemy lost twenty-four thousand men. The Prussian loss amounted to eighteen thousand. This day saw the pillars of the Prussian infantry cut down."

The routed Austrians fled for shelter behind the walls of Prague. The city, which contained one hundred thousand inhabitants, was quite unprepared for a siege. The garrison, daily expecting an Austrian army to march to its relief, held out with great firmness. The scene of misery witnessed in Prague was awful. An incessant storm of shot and shell fell upon the crowded dwellings. Conflagrations were continually bursting forth. There was no safety anywhere. Famine came; pestilence followed. Demons could not have inflicted more misery than the wretched inhabitants of Prague endured.

At length the banners of Marshal Daun appeared, waving over sixty thousand Austrians. The antagonists met, and fought with the utmost ferocity. The slaughter on both sides was awful. Frederick, almost frantic with grief, saw his battalions melting away before the batteries of the foe. Six times his cavalry charged; six times they were repulsed. Frederick was beaten. Sullenly he withdrew, leaving fourteen thousand behind him slain, or prisoners. With but twenty-five thousand men, their ranks shattered and bleeding, and their hearts despondent, Frederick retreated to the Fortress of Breslau in Silesia. An allied force of ninety thousand Austrians and French pursued them. Soon another terrific battle ensued. The Prussians, having lost eight thousand more men, were driven from Breslau.

It was now mid-winter. The allies supposed that Frederick was ruined. The Austrians spoke of his shattered bands with ridicule and contempt. Marvellous are the vicissitudes of war. On the 4th of December, 1757, the antagonistic hosts again met on the Plains of Lissa. Frederick had thirty thousand men; the allies, ninety thousand. The battle was short and decisive: it lasted only from the hour of noon to the going-down of the sun.

The Austrians were thoroughly routed. Seven thousand of their slain were strewed over the blood-stained snow. Twenty thousand were made prisoners. All their baggage, their military chest, one hundred and thirty-four pieces of cannon, and fifty-nine standards, fell into the hands of the victors. The Prussians paid for this victory five thousand lives.

Frederick, with triumphant banners, marched upon Breslau. The city capitulated, surrendering its whole garrison of eighteen thousand men and its supplies. The victor then turned upon the approaching Russians, and drove them out of the kingdom. He then advanced upon the Swedes: they fled precipitately to take shelter behind the walls of Stralsund. Thus terminated the **campaign of 1757.**

During the winter, both parties were recruiting their strength for the renewal of the fight. The returning sun of spring opened new woes for war-stricken Europe. The summer was passed in a series of incessant battles, sweeping over nearly the whole of Germany. In the battle of Hochkirchen, on the 14th of October, Frederick, in his turn, encountered a woful defeat. He retreated, leaving behind him nine thousand slain or prisoners, and a hundred and one guns. Nothing decisive was accomplished by the enormous expenditure of treasure, and the carnage and woe of this campaign. Thus ended the third year of this cruel and wasting war.

The spring of 1759 came. Maria Theresa was elated by her victories at the close of the last campaign. The allies redoubled their efforts. Catholic Germany generally rallied with religious zeal against heretical Prussia and England. England, a maritime nation, could afford Frederick but little assistance, save in money. Her gifts in that respect were small, amounting to but little over three millions of dollars a year. Indeed, England did but little, save to protect her own province of Hanover.

The armies of France, Austria, Poland, Sweden, and Russia, were now marching upon depopulated and impoverished Prussia. The allies represented a population of over a hundred millions. The population of Prussia was less than five millions. Thus Frederick had against him about twenty to one. With incredible exertions, the king had raised forty thousand troops. Early in June, he met eighty thousand of the allies near Frankfort on the Oder. Both parties were vanquished: first the allies in awful slaughter; then, by a sudden and unexpected turn in the tide of battle, the Prussians were overwhelmed.

Frederick, in the moment of supposed success, sent the following despatch to Berlin: "We have driven the enemy from his intrenchments. In two hours, expect to hear of a glorious victory."

The two hours of battle's hideous and hateful clamor passed away; and another courier was despatched with the appalling message, "Remove from Berlin with the royal family. Let the archives be carried to Potsdam, and the capital make conditions with the enemy."

Twenty-four thousand of the allies, and twenty thousand Prussians, fell on that bloody day. Two horses were shot beneath Frederick; and his clothes were pierced with many balls. In the darkness of the night, he retreated with the remnant of his troops. The allies had suffered so severely, that they did not attempt to pursue.

Disaster never disheartened Frederick: it only aroused anew his energies. With amazing vigor he rallied his scattered forces, dismantled distant fortresses, and brought their cannon into the field, and in a few days was at the head of twenty-eight thousand men to dispute the advance of the foe upon Berlin. Week after week, the thunders of war continued to echo over this wretched land. Winter came. The soldiers, on both sides, suffering more from famine, frost, and sickness, than from the bullets of the foe, could no longer remain in the open field. In the Austrian army, four thousand died in sixteen days from the inclemency of the weather. Thus terminated the campaign of 1759, the fourth year of this desperate conflict.

The spring of 1760 found both parties equally eager

for the renewal of the war. Maria Theresa was elate with hope. Frederick was inspired by despair: the veteran army of the Prussians was almost annihilated. The Prussian king had filled his broken ranks with peasants and boys, and any raw recruits whom he could force into the ranks by the energies of absolute power. With his utmost efforts, he could muster but seventy-five thousand men; and these, to use his own language, " were half peasants, half deserters from the enemy, — soldiers no longer fit for service, but only for show." The " deserters " were prisoners of war, whom Frederick had compelled to enlist under his banners.

The allies were marching upon him with two hundred and fifty thousand men. Against such unequal numbers, Frederick fought with energy and skill which filled Europe with wonder. Villages were burned; harvests were trampled under foot; fields were crimsoned with gore; widows and orphans starved on the dreary plains; and still there were no decisive results. On the whole, the campaign was in Frederick's favor. To the surprise of all, he had succeeded in thwarting the endeavors of the allies to crush him. Again the combatants retired to winter-quarters; and the fifth year of the war was ended.

Frederick, in his correspondence with his friends, confessed that his prospects were hopeless. He, however, resolved to struggle to the last, and to bury himself beneath the ruins of his kingdom. Having rejected Christianity, and having none of the consolations of religion to sustain him, he carried constantly with him a phial of poison, that, as a last resort, he might commit suicide.

The sixth campaign, that of 1761, proved uneventful.

Frederick fortified himself with so much skill at Kunersdorf, that the allies did not venture to attack him. They surrounded him in large numbers, as hounds surround a tiger at bay. There were many bloody skirmishes and sieges: large regions were devastated, and thousands perished in their misery. Frederick encountered severe reverses, and was, apparently, every month approaching nearer to his end. Despairing, yet resolute, when the storms of winter drove the allies from the field, the Prussians sought refuge in a camp near Leipsic. The sixth year of blood and woe had ended.

Frederick could no longer conceal his despondency. The English withdrew their subsidy: the Prussians declared that they could struggle no longer against such fearful odds. The allies were elated: it seemed manifest that one campaign more would finish their work, and that Prussia would lie helpless at their feet. In this dark hour, in a day as it were, the whole prospect became changed.

One individual chanced to be taken sick and die: that individual was Elizabeth, the Empress of Russia. She died on the 5th of January, 1762. Her death changed the fate of Europe. Peter III., who succeeded Elizabeth, hated Maria Theresa, and admired Frederick. He ordered his troops immediately to withdraw from the alliance, and sent them to the aid of Frederick. The Swedish court was so allied with that of Russia, that their troops also withdrew. Peter III. even solicited a position for himself in the Prussian army.

The change was as sudden as that caused by a turn in the kaleidoscope. Again there was a transient reverse. Peter III. was assassinated. His wife, the world-renowned Catharine II., ascended the throne: she dissolved the Prussian alliance, and ordered her troops to return to Russia. In the mean time, Frederick had roused the Turks against Austria. Before the Russians had left his camp, he attacked the Austrians with his accustomed impetuosity, and they were routed with great loss. Maria Theresa was now in dismay: her allies were leaving her; her treasury was exhausted. The Turks, sweeping all opposition before them, were ascending the Danube: Frederick, victorious, was enriching himself with the spoils of Saxony and Bohemia. On the 15th of February, 1763, peace was concluded. *Frederick retained Silesia.*

According to Frederick's computation, the conquest of the province had cost the lives of six hundred and seventy thousand of the allies, and one hundred and eighty thousand Prussians who had perished on the field of battle. The treasure expended and wasted in the desolations of war can never be estimated; neither can there be any accurate estimate of the hundreds of thousands of men, women, and children, who had perished of exposure, famine, pestilence, and misery. The population of Prussia had diminished five hundred thousand during the Seven-Years' War.

The day after the treaty of peace was signed, Frederick wrote to his friend D'Argens, "For me, poor old man that I am, I return to a town where I know nothing but the walls; where I find no longer any of my friends; where great and laborious duties await me; and where I shall soon lay my old bones in an asylum which can neither be troubled by war, by calamities, nor by the wickedness of men."

Under the energetic and sagacious administration of Frederick, Prussia rapidly recovered from its ruinous condition. "To form an idea," he writes, "of the general subversion, and how great were the desolation and discouragement, you must represent to yourself countries entirely ravaged, the very traces of the old habitations hardly discoverable: of the towns, some were ruined from top to bottom, others half destroyed by fire. Of thirteen thousand houses, the very vestiges were gone; there was no field in seed, no grain for the food of the inhabitants; noble and peasant had been pillaged, ransomed, foraged, eaten out by so many different armies, that nothing was now left them but life and miserable rags."

CHAPTER IV.

THE PARTITION OF POLAND, AND THE INVASION OF FRANCE.

NOTWITHSTANDING the acquisitions which Frederick had made to his domains, Prussia was still but a feeble kingdom, compared with the great monarchies of Austria, France, and Russia. To place Prussia upon any thing like an equality with these first-class powers, it was necessary for his Prussian majesty still more to enlarge his realms.

The kingdom of Poland occupied a territory of two hundred and eighty-four thousand square miles. It contained a population of twenty millions. Poland was surrounded by Austria, Russia, and Prussia. It is not certain with whom the idea originated, of dismembering this kingdom, — whether with the Russian empress, or with Frederick. The king was chosen by the nobles. Upon the death of Augustus, King of Poland, on the 5th of October, 1763, Catharine, by bribery, succeeded in placing upon the throne a handsome young Pole, Stanislaus Poniatowski, who had for some time been a very special favorite at her court. He was crowned King of Poland on the 7th of September, 1764.

Two or three years passed away of wars and insurrections, and all the usual tumult and woe which have characterized the progress of the nations. There were some secret interviews between the courts of Russia, Prussia, and Austria, in which it is supposed that the question of the dismemberment of Poland was agitated. Frederick, however, informs us that he at length sent to Catharine a sketch of a plan for partitioning several provinces in Poland; "to which," he says, "the court at Petersburg, intoxicated with its own outlooks on Turkey, paid not the least attention."[1]

Joseph, the son of Maria Theresa, had become emperor, through the agency of his mother, after the death of his father, the Emperor Francis. On the 25th of August, 1769, he visited Frederick, at Neisse. Under cloak of the festivities, the all-important question was discussed, of the partition of Poland, which was then in such a state of anarchy as to render any attempt at resistance hopeless. Another interview took place between the King of Prussia and the emperor, on the 3d of September, 1770, at Neustadt, near Austerlitz.

Not long after this interview, Frederick drew up a new plan of partition, which he presented to Russia and Austria. By this plan, which was adopted, Russia took eighty-seven thousand five hundred square miles. Austria received sixty-two thousand five hundred. The share which was allotted to Prussia was but nine thousand four hundred and sixty-four square miles. Small, in respect to territory, as was Prussia's share, it was regarded, in consequence of its position and the character of the region, equally valuable with the other portions.

In the carrying-out of these measures of partition, which the world has usually regarded as one of the most

---

[1] Œuvres de Frédéric, vi. 26.

atrocious acts of robbery on record, resort was had both to bribery and force. A common fund was raised by the three powers to purchase the acquiescence of the leading members of the Polish diet. Each of the confederate powers also sent an army to the frontiers of Poland to crush the distracted people, should any forcible resistance be attempted. Thus the deed was accomplished.

It would seem that the conscience of Maria Theresa recoiled from the political crime; but she was overborne by her son, the emperor, and by the imperious spirit of the prime-minister, Kaunitz. While, therefore, reluctantly she gave her assent to the measure, she issued the following extraordinary document: —

"When all my lands were invaded, and I knew not where in the world to be brought to bed in, I relied on my good right and the help of God. But in this thing, where not only public law cries to heaven against us, but also all natural justice and sound reason, I must confess never in my life to have been in such trouble. I am ashamed to show my face. Let the prince (Kaunitz) consider what an example we are giving to the world, if, for a miserable piece of Poland, we throw our honor and reputation to the winds. I see well that I am alone, and no more in vigor: therefore I must, though to my very great sorrow, let things take their course."[1]

In allusion to the same subject, Frederick writes, "A new career came to open itself to me; and one must have been either without address, or buried in stupidity, not to have profited by an opportunity so advantageous. I seized this unexpected opportunity by the forelock. By dint of negotiating and intriguing, I succeeded in

---

[1] "Hormayr, Taschenbuch, 1831, s. 66." — Cited by Dr. J. D. E. Preuss, historiographer of Brandenburg, in his Life of Frederick the Great, iv. 38.

indemnifying our monarchy for its past losses by incorporating Polish Prussia with my old provinces."

It was unquestionably a great benefit to the region, thus acquired, to be brought under the energetic administration of Frederick. "As Frederick's seven years struggle of war may be called superhuman, so was there also, in his present labor of peace, something enormous, which appeared to his contemporaries almost preternatural, — at times inhuman. It was grand, but also terrible, that the success of the whole was to him, at all moments, the one thing to be striven after. The comfort of the individual was of no concern at all."[1]

Frederick died, as he had lived, a dreary death of pain and hopelessness. He had no faith in the immortality of the soul, or in the existence of any God who takes an interest in the affairs of men. In the severe anguish of his dying-hours, he avoided any allusions to religious subjects. There is no royal road to the tomb. The sufferings of the dying monarch were very severe; but he bore them without a murmur. The king was unreasonably dissatisfied with his physicians, who could not relieve him from pain; and sent for the renowned Dr. Zimmerman of Hanover. In the following terms, Dr. Zimmerman describes the appearance of the king at his first interview: —

"When I entered the apartment of the king, I found him sitting in an elbow-chair, with his back turned toward that side of the room by which I had entered. He had on his head a large hat very much worn, ornamented with a plume of feathers equally ancient. His dress consisted of a cloak of sky-blue satin, all bedaubed

---

[1] Freytag, p. 397.

and tinged (of a brownish-yellow color) with Spanish snuff. He wore boots, and rested one of his legs, which was very much swelled, upon a stool; while the other hung down to the floor.

"When he perceived me, he pulled off his hat in a very civil and condescending manner, and in a mild tone of voice said, 'I return you many thanks, sir, for your kindness in coming hither, and for the speed with which you have performed your journey.'"[1]

At times, the king appeared exceedingly dejected. There could have been but little in the memory of the past to give him pleasure. The present was shrouded in the gloom of sickness in its most painful and revolting forms. The future opened before him but the abyss of annihilation. One day, as the doctor entered his room, the king greeted him with the words: —

"Doctor, I am an old carcass, fit only to be thrown to the dogs."

The doctor at length was compelled to leave his royal patient, and return to Hanover. "I left the king," he writes, "not only in a dangerous, but in a desperate condition, — with a confirmed dropsy, to all appearance an abscess in the lungs, and such a prostration of strength, that he could neither stand nor move without support."

In taking leave of Dr. Zimmerman, the king said, "Adieu, my good, my dear Mr. Zimmerman! I ask pardon of your patients for having deprived them of your assistance. I thank you for your kindness in staying with me so long. May you be always happy! Do not forget the old man you have seen here."

[1] Entretiens de Frédéric, Roi de Prusse, avec le Docteur Zimmerman.

For six weeks longer, the dying king remained in a state of constant suffering. The dropsy was in his stomach and chest. His limbs were greatly swollen, frequently bursting into loathsome and very offensive wounds. Asthma caused him to gasp for breath. He could not lie down by night or by day, but was confined to a wearisome position in his chair. Mirabeau, who was in Berlin at the time, writes, —

"The king has not been in bed for six weeks. The swelling augments. He sees it, but will not perceive what it is, or, at least, will not appear to do so. He talks as if it were a swelling accompanying convalescence. He is determined not to die if violent remedies can save him, but to submit to punctures and incisions to draw off the water."

It is not difficult, in youth, health, and prosperity, to reject the religion of Jesus; but when these dark, sad hours of the dying-chamber come, if one have not the consolations which Christianity proffers, the most dreadful and impenetrable gloom must overshadow the soul. One can scarcely conceive of a scene more utterly joyless and dismal than the dying-chamber of Frederick the Great.

On the 17th of August, 1786, at twenty minutes past two in the morning, he died, in the seventy-fifth year of his age, and the forty-sixth of his reign. There was one clause in his will which was judiciously disregarded. "He had directed himself to be buried near his dogs, in the gardens of Sans-Souci, — a last mark of his contempt for his own species. He was buried in a small chapel in the church of the garrison, at Potsdam, where, side by side, repose Frederick and his father, — the former in a coffin of block tin, the latter in one of copper, and equally without ornament of any kind."[1]

The Prussian territory had been nearly doubled under the reign of this extraordinary man. He left the crown to his nephew, his deceased brother's son. Frederick William II. commenced his reign in possession of a territory of 71,670 square miles, being but little larger than the State of Missouri. It contained nearly six million inhabitants. This little realm, proud of its military prestige, maintained a standing army of two hundred and twenty thousand men. This army consumed four-fifths of the revenues of the state.

Frederick William II. was a profligate and a weak man. He was a feeble ruler, and a wretched financier; speedily exhausting his treasury, and involving the kingdom in debt.

The French Revolution soon began, like a moral earthquake, to shake all the thrones in Europe. In the first partition of Poland, to which we have referred, there had still been a considerable portion of the kingdom left under its king, Poniatowski. The example of France had reached the wilds of Sarmatia. On the 3d of May, 1791, the Poles ventured to establish a republican constitution under monarchical forms. Perpetuating an *hereditary* monarchy, they proclaimed religious toleration, the emancipation of the *bourgeoisie*, and the progressive emancipation of the serfs.

Burke said of this movement, "In it humanity has every thing to rejoice and glory in. It is probably the most pure public good ever yet conferred on mankind. Ten millions of men were placed in a way

[1] Life of Frederick II., by Lord Dover, vol. ii. p. 328.

to be freed gradually, and therefore, to themselves, safely, not from civil or political chains, which, bad as they are, only fetter the mind, but from substantial personal bondage. Not one drop of blood was spilled; no insults on religion, morals, or manners."[1]

Prussia and Russia assumed that this constitution was bringing dangerous Jacobinism too near their thrones. They united their armies for a second dismemberment. In overwhelming numbers, their combined troops crossed the frontiers, and were cantoned in the provinces they had seized. Thus was Poland overrun by the armies of the two most powerful military monarchies in Europe.

The chivalric Poles were roused to energies of despair such as the world had never witnessed before. Kosciusko was chosen as military leader. With his brave band he retook Warsaw, driving out the Russian and Prussians. To recapture the city, Frederick William II. sent thirty thousand of his perfectly-drilled soldiers to co-operate with forty thousand Russian veterans sent by Catharine. After a series of bloody conflicts, Warsaw was taken by storm on the 4th of November, 1794. Amidst conflagrations, bombardments, shrieks, and death, the Polish battalions were driven into the Vistula. Ten thousand soldiers perished; ten thousand were taken prisoners; and twelve thousand of the inhabitants of Warsaw were put to the sword. Stanislaus was sent captive into Russia, where he died. The conquerors divided Poland between them.[2]

---

[1] Burke's Appeal to the Old Whigs. Works, vol. ii. p. 224.
[2] Alison's History of Europe, vol. i. p. 358.

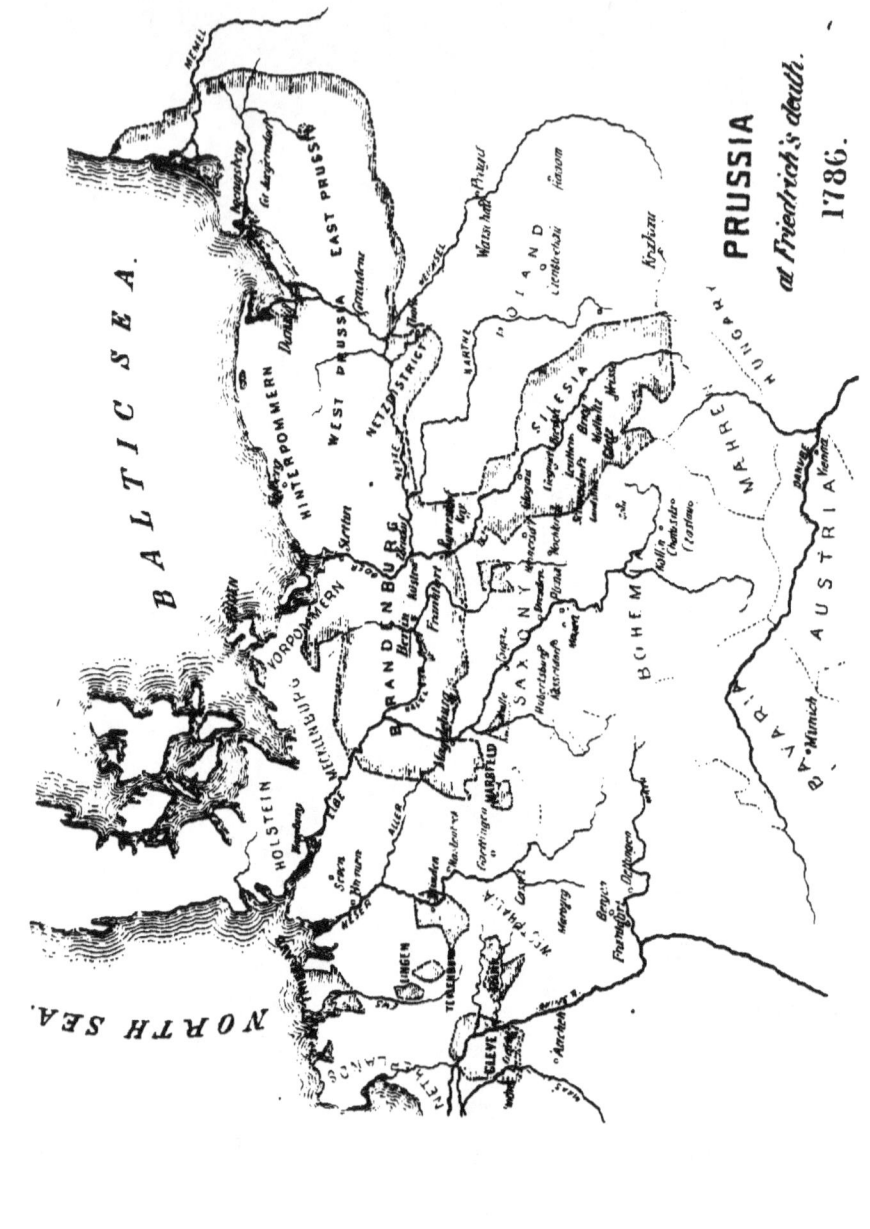

In reference to this great crime, the poet Campbell has written beautifully in his "Pleasures of Hope:" —

> "Oh bloodiest picture in the book of Time!
> Sarmatia fell unwept, without a crime;
> Found not a generous friend, a pitying foe,
> Strength in her arms, nor mercy in her woe;
> Dropped from her nerveless grasp the shattered spear;
> Closed her bright eye, and curbed her high career.
> Hope for a season bade the world farewell;
> And Freedom shrieked as Kosciusko fell."

Frederick William II., the King of Prussia, died at Berlin on the 16th of Nov. 1797. He did not leave behind him an enviable reputation in any respect. In the final partition of Poland, Prussia received twenty-one thousand square miles, with one million inhabitants. In all, Prussia had robbed Poland of fifty-seven thousand square miles, and two million five hundred and fifty thousand inhabitants.[1]

Frederick William III., son of the deceased king, who now ascended the throne, was twenty-seven years of age. Sir Archibald Alison, whose predilections are strongly in favor of kings and nobles, thus describes him: —

"His character and habits already presaged the immortal glories of his reign. Severe and regular in private life, he had lived, amid a dissolute court, a pattern of every domestic virtue. Married early to a beautiful and high-spirited princess, he bore to her that faithful attachment which her captivating qualities were so well fitted to excite, and which afterwards attracted the admiration, though they could not relax the policy, or meet

---

[1] Encyclopædia Americana.

the sternness, or excite a spark of chivalry in the cold and intellectual breast, of Napoleon." [1]

The young king wrested from the Countess Lichstenau, one of his deceased father's guilty favorites, many crown-jewels which were found in her possession, and a large portion of the enormous wealth which had been lavished upon her. She was assigned a retreat near Berlin, with a salary of three thousand dollars.

All the Continental monarchs were soon alarmed by the revolutionary principles which were so rapidly spreading throughout France. Prussia and Austria entered into a coalition to unite with the royalist party in France, crush out the popular movement with the tread of their armies, and restore the absolutism of the ancient *régime*. With that purpose they assembled an immense army at Coblentz, on the Rhine. The march of the invaders was commenced on the 25th of July, 1792.

The allied troops consisted of eighty thousand of the veteran soldiers of Prussia, and sixty-eight thousand Austrians.[2] These troops were placed under the command of the Duke of Brunswick. His mother was one of the sisters of Frederick the Great. His wife was the Princess Augusta of England.

In three great divisions, this army, one hundred and forty thousand strong, entered France. The Duke of Brunswick ascended the left bank of the Moselle, to march upon Paris by the way of Verdun and Chalons. His immense force, in all its immense array of infantry, cavalry, guns, and baggage, crowded forty miles of road.

Prince Hohenlohe, marching twenty miles on the left,

---

[1] Alison's History of Europe, vol. i. p. 473.

[2] Ibid., vol. i. p. 126; also Thiers' History of the French Revolution vol. i. p. 278.

pursued a route which passed through Thionville and Metz. Count de Clairfayt led his battalions on the right, by the Mézières and Sedan.

The Duke of Brunswick issued a proclamation, which at once became world-renowned, and which exasperated the popular party in France to the highest degree.

"Their majesties," said the duke in his famous manifesto, "the Emperor of Germany and the King of Prussia, having intrusted me with the command of the combined armies assembled by their orders on the frontiers of France, I desire to acquaint the inhabitants of that kingdom with the motives which have determined the measures of the two sovereigns, and the intentions by which they are guided.

"They wish to put an end to the anarchy in the interior of France; to stop the attacks against the throne and the altar; to re-establish the royal power; to restore to the king the security and liberty of which he is deprived, and to place him in a condition to exercise the authority which is his own.

"Such of the national guards as shall have fought against the troops of the two allied courts, and who shall be taken in arms, shall be treated as rebels, and punished as rebels to their king.

"The members of the departments, districts, and municipalities, shall be responsible, with their lives and property, for all misdemeanors, fires, murders, pillage, and acts of violence, which they shall suffer to be committed, or which they shall notoriously not strive to prevent in their territory.

"The inhabitants of the cities, towns, and villages, who shall dare to defend themselves against the troops of their imperial and royal majesties, and to fire upon them, either in the open field, or from the windows, doors, and apertures of their houses, shall be instantly punished with all the rigor of the law of war, and their houses demolished or burned.

"The city of Paris, and all its inhabitants, without distinction, are required to submit immediately, and without delay, to the king; to set that prince at full and entire liberty; and to insure to him, as well as to all the royal personages, the inviolability and respect which the laws of nature and nations render obligatory on subjects toward their sovereigns.

"Their imperial and royal majesties will hold personally responsible, with their lives, for all that may happen, to be tried militarily, and without hope of pardon, all the members of the national assembly, of the department of the district of the municipality, and of the national guard of Paris, the justices of the peace, and all others whom it may concern.

"Their majesties declare, moreover, on their faith and word as emperor and king, that if the Palace of the Tuileries is forced or insulted, that if the least violence, the least outrage, is offered to their majesties, the king and queen, and to the royal family, if immediate provision is not made for their safety, they will take exemplary and ever-memorable vengeance by giving up Paris to military execution and total destruction, and the rebels guilty of outrages to the punishments they shall have deserved," &c.[1]

"The greatest sensation," writes Prof. Smyth, "was produced in our own country of Great Britain, and all over Europe, by a manifesto like this, which went

---

[1] Thiers' History of the French Revolution, vol. i. p. 314.

in truth to say that two military powers were to march into a neighboring and independent kingdom, to settle the civil dissensions there as they thought best, and to punish by military law all who presumed to resist them. No friend to freedom could, for a moment, tolerate such a procedure as this."[1]

The result was, the Palace of the Tuileries was stormed by the exasperated populace of Paris; the royal family was taken captive, and incarcerated in the Temple; and soon both king and queen were led to the guillotine. Onward pressed the allies with resistless tramp. All opposition melted before their solid battalions. Thionville and Verdun were surrounded and captured. The victorious invaders crowded the defiles of the Argonne. The army of Dumouriez, sent to oppose them, was almost annihilated. Fugitives rushed into Paris, pale and breathless, declaring that no further opposition was possible.

Terrible was the consternation in Paris. France rose *en masse*. Every man on the popular side, pale with deathless resolve, grasped his arms. All who were suspected of being in alliance with the Prussians were mercilessly assassinated. The venerable Vergniaud uttered a word which nerved every arm.

" The plan of the enemy," said he, " is to march directly upon Paris, leaving the fortresses behind him. Let him do so: this course will be our salvation, and his ruin. Our armies, too weak to withstand him, will be strong enough to harass him in the rear. When he arrives, pursued by our battalions, he will find himself face to face with our Parisian army, drawn up in bat-

---

[1] Prof. Smyth's Lectures on the French Revolution, vol. ii. p. 326.

tle array under the walls of the capital. There, surrounded on all sides, he will be swallowed up by the soil which he has profaned."

The excesses committed in Paris against royalists in the blind frenzy of the hour are beyond the powers of any pen to describe. Dr. Moore, an English gentleman, who was an eye-witness, writes, —

"Amid the disorders which have taken place, it is impossible not to admire the generous spirit which glows all over the nation in support of its independence. No country ever displayed a nobler or more patriotic enthusiasm."[1]

On the 20th of September, 1792, the Duke of Brunswick encountered, to his surprise, a French army, strongly intrenched upon the heights of Valmy, near Chalons. Seventy thousand men, peasants and artisans, had rushed to those heights. For twenty days, the storm of battle raged there with tremendous fury. The young men from the shops and the fields fought from behind their ramparts with the bravery of veterans. From all parts of France, re-enforcements were hurrying to the scene of the conflict. The supplies of the invaders were cut off. Sickness decimated their camp. The freezing gales of winter were at hand. In deep humiliation, the Prussians broke up their camp on the 15th of October, and retired to their fortresses on the Rhine. They left behind them twenty-five thousand, who had perished of sickness, the bullet, and the sword.

"The force," writes Alison, "with which the Prussians retired, was about seventy thousand. Their retreat was conducted in the most imposing manner; tak-

---

[1] Journal of Sir John Moore, vol. i. p. 160.

ing position, and facing about, on occasion of every halt. They left behind them, on their route, most melancholy proofs of the disasters of the campaign. All the villages were filled with the dead and dying. The allies had lost by dysentery and fevers more than a fourth of their numbers."

CHAPTER V.

PRUSSIA AND THE FRENCH REVOLUTION.

AS the allied army retreated, after its defeat at Valmy, in September, 1792, Gen. Dumouriez pursued a division of twenty-five thousand Austrians under Gen. Clairfayt. On the 4th of November he overtook the fugitives, strongly intrenched upon the heights of Jemappes, near Mons. One day was employed in concentrating the French forces and arraying the batteries. Twenty-five thousand men were behind the ramparts: sixty thousand advanced to storm them. Early in the morning of the 6th, the cannonade began: a hundred pieces of artillery opened their thunders. All day long, war's fierce tornado, with its whirls, its eddies, and its onward rush, swept the field. The Austrians were routed. In broken bands they fled, having lost fifteen hundred prisoners, and four thousand five hundred in killed and wounded.

"The sensation," writes Thiers, "produced by this important battle, was prodigious. The victory of Jemappes instantaneously filled all France with joy, and Europe with new surprise. Nothing was talked of but the fact of the coolness with which the Austrian artillery had been confronted, and the intrepidity displayed in storming their redoubts. The danger and the victory were even exaggerated; and throughout all Europe the faculty of gaining great battles was again awarded to the French."[1]

The Duke of Orleans (subsequently King Louis Philippe), at that time a young man, known as the Duke of Chartres, greatly signalized himself by his bravery in this conflict. The French armies now swept triumphantly towards the Rhine, driving their foes before them. Cheered by these victories, the convention in Paris, on the 19th of November, 1792, issued the decree, —

"That they would grant fraternity and succor to every people who were disposed to recover their liberty; and that they charged their generals to give aid to all such people, and to defend all citizens who had been or might be disquieted in the cause of freedom."

This decree was followed by another, on the 15th of December, declaring that France would proclaim, in all the provinces it conquered, "the sovereignty of the people, the suppression of all the constituted authorities, of all feudal and territorial rights, of all the privileges of nobility, and exclusive privileges of every description."[2]

The people were invited to meet, and organize new republican governments founded on popular suffrage. By these defeats, the Prussians were placed in a very deplorable condition. Winter was at hand; disease was making dreadful ravages in their camps; republican principles were penetrating even the ranks of the army. A flag of truce was sent by Frederick William III. to

---

[1] Thiers' History of the French Revolution, vol. ii. p. 10.
[2] Jomini, Histoire des Guerres de la Révolution, ii. 264.

confer upon terms of compromise. Dumouriez wrote to the French Government, —

"The proposals of the King of Prussia do not appear to offer a basis for negotiation; but they demonstrate that the enemy's distress is very great. I am persuaded that the King of Prussia is now heartily sorry in being so far in advance, and that he would readily adopt any means to extricate himself from his embarrassments."[1]

The negotiations for peace were not successful.

During the winter, the allies gathered their forces anew; and, in the spring, Frederick William commenced another campaign by besieging the French fortress of Mayence, on the left bank of the Rhine. The King of Prussia brought forward fifty-five thousand men; and Austria sent enough troops to swell the number to eighty thousand. The French had about the same number in the Valley of the Moselle and in their fortresses on the Rhine.

The King of Prussia crossed the river, without opposition, at a point a little below Mayence, and invested the city from both sides of the Rhine. The garrison consisted of twenty thousand men. The investment commenced in April, 1793.

The city of Mayence, nearly opposite the mouth of the River Mayne, was even then a very strongly fortified place. The King of Prussia, in person, conducted the siege. There were the usual scenes of bombardment, tumult, and blood, storming-parties repulsed, and *sorties* driven back. Two hundred pieces of artillery played upon the fortress; while floating batteries, placed upon

---

[1] Dumouriez' despatch to the French Government.

the Rhine, threw into the streets an incessant storm of shells.

"Distress was at its height. Horseflesh had long been the only meat the garrison had. The soldiers ate rats, and went to the banks of the Rhine to pick up the dead horses which the current brought down with it. A cat sold for six francs; horseflesh, at the rate of forty-five sous per pound. The officers fared no better than the soldiers. Gen. Albert Dubayet, having invited his staff to dinner, set before it, by way of a treat, a cat, flanked by a dozen mice.

"Communications were so completely intercepted, that, for three months, the garrison was wholly ignorant of what was passing in France. The Prussians, who had practised all sorts of stratagems, had false "Moniteurs" printed at Frankfort, stating that Dumouriez had overthrown the Convention, and that Louis XVIII. was reigning with a regency. The Prussians placed at the advanced posts transmitted these false "Moniteurs" to the soldiers in the French garrisons.

"At length the distress became so intolerable, that two thousand of the inhabitants solicited permission to depart. Albert Dubayet granted it; but, not being received by the besiegers, they remained between two fires, and partly perished under the walls of the place. In the morning, soldiers were seen bringing in wounded infants wrapped in their cloaks."[1]

On the 25th of July, the starved garrison was compelled to capitulate. The King of Prussia allowed the troops to march out with their arms and baggage. They simply engaged not to serve, for a year, against the allies.

[1] Thiers' French Revolution, vol. ii. p. 250.

But Frederick William III. had now become weary of the war. He would have abandoned the enterprise; but England came forward with liberal promises of gold. England, uniting with Holland, agreed to pay the King of Prussia two hundred and fifty thousand dollars a month, and also to meet all the expenses of bread and forage for the Prussian army. There was also granted the Prussian king a gratuity of one million five hundred thousand dollars to aid him in commencing operations, with the promise of five hundred thousand dollars upon his return to the Prussian States.

In consideration of this subsidy, Frederick William agreed to furnish sixty-four thousand five hundred men to the coalition; of which coalition, England was now the acknowledged head. The Prussian army was to be under a Prussian commander. All the conquests made of French territory were to belong jointly to England and Holland.[1]

"The discontent of the Prussian troops," writes Alison, "was loudly proclaimed when it transpired that they were to be transferred to the pay of Great Britain. They openly murmured at the disgrace of having the soldiers of the great Frederick sold like mercenaries to a foreign power. The event soon demonstrated that the succors stipulated from Prussia would be of the most inefficient description."

The conflict raged on the Rhine, month after month, with varying success. Gen. Kleber, who was in command of the French forces, driving the allies before him, crossed the Rhine, and carried the horrors of war into the territory of the enemy. Ere long he encoun-

---

[1] Thiers' French Revolution, vol. iii. p. 18.

tered overwhelming numbers, and was compelled to retreat across the Rhine, back into France. Again, reenforcements arriving, the French republicans assumed the offensive, and carried the war across the river to the right bank. Thus the blood-red tides of battle ebbed and flowed.

This majestic stream, the Rhine, which had so long been the boundary of the Roman Empire, mainly separated the antagonistic armies from the Alps to the ocean. The allies had an immense advantage in still holding the strong fortress of Mayence, which they had captured on the French side of the Rhine; but as the republican troops gained victory after victory, and Prussia itself was threatened with invasion by the tricolor flag, Frederick William, disheartened and trembling, again resolved to withdraw from the alliance.

Republican France had so roused herself, that she had twelve hundred thousand men under arms. All the important military points on the Rhine were in their possession. Holland was organizing as the Republic of the United Provinces, and entering into alliance with the French Republic.

Frederick William III. sent a commissioner to the headquarters of the French commander to propose peace. The commissioners met at Basle; and on the 5th of April, 1795, peace was concluded with Prussia. The French agreed to evacuate all the provinces they had conquered on the right bank of the Rhine. The Prussian king pledged himself to friendly relations with the French Republic.

Still England, Austria, and Naples continued the war for three years longer. The French armies, having encountered some repulses in the conflict with the Austrians, occupied the left bank of the Rhine, and, with that broad and rapid river for their protection, warded off invasion from Germany. Immense French victories gained by the young general, Bonaparte, over the Austrians in Italy, led to a convention at Rastadt to confer upon terms of peace. We give the substance of these negotiations as stated by M. Thiers. The intelligent reader will be deeply interested in comparing the claims of France and the reply of Germany in 1798 with the claims of Germany and the reply of France in 1870.

France demanded, not only that the line of the Rhine should be the recognized frontier between the two countries, but that France should also have possession of all the islands in the Rhine, which were very important in a military point of view. France also demanded Kehl and its territory, opposite to Strasburg; and Cassel and its territory, opposite Mayence; and that fifty acres of land on the German side of the Rhine, facing the old bridge of Huningen, should be transferred to the Republic. In addition to this, France insisted that the important fortress of Ehrenbreitstein, nearly opposite Coblentz, should be demolished. These concessions, it was asserted, were essential to protect France from the menace of Germanic invasion.

The deputation of the German Empire, on the other hand, replied, that the River Rhine was the natural boundary between the two nations, offering equal security to both; that, if France were to keep all the offensive points, this security would cease to exist for Germany. They proposed, as the real boundary, the channel of the main branch of the river, — all the islands on the right of that line to belong to Germany; all on the left, to France. The deputation was not willing that France should retain any offensive points on the river, while Germany was to lose them all.[1]

After long negotiation, the obviously reasonable German proposition was accepted. The main channel of the River Rhine was declared to be the boundary between France and Germany. This important treaty was signed in September, 1798.

The establishment of, first the consulate, and then the empire, in France, increased rather than diminished the exasperation of the old feudal monarchies. Under these new organizations, the republican doctrine of equal rights for all men was retained. Hereditary nobility was rejected, at first entirely rejected, and then but partially revived. Titles of honor were conferred as the reward of merit only. The doctrine of the " divine right" of kings was utterly repudiated; and the powers of government were based upon popular suffrage.

The feudal kings and nobles of Europe were not to be deceived by a name. The fact that the Republic called itself an Empire, and that the elected executive was called Imperator, instead of President, rendered republicanism, thus arrayed, as formidable as ever. The principles avowed were in direct antagonism with all the old *régimes:* consequently, coalition after coalition was organized against these democratic principles, whatever names they might assume.

The antagonism which had so long existed between Prussia and Austria was one of the influences which induced Frederick William III. to withdraw from the alliance against France. During the ten years of

---

[1] Thiers' History of the French Revolution, vol. iv. p. 205.

peace which Prussia enjoyed, the kingdom had rapidly increased in population and wealth. The vicissitudes of war had thrown a large portion of the commerce of Germany into its hands. The population had increased to nine million five hundred thousand souls; its net income amounted to about fifty million dollars; its standing army numbered two hundred thousand highly-disciplined troops.[1]

"The Prussian capital was one of the most agreeable and least expensive in Europe. No rigid etiquette, no rigid line of demarcation, separated the court from the people. The royal family lived on terms of friendly equality, not only with the nobility, but with the leading inhabitants of Berlin. An easy demeanor, a total absence of aristocratic pride, an entire absence of extravagance or parade, distinguished all the parties given at court; at which the king and queen mingled on terms of perfect equality with their subjects.

"Many ladies of rank, both in Paris and London, spent larger sums annually on their dress than the Queen of Prussia. None equalled her in dignity and grace of manner and the elevated sentiments with which she was inspired. Admiration of her beauty, and attachment to her person, formed one of the strongest feelings of the Prussian monarchy."[2]

The King of Prussia was the first of the monarchs, among the great powers, who recognized the empire in France. When, in 1804, Russia, in coalition with Austria and England, was preparing to send down her Muscovite legions into France, Frederick entered into an agreement with the French Empire to maintain a

---

[1] Bignon, Histoire de France depuis le 18me Brumaire, t. ii. p. 293.
[2] Alison's History of Europe, vol. ii. p. 288.

strict neutrality, and not to permit Russian or any other foreign troops to cross her territories.

Early in the spring of 1805, England, Austria, and Russia formed a new coalition against France, into which Sweden, Hanover, Sardinia, and Naples were soon drawn. The united army of the allies was to number five hundred thousand men.

"It was a great object," writes Sir Archibald Alison, "if possible, to unite Prussia in the alliance. For this purpose, M. Noviltzoff was despatched to Berlin. Notwithstanding all the efforts of England and Russia, it was found impossible to overcome the leaning of Prussia towards the French interest. The real secret of this partiality was the effect of the glittering prize, which her ministers had long coveted, in the electorate of Hanover. The Prussian Government could never divest itself of the idea, that by preserving a dubious neutrality, and reserving her interposition for the decisive moment, she might, without danger, add that important acquisition to her domains.

"The Prussian ministers at length openly broached the project of taking provisional possession of that electorate, 'as the union of the Continental dominions of his Britannic Majesty to Prussia is of such consequence to that monarchy, that it can never relinquish the prospect of gaining such an acquisition, providing it can be done without compromising the character of his Majesty.'

"The king at length put the question, 'Can I, without violating the rules of morality, without being held up in history as a king destitute of faith, depart, for the acquisition of Hanover, from the character which I have hitherto maintained?'

"It was easy to see in what such contests between duty and interest would terminate. Before the middle of August, the Prussian cabinet intimated to the French minister at Berlin their willingness to conclude a treaty of alliance, offensive and defensive, with the French Government, on the footing of the annexation of Hanover to their dominions. Subsequent events prevented the treaty being signed, and saved Prussia from this last act of cupidity and infatuation."[1]

During all this time, there was a strong minority in Prussia in favor of war, against the rapidly-spreading liberal opinions of France. The Queen Louisa and Prince Louis were prominent in this party. A French army-corps had marched through a corner of Anspach, thus violating the territory of Prussia. Though immediate apology was made, "the cabinet at Berlin," writes Alison, "had taken umbrage to an extent which could hardly have been anticipated, and which was greatly beyond the amount of the injury inflicted.

"Matters were in this inflammable state when the Emperor Alexander arrived at Berlin, and employed the whole weight of his great authority, and all the charms of his captivating manners, to induce the king to embrace a more manly and courageous policy. Under the influence of so many concurring causes, the French influence rapidly declined.

"On the 3d of November, 1805, a secret convention was signed between the two monarchs, for the regulation of the affairs of Europe, and to erect a barrier against the encroachments of France.

"The conclusion of this convention was followed by

---

[1] Alison, vol. ii. p. 322.

a scene as remarkable as it was romantic. When they signed it, both were fully aware of the perilous nature of the enterprise on which they were adventuring. The Archduke Anthony had arrived two days before with detailed accounts of the disastrous result of the combats around Ulm.

"Inspired with a full sense of the dangers of the war, the ardent and chivalrous mind of the queen conceived the idea of uniting the two sovereigns by a bond more likely to be durable than the mere alliance of cabinets with each other. This was to bring them together at the tomb of the great Frederick, where, it was hoped, the solemnity and recollections of the scene would powerfully contribute to cement their union.

"The emperor, who was desirous of visiting the mausoleum of that illustrious hero, accordingly repaired to the church of the garrison at Potsdam, where his remains are deposited; and at midnight the two monarchs proceeded together, by torchlight, to the hallowed grave. Uncovering when he approached the spot, the emperor kissed the pall; and taking the hand (sword?) of the King of Prussia, as it lay on the tomb, they swore an eternal friendship to each other, and bound themselves by the most solemn oaths to maintain their engagements inviolate in the great contest for European independence in which they were engaged.

"A few hours after, Alexander departed for Gallicia, to assume, in person, the command of the army of reserve, which was advancing through that province to the support of Kutusoff. Such was the origin of that great alliance, which, though often interrupted by misfortune, and deeply checkered with disaster, was yet destined to be brought to so triumphant an issue, and ultimately wrought such wonders for the deliverance of Europe." [1]

Before the Prussians had brought their two hundred thousand troops into the field, the French armies, under Napoleon, had captured Vienna, and had almost annihilated the Prussian army in the great victory of Austerlitz. Prussia had, as yet, made no declaration of war. The treaty was kept a profound secret. The 15th of December, 1805, was the appointed day in which war was to be declared against France, and hostilities were to commence. The result we give in Sir Archibald Alison's words, somewhat abbreviated.

The Prussian minister, " Haugnitz, had come to Vienna to declare war against Napoleon; but the battle of Austerlitz had totally deranged their plans. The armistice had completely detached Austria from the coalition. The severest morality could not condemn a statesman who sought to withdraw his country from a contest which now appeared hopeless. But, not content with this, Haugnitz resolved to go a step farther.

" On the breaking-up of the confederacy into which he had just entered, he determined to secure a part of the spoils of his former allies, and, if he could not chase the French standards beyond the Rhine, at least wrest from England those Continental possessions which she now appeared in no condition to defend.

" With matchless effrontery, he changed the whole object of his mission; and when admitted into the presence of Napoleon, after the victory, congratulated him upon his success, and proposed a treaty, the basis of which should be the old project of annexing Hanover to the Prussian dominions.

---

[1] Alison's History of Europe, vol. ii. p. 357.

"Although Napoleon had not received full accounts of the treaty of the 3d of November, he was aware of its substance. Upon receiving Hauguitz, therefore, he broke out into vehement declamation against the perfidy of the Prussian cabinet; informed him that he was acquainted with all their machinations; and that it now lay with him alone, after concluding peace with Austria, to turn his whole forces against Prussia; wrest from them Silesia, whose fortresses, unarmed and unprovisioned, were in no condition to make any defence; excite an insurrection in Prussian Poland, and punish them in the most signal manner for their perfidy.

"Reasons of state, however, he added, sometimes compelled sovereigns to bury in oblivion the best founded cause of animosity. On this occasion, he was willing to overlook their past misconduct, and ascribe it entirely to the efforts of England; but this could be only on one condition,—that Prussia should at length abandon its doubtful policy, and enter, heart and hand, into the French alliance. On these terms, he was still willing to incorporate Hanover into their dominions, in exchange for some of its detached southern possessions, which were to be ceded to France and Bavaria.

"Overjoyed at the prospect thus afforded of extricating his country, not only without loss, but with great accession of territory, Hauguitz at once accepted the stipulations. It was agreed that Prussia should enter into an alliance with France, and receive, besides the margraviate of Baireuth, the whole electorate of Hanover, in full sovereignty, as well as all the other Continental dominions of his Britannic Majesty."[1]

[1] Alison's History of Europe, vol. ii. p. 394.

This treaty was signed on the 15th of December, 1805, — the very day on which Prussia was to have commenced hostilities against France. The indignation which this transaction excited in Great Britain was intense. Mr. Fox, who was then minister, said in his place in parliament, "The conduct of Prussia is a union of every thing that is contemptible in servility with every thing that is odious in rapacity."[1]

[1] Parliamentary Debates, vi. 891.

CHAPTER VI.

PRUSSIA OVERWHELMED.

LOUISA, the Queen of Prussia, was, intellectually, far the superior of her husband. She saw clearly that the principles of the French Revolution, organized in the empire of France, if unchecked, would inevitably undermine the Prussian and all other feudal thrones. The war-party in Berlin, with the queen and Prince Louis at its head, were unmeasured in their vituperation of this alliance with France. Their remonstrances, however, were of no avail.

The annexation of Hanover to Prussia gave to that kingdom an increase of territory amounting to fourteen thousand eight hundred square miles (equal to about twice the State of Massachusetts), and increased the population by over a million. The course, however, which Prussia pursued, was so vacillating, that "all sincere friendship had become impossible between Prussia and France. Prussia was regarded as a suspected power, whose hollow friendship had ceased to have any value." [1]

England was greatly exasperated. The Prussian harbors were immediately declared in a state of blockade,

---

[1] Bignon, Histoire de France, t. v. p. 223.

and an embargo laid upon all vessels of that nation in the British harbors.

"An order of council," writes Alison, "was soon after issued, authorizing the seizure of all vessels navigating under Prussian colors. And such was the effect of these measures, that the Prussian flag was instantly swept from the ocean; and, before many weeks had elapsed, four hundred of its merchant-vessels had found their way into the harbors of Great Britain." [1]

Queen Louisa and Prince Louis were still consecrating all their energies to bring Prussia into co-operation with England, Russia, and Austria, in antagonism to the principles of the French Revolution, which were now being borne widely through Europe on the imperial banners. Suddenly Prussia changed front, renounced the alliance with France, and commenced vigorous hostilities against the French Empire. We give the reasons for this change as expressed by Sir Archibald Alison:—

1. France had overturned the constitution of the Germanic Empire, and, by the newly-formed confederation of the Rhine, had made Germany essentially tributary to the French Empire.

2. The Queen and Prince Louis did not appeal in vain to the patriotic spirit of the nation. "The inhabitants of that monarchy, clear-sighted and intelligent beyond almost any other, as well as enthusiastic and brave, perceived distinctly the gulf into which they were about to fall. One universal cry of indignation burst forth from all ranks. The young officers loudly demanded to be led to the combat: the elder spoke of the glories of Frederick and of Rosbach. An irresistible current swept away the whole nation.

[1] Alison, vol. ii. p. 425.

"3. But all these causes of complaint, serious as they were, sank into insignificance compared to that which arose when it was discovered by M. Lucchesini, the Prussian ambassador at Paris, that France had entered into negotiations with England, on the footing of the restitution of Hanover to its lawful sovereign; that, while continually urging the cabinet at Berlin to look for indemnities for such a loss on the side of Pomerania, Napoleon had engaged to Russia to prevent them from depriving the King of Sweden of any part of his German dominions; and that, while still professing sentiments of amity and friendship to Frederick William, he had offered to throw no obstacles in the way of the re-establishment of the kingdom of Poland, including the whole of Polish Prussia, in favor of the Grand Duke Constantine.

"Irritated beyond endurance by such a succession of insults, and anxious to regain the place which he was conscious he had lost in the estimation of Europe, the King of Prussia put his armies on a war-footing; despatched M. Krusemark to St. Petersburg, and M. Lacobi to London, to endeavor to effect a reconciliation with these powers; opened the navigation of the Elbe; concluded his difficulties with the King of Sweden; and caused his troops to defile in the direction of Leipsic.

"The torrent of public indignation at Berlin became irresistible. The war-party overwhelmed all opposition. In the general tumult, 'the still small voice' of reason, which counselled caution and preparation in the outset of so great an enterprise, was overtossed. Prince Louis and his confederates openly boasted, that Prussia, strong in the recollection of the great Frederick and the discipline he had bequeathed to his followers, was able, single-handed, to strike down the conqueror of Europe. Warlike and patriotic songs resounded, amidst thunders of applause, at the theatres; and the queen roused the general enthusiasm to the highest pitch by displaying her beautiful figure on horseback in the streets of Berlin, at the head of the regiment of hussars, in the uniform of the corps."[1]

The Prussian armies, numbering two hundred thousand, entered the heart of Saxony. Frederick William compelled the King of Saxony to join the alliance. "Our cause," he said, "is the common cause of legitimate kings. All such must aid in the enterprise."

The young emperor, Alexander of Russia, anxious to efface the stain of Austerlitz, was hastening by forced marches over the wilds of Poland, with two hundred thousand veteran troops in his train. The invincible fleet of England crowded the shores of the Mediterranean and of the Channel.

At midnight on the 24th of September, 1806, Napoleon entered his carriage at the Tuileries to join his army in the Valley of the Rhine. In his parting message to the senate, he said, "In so just a war, which we have not provoked by any act, by any pretence, the true cause of which it would be impossible to assign, and where we only take arms to defend ourselves, we depend entirely upon the support of the laws, and upon that of the people, whom circumstances call upon to give fresh proofs of their devotion and courage."

"Napoleon," says Alison, "had no gallantry or chivalrous feeling in his breast. In his first bulletin he wrote, 'The Queen of Prussia is in the army, dressed

---

[1] Alison, vol. ii. p. 428.

as an Amazon, bearing the uniform of the regiment of dragoons, writing twenty letters a day to spread the conflagration in all directions. We seem to behold Armida in her madness, setting fire to her own palace. After her follows Prince Louis of Prussia, a young prince full of bravery and courage, hurried on by the spirit of party, who flatters himself he shall find a great renown in the vicissitudes of war. Following the examples of these illustrious persons, all the court cries, 'To arms!' but when war shall have reached them, with all its horrors, all will seek to exculpate themselves from having been instrumental in bringing its thunders to the peaceful plains of the North.'

"Such," continues Sir Archibald Alison, "was the language in which Napoleon spoke of the most beautiful princess in Europe."

By skilful manœuvres, the whole French army, in a few days, having crossed the Rhine, were thrown into the rear of the Prussians, thus cutting off all their supplies. Victory seemed no longer doubtful. Under these circumstances, the emperor wrote as follows to Frederick William:—

"Sire, I am now in the heart of Saxony. Believe me, my strength is such, that your forces cannot long balance the victory. But wherefore shed so much blood? to what purpose? Why should we make our subjects slay each other? I do not prize a victory which is purchased by the lives of so many of my children. If I were just commencing my military career, and if I had any reason to fear the chances of war, this language would be wholly misplaced. Sire, your Majesty will be vanquished: you will have compromised the repose of your life and the existence of your subjects, without the shadow of a pretext. At present you are uninjured, and may treat with me in a manner conformable with your rank. Before a month has passed, you will treat, but in a different position. I am aware that I may, in thus writing, irritate that sensibility which belongs to every sovereign; but circumstances demand that I should use no concealment. I implore your Majesty to view in this letter nothing but the desire I have to spare the effusion of human blood. Sire, my brother, I pray God that he may have you in his worthy and holy keeping. Your Majesty's good brother, "NAPOLEON."

"Finding affairs," writes Alison, "in a situation so much more favorable than he could have anticipated, Napoleon, to gain additional time to complete the encircling of his antagonist, despatched an officer of his household with proposals of peace to Frederick William." Whatever may have been the motives which dictated the pacific overture, no reply was returned to the letter. Though the despatch was intrusted to a Prussian officer, it is said that the king did not receive it until the morning of the battle of Jena.

On the morning of the 14th of October, the two hostile armies met, face to face, on the plains of Jena and Auerstadt. The two battle-fields were at the distance of but a few miles from each other. On each side the soldiers were equally brave, equally inured to war, and were led by able generals. Immediately there was commenced one of the most awful storms of battle which has ever desolated this globe. For eight hours the struggle continued, with the summoning of all possible human energies. About mid-day, the

Prussian commander felt sanguine of victory. He despatched the following order to one of his generals:—

"Send all the force you can to the chief point of attack. At this moment, we beat the enemy at all points. My cavalry has captured some of his cannon."

A few hours later, the whole aspect of the field was changed. The tide of disaster was surging in upon the Prussian general from all directions. The following almost frantic despatch was sent to his reserve:—

"Lose not a moment in advancing with your yet unbroken troops. Arrange your columns so that through their openings there may pass the broken bands of the battle. Be ready to receive the charges of the enemy's cavalry, which in the most furious manner rides on, overwhelms and sabres the fugitives, and has driven into one confused mass the infantry, cavalry, and artillery."

Night came. The Prussian army was destroyed. It was no longer a battle, but a massacre. All order was lost, as the Prussians, a rabble rout, fled like an inundation from the field. The king himself narrowly escaped being made prisoner. In the gloom of night, and almost alone, he leaped hedges and fences, and plunged through field and forest, to effect his escape. Prince Louis fell in one of the conflicts which ushered in the great battle, his head being split open by a sabre blow.

The Prussians lost, during this disastrous day, twenty thousand in killed and wounded; and twenty thousand were taken prisoners. In nothing was the military genius of Napoleon more conspicuous than in the vigor and ability with which he pursued a vanquished foe.

In less than fourteen days, every remnant of the Prussian army was taken, and all the fortresses of Prussia were in the hands of the French.

Frederick William III. fled to the confines of Russia to seek protection behind the bayonets of the troops of Alexander.

Prussia was struck as by a thunderbolt. The history of the world presents no other example of such a power being so speedily and so utterly destroyed. In one month after the emperor left the Tuileries, the feat was accomplished. An army of two hundred thousand men was killed, captured, or dispersed. Fortresses hitherto deemed impregnable had been compelled to capitulate. Napoleon was reposing in the palace of the Prussian king at Berlin, while the French army was encamped in the streets and squares of the city. Prussia was a captive in the hands of France, bound hand and foot.

By what is called the right of conquest, Prussia now belonged to France. Monarchical Europe heard these tidings with amazement and dismay.

Wherever the French army appeared, it was the propagator of the revolutionary doctrines of "equal rights for all men." Every soldier in the ranks was animated by the conviction, that all the avenues of honor and of wealth were open before him; that merit, not birth, was the passport to distinction. Many of the Prussian officers appreciated the tremendous power with which the doctrine of equality invested the French soldier.

One of them wrote, in a letter which was intercepted, "The French, in the fire, become supernatural beings: they are urged on by an inexpressible ardor, not a trace of which is to be discovered in our soldiers. What can be done with peasants who are led into battle by nobles to encounter every peril, and yet have no share in the honors or rewards?"

The King of Saxony, as we have mentioned, had been compelled to join Prussia against France. Such is the fate of the minor powers. Immediately after the great battle, the emperor assembled the Saxon officers in one of the halls of the University of Jena.

"I know not why," he said to them, "I am at war with your sovereign. He is a wise, pacific prince, deserving of respect. I wish to see your country rescued from its humiliating dependence upon Prussia. Why should the Saxons and the French, with no motives for hostility, fight against each other? I am ready, on my part, to give you a pledge of my amicable disposition, by setting you all at liberty, and by sparing Saxony. All I require of you is, no more to bear arms against France."

The officers, with many expressions of gratitude, departed for Dresden; and Saxony immediately withdrew from the coalition. But the armies of Russia, two hundred thousand strong, rapidly advancing, were still to be encountered.

"It was shortly after having detached Saxony from the Prussian, and united it to his own alliance, that Napoleon received an answer from the King of Prussia to the illusory proposals of accommodation made by him before the battle of Jena, and which that unhappy monarch easily caught at after that disaster, as the only light which seemed to break upon his sinking fortunes."[1]

[1] Alison, vol. ii. p. 455.

The emperor replied, that he had then no time to negotiate upon the terms of a final peace; that the campaign was but just begun, and that he must await its issue. He, however, entered into an armistice with a foe who was disarmed and bound, and entirely at his mercy.

The French army then pressed forward, through December storms, for the banks of the Vistula. There they encamped for the winter. On the 7th of February, 1807, the terrible battle of Eylau was fought. Immediately after this great victory, the French emperor wrote to the King of Prussia as follows: —

"I desire to put a period to the misfortunes of your family, and to organize, as speedily as possible, the Prussian monarchy. Its intermediate power is necessary for the tranquillity of Europe. I desire peace with Russia; and, provided the cabinet of St. Petersburg has no designs upon Turkey, I see no difficulty in obtaining it. Peace with England is not less essential with all nations. I shall have no hesitation in sending a minister to Memel, to take part in a conference of France, Sweden, England, Russia, Prussia, and Turkey; but as such a congress may last many years, which would not suit the present condition of Prussia, your Majesty therefore will, I am persuaded, be of opinion, that I have taken the simplest method, and one which is most likely to secure the prosperity of your subjects. At all events, I entreat your Majesty to believe in my sincere desire to re-establish amicable relations with Russia and England."

These overtures the allies peremptorily rejected. The King of Sweden wrote to the King of Prussia, —

"I think that a public declaration should be made in

favor of the legitimate cause of the Bourbons by openly espousing their interests, which is plainly that of all established governments. My opinion on this point is fixed and unalterable." [1]

In reference to these proposals of peace made by the Emperor of the French, Alison says that the Russian general strongly advised Frederick William not to treat. He urged, that the fact of Napoleon proposing an armistice, after so doubtful a battle as that of Eylau, was the best evidence that it was not for the interest of the allies to grant it. Napoleon, being thus foiled in his endeavors to arrest the war by negotiation, gathered up his strength to conquer a peace with his sword.

Scarcely had the snows of winter begun to melt, ere the French army commenced its march northward from the banks of the Vistula to the Banks of the Niemen. A campaign of ten days, which culminated in the great French victory of Friedland, secured the following results: —

The French took one hundred and twenty pieces of cannon, seven colors, and killed, wounded, or captured sixty thousand Russians. They took from the hostile army all its magazines, its hospitals, its ambulances, the fortress of Königsberg, with three hundred vessels which were in that port, laden with all kinds of military stores, and one hundred thousand muskets, which England was sending to the aid of the Russians.[2]

Frederick William was with Alexander at the time of this terrible defeat of the Russian arms. The conference at Tilsit, between the Emperor of France and the Emperor of Russia, ensued.

[1] Mémoires d'un Homme d'État (Prince Hardenberg), t. ix. p. 396.
[2] Bignon, Histoire de France depuis le 18me Brumaire, t. vi. p. 311.

"France," says Alison, "had nothing to demand of Russia, except that she should close her ports against England; Russia nothing to ask of France, but that she should withdraw her armies from Poland, and permit the emperor to pursue his long-cherished projects of conquest in Turkey."[1]

The two emperors speedily agreed upon terms of peace. The poor King of Prussia was quite disregarded in these arrangements.

"The King of Prussia arrived two days after in Tilsit, with his beautiful and unfortunate queen, and the ministers on both sides,—Talleyrand on the part of France, and Marshal Kalkreuth on that of Prussia. But they were of little service; for such was the extraordinary length to which the intimacy of the two emperors had gone, that not only did they invariably dine and pass the evening together, but almost all the morning conferences, during which the destinies of the world were arranged, were conducted by them in person."[2]

"Had the Queen of Prussia arrived earlier at our conferences," says Napoleon, "it might have had much influence upon the result of our negotiations; but, happily, she did not make her appearance till all was settled. As soon as she arrived, I went to pay her a visit. She was very beautiful, but somewhat past the first flower of youth. She received me in despair, exclaiming, 'Justice, justice!' and throwing herself back with loud lamentations. I at length prevailed on her to take a seat; but she continued, nevertheless, her pathetic entreaties.

[1] Alison, vol. ii. p. 541.
[2] Mémoires de Savary, Duke of Rovigo, t. iii. p. 77.

"'Prussia,' said she, 'was blinded in regard to her power. She ventured to enter the lists with a hero, oppose herself to the destinies of France, and neglect its fortunate friendship. She has been severely punished for her folly. The glory of the great Frederick, the halo his name spread round our arms, had inflated the heart of Prussia. They have caused her ruin.'

"Magdeburg," continues the emperor, "was the object of her entreaties; and when Napoleon, before dinner, presented her with a beautiful rose, she at first refused it, but immediately after took it with a smile, adding, 'At least with Magdeburg.'

"'I must observe to your Majesty,' replied the emperor, 'that it is I who give, and you only who must receive.'

"The Queen of Prussia," Napoleon continues, "unquestionably possessed talents, great information, and singular acquaintance with affairs. She was the real sovereign for fifteen years. In truth, in spite of my address and utmost efforts, she constantly led the conversation, returned at pleasure to her subject, and directed it as she chose, but with so much tact and delicacy, that it was impossible to take offence."[1]

The Queen of Prussia was most bitterly disappointed at the terms of the treaty which her husband felt constrained to sign. The losses of Prussia, by this treaty, were enormous. Frederick William had about one-half his kingdom restored to him. The portion which Prussia had wrested from Poland was organized into a Polish state, called the Duchy of Warsaw. The provinces of Prussia upon the left bank of the Elbe were formed

[1] Napoleon at St. Helena, by John S. C. Abbott, pp. 271, 272.

into the kingdom of Westphalia. The kingdom of Prussia was reduced from about nine million of inhabitants to about five millions. Her revenue of twenty-four million dollars was diminished to fourteen million dollars. The fortresses left her, whether in Silesia or on the Oder, remained in the hands of France as security for the payment of the war-contributions.[1]

"At the same time," writes Alison, "enormous contributions, amounting to the stupendous, and, if not proved by authentic documents, the incredible sum of twenty millions sterling, were imposed on the countries which had been the seat of war between the Rhine and the Niemen. This grievous exaction completely paralyzed the strength of Prussia, and rendered her, for the next five years, totally incapable of extricating herself from that iron net in which she was enveloped by the continued occupation of her fortresses by the French troops."[2]

[1] Bignon's Histoire de France, t. vi. p. 35.   [2] Alison, vol. ii. p. 547.

CHAPTER VII.

FREDERICK WILLIAM III. AND THE NEW COALITION.

FREDERICK WILLIAM of Prussia, though of moderate abilities, seems to have been an honest and humane man. The following touching proclamation, which he issued to the inhabitants of his lost provinces, won for him the esteem of every generous heart in Europe: —

"Dear inhabitants of faithful provinces, districts, and towns, my arms have been unfortunate. Driven to the extreme boundaries of my empire, and having my powerful ally conclude an armistice, and sign a peace, no choice remained to me but to follow his example. That peace imposed on me the most painful sacrifices. The bonds of treaties, the reciprocal ties of love and duty, the fruit of ages of labor, have been broken asunder. All my efforts (and they have been most strenuous) have proved in vain. Fate ordains it. A father is compelled to depart from his children. I hereby release you from your allegiance to me and my house. My most ardent prayers for your welfare will always attend you in your relations to your new sovereigns. Be to them what you have ever been to me.

Neither force nor fate shall ever sever the remembrance of you from my heart." [1]

The grief of the unhappy Queen of Prussia wore so heavily upon her spirits, that she soon sank into the grave, when but thirty-nine years of age. She, above all others, had instigated the war; and she could not brook the ruin which she had thus brought upon her country and her house. Her life was indeed a sad one, full of trouble. Her virtues were her own: her faults were to be attributed to her education and the times.

The kingdom of Frederick the Great had apparently met with an irreparable blow; but the king, Frederick William III., instead of sinking in despair, nobly roused himself to additional exertions to develop the wealth and resources of his diminished realms. The calamity which had befallen Prussia, in the end proved a blessing. A new era of freedom and equality dawned upon the realm, which had hitherto been governed by absolute power.

The illustrious Baron Stein, in the retirement of his estates, had pondered the great questions which were now agitating Europe. His mind, greatly liberalized, had become deeply convinced of the necessity of political reform. Upon being appointed minister of the interior, he issued an ordinance, conferring upon peasants and burghers the right, hitherto confined to the nobles, of acquiring and holding landed property. The nobles, in their turn, were permitted, without losing caste, to engage in pursuits of commerce and industry. Every species of slavery and of feudal servitude was forever abolished. The inhabitants of cities were allowed to choose councillors, who should regulate all

[1] Scott's Napoleon.

local and municipal concerns. Thus the disasters which Prussia had encountered led her to relax the fetters of the feudal system, and vigorously to commence the introduction of republican reforms.[1]

Gen. Scharnhorst was appointed minister of war. "In him," says Alison, "a blameless life and amiable manners were combined with the purest patriotism and the soundest judgment. Exalted attainments were undisfigured by pride."

Gen. Scharnhorst, following the admirable example of Baron Stein, threw open to the common soldiers the higher offices of the army, from which they had hitherto been excluded. He abolished those degrading corporal punishments under which the self-respect of the soldier had wilted. He also abolished those invidious distinctions, which, by exempting the aristocratic classes from the burden of military service, caused its weight to fall more severely upon those who were not relieved.

By the engagements with France, it was stipulated that Prussia should not keep on foot an army of more than forty-two thousand men. The letter of this agreement was kept, while its spirit was evaded, by never having more than the agreed number at once in arms. The young recruits, having been thoroughly drilled, were sent to their homes; and others took their places: thus, while but forty thousand were enrolled, there were soon more than two hundred thousand thoroughly trained to arms.

In the year 1812, Napoleon commenced his fatal campaign to Moscow. The latter part of December,

---

[1] Mémoires d'un Homme d'État (Prince Hardenberg), t. ix. p. 400.

the tidings of the utter disaster which had overwhelmed the French armies reached Berlin. The opponents of the French alliance, still numerous in Prussia, were clamorous for a general uprising, to attack the French in the disorder, the misery, and the helplessness of their retreat; but the king, and his able minister Hardenberg, remained faithful to their treaty-obligations. Great anxiety was felt in Paris in consequence of the past fickleness of Prussia: but Augereau, the French minister at Berlin, wrote to the French Government, that France had no cause for anxiety; that the Berlin cabinet would remain firm to the French alliance.[1]

Still the opponents of France were unwearied in their endeavors to change the policy of the government, and enter into an alliance with Russia. One of the Prussian generals, De York, treacherously entered into a secret treaty with a Russian general to do nothing to oppose the advance of the Russian troops in their pursuit of the French. He excused himself for this act of perfidy by the declaration that the French were so utterly routed, and his own forces so weak, that in this way only could he save his army-corps from destruction. In a despatch to the King of Prussia, he stated, —

"Now or never is the time for your Majesty to extricate yourself from the thraldom of an ally whose intentions in regard to Prussia are veiled in impenetrable darkness, and justify the most serious alarm. That consideration has guided me: God grant it may be for the salvation of the country!"[2]

[1] Augereau to Berthier, Dec. 22, 1812.
[2] Baron Fain, Campagne de 1814, t. ii. p. 209.

"Never," writes Alison, "was a monarch more embarrassed by a step on the part of a lieutenant than the King of Prussia was on this occasion. His first words were, 'Here is enough to give one a stroke of apoplexy.' Deeply impressed with the sanctity of his existing treaties with France, and feeling, as every man of honor would, that the obligation to maintain them inviolate was only rendered the more stringent by the disasters which had overwhelmed the imperial armies, he saw clearly that the agitation in his dominions was such, that it was not improbable that the people would ere long take the matter into their own hands, and, whatever the government might do, join the Russians as soon as they advanced into the Prussian territory."[1]

Oppressed by these embarrassments, the king remained faithful to his treaty-obligations. Gen. De York was ordered under arrest. His command of fifteen thousand men was conferred on Gen. Kleist, who was ordered to take his contingent as rapidly as possible to the aid of the retreating French. At the same time, Prince Hardenberg submitted to the French ambassador at Berlin, with the approval of the king, a proposal to consolidate the union between Prussia and France by the marriage of the Prince Royal of Prussia with a princess of the family of the French emperor. Frederick William engaged, under these circumstances, to raise the Prussian contingent in the service of France to sixty thousand men.[2]

Frederick William wrote to the French minister, the Duke of Bassano, on the 12th of January, 1813, —

"Tell the emperor, that, as to pecuniary sacrifices,

---

[1] Alison, iv. 40.   [2] Baron Fain, Campagne de 1814, t. i. p. 207.

they are no longer in my power; but that, if he will give me money, I can raise and arm fifty thousand or sixty thousand men for his service. I am the natural ally of France. By changing my system of policy, I should only endanger my position, and give the emperor grounds for treating me as an enemy. I know there are fools who regard France as struck down; but you will soon see it present an army of three hundred thousand men as brilliant as the former." [1]

Early in January, 1813, the Russian armies, pursuing the retreating French, entered the Prussian territory. Proclamations were scattered broadcast, urging the inhabitants of Prussia to rise, and join in the war against France. The Russians rapidly took possession of the fortresses of Prussia. On the 4th of March, the advance guard of Cossacks entered Berlin; and, on the 11th, Berlin became the headquarters of the Russian army. Still the Prussian monarch, who had retired to Breslau, remained firm in his allegiance to France.

On the 15th of May, 1813, the Prussian minister, Hardenberg, wrote to the French minister, St. Marsau, —

"The system of the king has undergone no alteration. No overtures, direct or indirect, have been made to Russia. If the emperor approves the steps which have been taken to secure the neutrality of Silesia, and will grant some pecuniary assistance to Prussia, the alliance could be contracted more closely than ever. Nothing but despair will throw Prussia into the arms of Russia." [2]

"There can be no doubt," writes Alison, "that these protestations on the part of the Prussian monarch were

---

[1] Baron Fain, t. i. p. 213. [2] Mémoires d'un Homme d'État, t. xii. p. 32.

sincere; and that it only lay with Napoleon, by giving him some pecuniary assistance, to secure the cabinet of Berlin in the French alliance, and gain an auxiliary force of sixty thousand men to aid him in defending the course of the Elbe."[1]

But it was obvious to the emperor, that Prussia, overrun by the triumphant armies of Russia, would be compelled to join in the coalition against France. He judged correctly. The anti-French party, sustained by the Russian armies, rapidly increased in influence. Secret negotiations were opened between them and the Russian general. At length a treaty was formed, called the "Treaty of Kalisch," to which Frederick William was induced, with great difficulty, to give his assent.

By this treaty, an alliance, "offensive and defensive," was formed between the Emperor of Russia and the King of Prussia to prosecute the war with France. Prussia agreed to bring eighty thousand men into the field, independent of the garrisons in the fortresses. Neither party was to make peace without the consent of the other: jointly, they were to do every thing in their power to induce Austria to join the alliance, and to induce England to afford pecuniary aid to Prussia. The Emperor of Russia engaged never to lay down his arms until all the possessions wrested from Prussia in the campaigns of Jena and Auerstadt were restored. The treaty was to be kept secret from France for two months, while privately communicated to England, Austria, and Sweden.[2]

"Frederick William," writes Alison, "who was only brought to accede to this treaty with the utmost diffi-

[1] Alison, vol. iv. p. 45.
[2] Martin's Collections de Traité de Pays, sup. iii. 284.

culty, was well aware that his political existence was thenceforth bound up in the success of Russia in the German war. His first words, after agreeing to the alliance, were, 'Henceforth, gentlemen, it is an affair of life and death.' Great pains, accordingly, were taken to conceal the treaty from the knowledge of the French ambassador: but, notwithstanding every effort, its existence soon transpired; and it was thought unnecessary to dissemble any longer. The French Government, informed of these facts, which were not unexpected, replied to the Prussian minister, —

"'As long as the chances of war were favorable to us, your court remained faithful to its engagements; but scarcely had the premature rigors of winter brought back our armies to the Niemen than the defection of Gen. De York excited the most serious suspicions. His Majesty the Emperor of France prefers an open enemy to an ally always ready to abandon him. A power whose treaties are considered binding only so long as they are deemed serviceable can never be either useful or respectable. The finger of Providence is manifest in the events of last winter. It has produced them, to distinguish the true from the false friends of humanity. His Majesty feels for your situation, M. Baron, as a soldier and a man of honor, on being obliged to sign such a declaration.'"[1]

The Emperor of France, speaking upon this subject at St. Helena, said, —

"The King of Prussia, in his private character, is a good, loyal, and honorable man; but, in his political capacity, he was unavoidably forced to yield to necessity.

[1] Baron Fain, t. i. p. 260.

You were always the master with him when you had force on your side, and the hand uplifted."[1]

Frederick William issued a proclamation, informing his subjects, that, if they would volunteer their services, he would, as a reward, confer upon them a constitution securing to them many civil rights.[2] Universal enthusiasm pervaded the nation. In the terrible conflict which ensued, the Prussian troops took a conspicuous part.

At Waterloo, it was the appearance of Blucher with sixty-five thousand Prussians, late in the day, upon the field, which secured the victory of the allies, the overthrow of the French Empire, and the re-establishment in France of the old *régime* of the Bourbons.

"It is almost certain," says Gen. Jomini, "that Napoleon would have remained master of the field of battle, but for the arrival of sixty-five thousand Prussians in his rear."

The Prussian army returned in triumph to Berlin. And now the people demanded the promised constitution; but the Emperor of Austria interposed.

"I cannot allow," he said, "free institutions so near my throne. They will excite disaffection among my subjects. I shall therefore consider the granting of a constitution as a declaration of war against me."

The Emperor of Russia also issued an equally imperative remonstrance. Thus the king forfeited his pledge, being unable to redeem it without involving his kingdom in a desolating and hopeless war.

When the allies met at Vienna to partition out

---

[1] Las Casas, ii. 305.
[2] "This was a gigantic contest; for his enemies, by deceiving their subjects with false promises of liberty, had brought whole nations against him." — *Napier's War in the Peninsula*, vol. iv. p. 205.

Europe among them, they were not generous in their treatment of Prussia. Though the kingdom was considerably enlarged, the treaties of 1815 did not give compactness to her irregular territory. The kingdom was divided into two very unequal parts, — the eastern and the western, — separated by the German States of Hesse, Hanover, and Brunswick. With but a third of the population of France, Prussia had seven hundred miles more of frontier to guard. One extremity of Prussia reached the walls of the French fortress of Thionville, on the Moselle, far west from the Rhine; while the other extremity was bordered by the Memel and the Niemen. There were, in reality, three Prussias, — one in Poland, one in Germany, and one on the Rhine.[1]

After these terrible convulsions, Europe, exhausted, enjoyed repose for many years. Nothing occurred in Prussia particularly calling for historic notice. In the year 1840, Frederick William III. died, in the sixty-sixth year of his age. His reign was long, exceedingly disastrous at its commencement; and though, at its close, he left Prussia apparently prosperous and happy, the fires of approaching revolution were slumbering beneath the surface.

The sceptre passed to the king's son, Frederick William IV. To the surprise and consternation of the king and court, at the time of his coronation, the Prussian diet passed a motion, by a majority of ninety to five, requesting the king to grant a new law for the organization of the provincial diets, by which *the national representation should be chosen by the people*, in accordance with the royal declaration of 1815, which had never yet been fulfilled.

---

[1] Encyclopædia Americana.

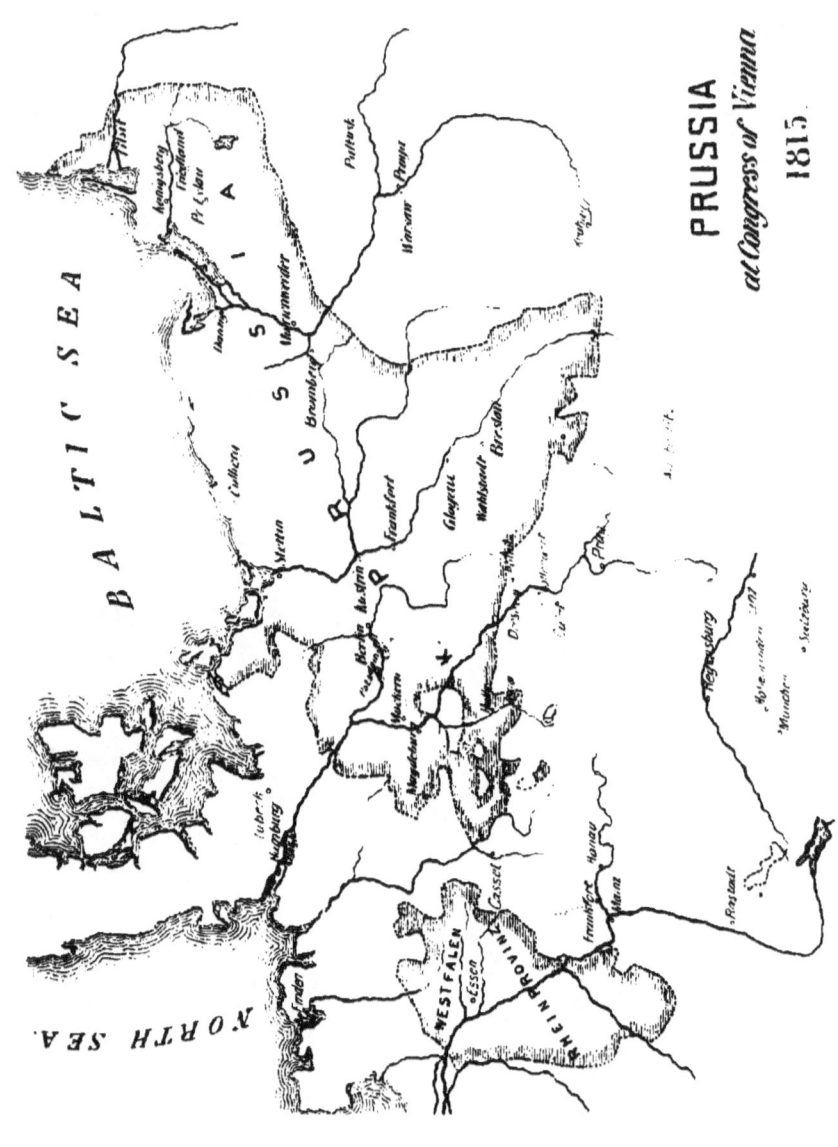

After an embarrassing delay, the king declared that "he would never consent to a general popular representation, but that he would pursue a course in accordance with historical progress, and suited to German nationality." [1]

Republican principles were now bursting forth in all directions throughout the kingdom of Prussia. There were loud demands that the censorship of the press should be abolished, that a general parliament of the whole kingdom should be convoked, and that there should be publicity of debates. This fermentation of liberty was peculiarly active in the Rhine provinces. There was now a steady, constant struggle for many years, without revolutionary violence, — on the part of the people for reform, and on the part of the court to check the progress of liberal ideas.

At length, in the year 1847, the demand for a representative government had become so loud and universal, that the royal cabinet could no longer venture to resist. On the 3d of February an edict was issued, convoking a general assembly of the States of Prussia. This was an immense step in the path of popular liberty. But still the spirit of the court was manifest in the royal speech at the opening of the assembly.

"I have convoked this assembly," said the king, "to make myself acquainted with the wants of the people; but the government will not be changed in its essence. The absolute monarchy has only become *consulting*. I do not deem it for the interest of my people to adopt a proper representative government. I consider it my duty to resist the levelling and innovating spirit of the

---

[1] Annual History, vol. xxiii. p. 422.

age. I will never permit a charter to intervene between me and the duty I owe my people. I will never yield to the rule of majorities, and will resist to the last extremity the ruinous democratic designs which are the disgrace and peril of the age." [1]

A stormy debate, of course, followed these bold declarations. There were three hundred and fifty-three members of the assembly. Even in this body, the royal party — that is, the party in favor of absolute government — was so strong, that only by a majority of fifty-three could a vote be carried in favor of a constitution. Germany consisted of a conglomeration of a large number of States, consisting of kingdoms, electorates, duchies, and principalities. Each State was independent in the regulation of its local affairs, but bound in offensive and defensive alliance with the great confederation. Austria had long been the predominating power in this league. Though the crown of the Germanic Empire was elective, it had for some time been almost hereditary in the royal family of Austria. Prussia had become exceedingly jealous of the domination of Austria.

A party had arisen in Germany, as in Italy, calling for unity. Germany contained a population of forty million inhabitants, and had two thousand walled cities. It was affirmed, that, by concentration and unity like that which existed in France and Russia, Germany might become the controlling power in Europe. There were many leading minds in Prussia in favor of this unification, hoping by diplomatic intrigue to secure the imperial crown of United Germany for the King of Prussia.

[1] Annual History, vol. xxx. p. 325.

On the 18th of March, 1848, Frederick William IV. issued a royal proclamation, in which he said, —

"Above all, we demand that Germany shall be transformed from a confederation of States into *one federal State*. We demand a general military system for Germany; and we will endeavor to form it after that model under which our Prussian armies reaped such unfading laurels in the War of Independence. We demand that the German army be assembled under one single federal banner; and we hope to see a federal commander-in-chief at its head," &c.

This remarkable document placed the King of Prussia at the head of the party in favor of German unity, which was then considered the liberal or popular party. Austria was by no means disposed thus to yield her supremacy. The ultra democrats of the liberal party regarded this movement of the Prussian king as a mere feint to gain power which he would wield against them.

On the evening of March 19, 1848, — the day after the issuing of the proclamation, — there was an immense gathering of the populace in King Street, opposite the palace, in Berlin, to testify their gratitude to the monarch who had thus apparently espoused their cause. When the king appeared upon the balcony, the sky was rent with their acclamations.

A squadron of cavalry and a body of infantry were drawn up under the windows of the palace to preserve order. The disaffected party wished to provoke the hostility of the people against the government by exciting a collision between the citizens and the royal troops. With this design, in the midst of the tumult caused by the immense gathering, some pistol-shots were fired at the troops; and an eager party commenced throwing up barricades.

The cavalry, without drawing their swords or making a charge, moved their horses forward, upon the walk only, to clear the square. Either by design or accident, two muskets were discharged from the ranks of the infantry into the retreating mass of the populace. The response was a general discharge of fire-arms upon the soldiers from numerous insurgents who had come prepared for that purpose.

The insurrection proved to be very formidable. The students of the university, as brave as they were intelligent, were at its head. A battalion of the guard soon joined them.

" The cavalry now drew their sabres, and charged the mob in good earnest. A sanguinary conflict ensued; for the insurgents had among them a great number of old soldiers as well trained to arms as the royal troops, and the students combated with the utmost resolution. The conflict continued until nightfall, and even long after it had become dark, by the light of the burning houses, several of which were broken into, and, after being sacked, were set on fire by the inhabitants.

" Overwhelmed with terror at this calamitous event, which cost sixty persons their lives, besides four times that number wounded, the king issued a proclamation, addressed to ' My beloved Berliners,' in which he expressed the utmost regret at the events which had occurred, and declared that the conflict had arisen from accident and the shots first fired from King Street."[1]

[1] Alison, vol. viii. p. 413.

The king was an ultra absolutist. His cabinet was in perfect sympathy with him in his hatred of popular liberty. The more intelligent of the liberal party understood full well that the king, in advocating German unity, sought only to consolidate the powers of despotism. He wished to become emperor of united Germany, that he might sway a sceptre of unrestrained power like that wielded by the Sultan of Turkey and the Czar of Russia. He could thus easily silence the clamors of the people for reform. But the king was greatly alarmed by the indication the insurrection gave of the most formidable opposition to his views. There was infinite danger that the *insurrection* would become *revolution* unless he instantly retraced his steps.

"The next morning, the king gave token of his submission by accepting the resignation of his whole ministers, who were immediately succeeded by a new cabinet, composed of known liberals.

"On the 20th, a general amnesty was proclaimed; and the whole persons in custody on account of the insurrection were liberated without bail; and two additional ministers were appointed, known to belong to the most advanced liberals. On the 22d, the bodies of the citizens who had been killed in the affray on the evening of the 18th were paraded with great pomp before the royal palace; and the king was obliged to submit to the humiliation of inclining his head before the lifeless remains of those who had perished under the sabres of his guards. At the same time, the king published a decree appointing a national guard in the capital, and ordered the royal troops to leave the city; and after riding through the streets in the German uniform, in the course of which he made repeated protestations of his anxious desire for German freedom, he issued two proclamations, in which he openly announced his intention of putting himself at the head of the restored and united German nation."[1]

[1] Alison, vol. iii. p. 413.

CHAPTER VIII.

STRUGGLES FOR LIBERTY.

IT is a great mistake to suppose, that, in the great conflicts which have agitated the monarchies of Europe, there has been a clearly-marked line of division between the oppressed people on the one side, and the despotic kings and courts on the other. The people have been in antagonism between themselves; and often the large majority have been in favor of the old feudal despotisms. The people in Prussia were thus divided. The Catholic party, which was quite numerous, and which embraced a large part of the peasantry, strongly opposed the liberal movement. The Poles were mostly in favor of it. As a general rule, the liberals, as they were called, were confined to the large towns. The peasantry were opposed to change.

While Prussia was in this state of agitation, the newly-appointed assembly met, on the 2d of April, to draw up a constitution. The king, in opening the assembly, said, —

"His Majesty has promised a real constitutional charter, and we are assembled to lay the foundation-stone of the edifice. We hope that the work will proceed rapidly, and that it will perfect a constitution *for the whole German race.*" The following were the fundamental principles of the constitution, presented by the king, and adopted by the assembly: —

1. Every householder twenty-four years of age was entitled to a vote for representation in the lower house.

2. Every five hundred voters could choose an elector.

3. Every householder thirty years of age was eligible as a deputy.

4. Two deputies were to be chosen by every sixty thousand inhabitants.

The king also promised to lay before them a bill providing for freedom of the press, personal liberty, the right of meeting and petitioning, the publicity of judicial proceedings, trial by jury, and equal civil and political rights for all persons.

These regulations referred to Prussia alone, and could bind no other State of Germany. Still the agitation in Prussia extended throughout all the German States.

The legislature was to consist of two houses. The first, or senate, was composed of the princes of the blood royal, and sixty peers appointed by the king; and also of one hundred and eighty members, to be chosen by the people. The dignity of the sixty peers was hereditary. The others were chosen for eight years. No commoner could be chosen who was not in receipt of an income of two thousand five hundred dollars.

The members of the lower house were to be elected for four years, and were subject to no property qualification. This constitution, though a great advance from the absolutism of the past, did by no means satisfy the democratic leaders. During the whole summer, there were excited gatherings of the people, and violent and inflammatory debates. There were mobs in the streets of Berlin, and many acts of violence were perpetrated.

Under these circumstances, the king resolved on very energetic repressive measures. Assuming the pretence of a general review of the royal forces, fifty thousand troops were assembled at Potsdam. Gen. von Wrangel, a very determined royalist, was appointed to command them. The review took place on the 22d of September, 1848. In an order of the day, the general thus addressed the troops: —

"The king has honored me with the highest proof of his confidence in giving me command of all the troops. I will establish order when it is disturbed. The troops are stanch, their swords are sharpened, and their muskets are loaded. It is not against you, men of Berlin, that this is done, but to protect you. Grass is growing in your streets. Your houses are empty. Your shops are full of goods, but void of purchasers. This must be changed; and it shall be changed. I swear it to you; and a Wrangel never yet failed in keeping his word."

The Burgher Guard, a body somewhat corresponding with our militia, were in sympathy with the people. Though this was the natural force to be called upon to preserve order in the city, it could not be relied upon by the king. In a discussion which took place upon the articles of the constitution, it was decided, by a vote of two hundred and seventeen to one hundred and thirty-four, that, in the title given to the king, the words, " by the grace of God," should be omitted. This was very distinctly announcing the democratic principle, that the king's sole title to the throne was the *will of the people*.

Nearly all branches of business were thrown into

confusion by these distractions and agitations. The chief manufactories were closed. Thousands were without employment and without bread. The assembly, chosen by popular suffrage, had a decided majority in favor of reform. This majority kept up a constant warfare against the king and court, confident of support, should it be needed, from the Burgher Guard and the populace at Berlin.

On the 31st of October, 1848, the assembly passed a resolution, "that all Prussians are equal before the law; that neither privileges, titles, nor rank, are to exist in the State; and that *the nobility are abolished.*" In fact, the democratic clubs now governed the assembly, controlling its measures by the menaces of the mob. "Not content with the majority which they already possessed in the assembly, the mob from without, with the avowed purpose of intimidating the conservative members, broke into its hall, amply provided with ropes, nails, and nooses, as a preparation for summary hanging."[1]

The king speedily developed the resolute measures he had decided to adopt. He dismissed his liberal ministry, and appointed, defiantly, an administration of the most decided conservatists. It was certain that a collision would soon occur. The king, having inaugurated the new ministry, sent in a royal decree to the assembly, stating that the insubordination in the streets of Berlin was such, that he transferred the sittings to Brandenburg.

A scene of fearful violence ensued. The monarchical party, fifty in number, withdrew with the president.

---

[1] Alison, vol. viii. p. 423.

The rest, in a state of intense excitement, passed a series of indignant remonstrances, and declared themselves in permanence. Thirty of the members remained in the house all night.

The next morning, as the members began to arrive, they found the building surrounded by royal troops, who were ordered to allow any one to go out, but none to go in. The Burgher Guard warmly espoused the cause of the assembly. The majority, two hundred and twenty-five in number, which remained after the withdrawal of the monarchical members, re-assembled, at an early hour next morning, in the hall of the Schützen Gild. Before daylight, a numerous body of the Burgher Guard, well armed, had met around that hall for the protection of the assembly.

The king immediately issued a proclamation, dissolving the Burgher Guard, and ordering them to give up their arms. No attention was paid to the order. The order was reiterated more peremptorily; thirty thousand royal troops were brought into the city; and Berlin was declared in a state of siege. As there were but fifteen thousand Burgher Guards, and the royal troops were incomparably better disciplined, the Guard dispersed, and a bloody contest was avoided.

The next day, the assembly again met in the Schützen Gildhall. An officer from Gen. Wrangel ordered them to disperse as an illegal assembly. "Never, till forced by arms!" was the cry of the assembly. The vice-president was in the chair. A body of soldiers entered. Four officers quietly lifted up the chair upon which the vice-president was seated, and carried it, with its occupant, into the street. The members followed in a state of great exasperation.

The assembly made several other efforts to meet; but it was always dispersed by the soldiery, without bloodshed. The months rolled on, fraught with intrigue, agitation, peril, and distress. The people, in their blindness, were often warring against their own interests. The court was struggling to retain the despotic power which had descended to it through the dreary ages.

Throughout all the States of Germany, there had been a struggle between the democratic and monarchical party in reference to the choice of the Emperor of the German Confederacy. The democrats wished to have any man of ability eligible: the monarchists wished to confine the choice to one of royal blood.

In the diet at Frankfort, in 1849, it was voted, by 258 to 211, that the choice should be limited to one of the ruling sovereigns of Germany. It was then moved that the imperial crown should be offered to the King of Prussia. After an exciting debate of eleven days upon this subject, it was announced, by a vote of 290 out of 558, that the King of Prussia was chosen emperor.

"The time was when this flattering offer would have been joyfully accepted; but time had worked many changes. The imperial crown, as now tendered, was very different from the imperial crown as originally coveted. Being elective, it more nearly resembled the presidency of America, or the empire of imperial Rome, than the old Germanic diadem.

"Austria had openly declared against the union of all the confederacy under one head; and there could be little doubt that the acceptance of the imperial crown by Frederick William would at once bring on a war with that power, backed by Russia, with whom she was now in closest alliance. Influenced by these considerations, the king determined to decline the proffered honor." [1]

The new constitution prepared by the general assembly at Frankfort was rejected by Austria, Bavaria, Hanover, and Saxony. It was, however, received by twenty-one of the lesser States of Northern Germany. These minor States concurred, by a collective vote, in an address to the King of Prussia, urging him to accept the proffered dignity.

All Germany was thrown into confusion by these discussions; and there were insurrections, which were only quelled by the sword. It was manifest that the constitution of Frankfort could not be accepted. The Kings of Prussia, Hanover, and Saxony, met, and drew up, with great precision, a constitution of a hundred and ninety articles. By this arrangement, the imperial crown was made hereditary in the Prussian monarchy. The liberals, in derision, called this the "Constitution of the Three Kings." Neither Austria nor Bavaria would accept it. Thus it failed.

While the King of Prussia was thus struggling to gain the ascendency in Germany, the spirit of revolution continued to agitate his kingdom. A new chamber of deputies was chosen, which consisted strongly of democrats. The representatives boldly declared themselves against the government. The challenge thus thrown down was accepted by the court. On the 29th of April, 1849, a circular was addressed by the Prussian cabinet to all the States of Germany. In this it was said, —

[1] Alison, vol. viii. p. 431.

"Prussia engages to oppose the revolutionary agitation of the times with the utmost energy, and promises to furnish the other governments with timely assistance for the same purpose. The danger is a common one. Prussia will not betray its mission to interfere, in the hour of peril, wherever and in any manner it may deem necessary. It is convinced that a limit must be put to the revolution of Germany. This cannot be effected by mere passive resistance: it must be done by active interference." [1]

Thus the King of Prussia endeavored to place himself at the head of the party opposed to reform; and thus he called upon all throughout Germany, who were in sympathy with his views, to rally to his support. He wished for a united Germany, that he might consolidate the powers of absolutism, and, with the tramp of his armies, crush out the revolutionary spirit. The liberals wished for a united Germany, that republican freedom might work in unison, and that their nation might be brought more in harmony with the United States of America.

The king invited a congress of all the German princes to meet in Berlin in May, 1849. Twenty-two of the minor princes came; but Austria, Bavaria, Wurtemberg, and Saxony declined the invitation. The assembly was a failure.

An American gentleman, who was in Berlin at that time, gives the following interesting account of the scenes which he witnessed. This was in 1848, when William I. was not yet king, but only crown prince, the king's brother. We give the narrative in his words, though abbreviated: —

[1] Annual Register, 1849, p. 840.

"The king, in those days, was his poor Majesty Clicquot, as he was called,—a man not without literary cultivation, of a great deal of maudlin sentimentality, and a prodigious capacity for drinking champagne; but champagne and political sentimentality were his bane and ruin. It was a great pity both for him and his country; but his Majesty was not respected.

"For many days, in Berlin, there had been thunder in the air. It was evident that something impended. The reading-rooms along the pleasant street, Unter den Linden, and all the *bier lokals*, were full of attentive students of the papers, who discussed the chances of events. At length, the final news came.[1] The first thing that we heard in Berlin was, that the government was ready, and had plenty of soldiers. Probably it knew the necessity: for the city had an air of suppressed excitement; and the feeling was such, that troops of the cavalry of the paternal government paraded the streets at night to help everybody keep quiet.

"But the amazing and sudden success of the revolution in France put all the crowned heads of Europe in a panic; and they began to make concessions to the people. It was pitiful to see, because it implied a kind of conscious robber relation between the rulers and the nations. The kings seemed like pirates who had been overtaken, and, in mortal terror at the probable consequences of their crimes, proposed to disgorge their plunder. They professed willingness to restore large shares of the treasures of liberty that they had stolen; and were evidently much more conscious, at that moment, of the power of the people, than of their 'God-given' authority. King

---

[1] The news of the revolution in France of 1848, rumors of which had already spread through all Europe, creating intense excitement.

Clicquot went with the rest, and promised well: there should be a constitution, and all the modern improvements, added to the political edifice of Prussia. There were optimists in those startling days, who thought that Europe was to be republicanized by the mere force of reason; and that kings were about gracefully to own themselves in the wrong, and to retire.

"But suddenly, one Saturday afternoon in Berlin, the mere force of reason gave way. The writer was dining with some student friends at the old Belvidere. While we were yet dining, anxious faces appeared; and we were told that trouble was brewing. A crowd of people had been to the royal palace to demand arms, and they had been refused. The revolution was coming: the tidal wave was even now lifting us. We all arose, and went out. A huge concourse of men was swiftly swarming from the palace into the broad street. As it passed along like a dark cloud, covering every thing with shadow, doors and windows were closed; and shop-keepers hurried to make all fast. Before the palace of the Prince of Prussia, his present Majesty King William, a carriage was standing; and, the moment the crowd had passed, the Princess of Prussia, the present queen, and a beautiful woman, came out with children, and stepped quickly into the carriage, which drove off rapidly toward the king's palace. The crowd swept on; and the leaders of revolution knew that the hour had come.

"As we strolled curiously along, we saw men with clubs and iron bars, hurrying by, evidently, to a rendezvous; and officers on horseback clattered through the streets, which all carriages had deserted. The leaders knew that no time could be safely lost; and by three o'clock barricades were rising in the chief streets that led into Unter den Linden. We turned into our room in the Friedrich Strasse, and at the same moment saw from the window that a crowd had brought the materials to build a barricade just beneath it.

"The barricade was soon built; and the sound of firing grew heavier and nearer. We heard the approach of soldiers advancing upon the barricade. At the same moment, the sloping roof of the house opposite the window began to heave, and was finally burst through by the iron bars of the insurgents, who, completely protected by the eaves from the fire of the soldiers in the street, could throw down upon them every kind of deadly missile. But the clear voice of the commanding officer ordered, loud enough for all on the neighboring houses to hear, that the troops should fire upon every person who appeared at a window; and he sent a detachment into the opposite house. The barricade was then assaulted and carried. But for hours the alarm-bells rang, and the sharp volleys of musketry rattled, and the dull heavy cannon thundered and shook the air. A great battle was going on in the city. The moon shone; the white clouds drifted through the sky; and there was no other sound than that of the bells, the muskets, and the cannon.

"The next day, the city was like a city that had been carried by assault. The soldiers had taken the barricades, and held the streets. But there was a universal feeling that the people were strong enough to bring King Clicquot to terms; and there was bitter hatred of the Prince of Prussia, who had counselled and directed the operations of the night. The king issued a sentimental proclamation to his *liebe Berliner* (his dear Berlinese). But the dead were carried to the royal palace, and brought into the court; and his poor Majesty was compelled to come to the window and look upon his subjects, whom he was plainly told that he had murdered. He wept and promised; and it was understood that his brother sharply reproached him for not maintaining his prerogative by the grace of God. But there was a kind of national guard organized and armed. There was a solemn and triumphal funeral of the dead; and Humboldt walked in the procession among the national mourners. There was a little feeble talk of Clicquot as Emperor of Germany; but, after the ludicrous and brief empire of the Archduke John, the last of poor Clicquot's wits ebbed away. Robert Blum, the popular leader, had been shot; and the Prince of Prussia, becoming king, stoutly held that he owed his crown to God, and was responsible to him, and not to the people." [1]

[1] Harper's Magazine, November, 1870.

CHAPTER IX.

KING WILLIAM I.

THUS the tumult of affairs continued, ever varying, and yet ever essentially the same, until the year 1857. The king, Frederick William IV., then gave indubitable evidences of insanity: it consequently became necessary for him to withdraw from the government. As he had no children, his next brother, William, was declared regent. William was exceedingly unpopular, in consequence of his openly-avowed advocacy of absolutism, and his implacable hostility to popular reform. For four years, the Crown Prince, William, reigned as regent; then, upon the death of his brother, he was crowned king on the 2d of January, 1861.

William I., who now occupies the throne, was the second son of Frederick William III. He was born on the 22d of March, 1797. In 1829, he married the Duchess Catharine of Saxe-Weimar. He has two children. The eldest, the Crown Prince, Frederick William Nicholas Charles, was born Oct. 18, 1831. He was married to Victoria, Princess Royal of Great Britain, on the 25th of January, 1858. The younger child, the Princess Louisa Maria, was born

Dec. 3, 1838; and married, on the 20th of September, 1856, the Grand Duke Frederick of Baden.

The coronation of the king took place in the ancient town of Königsberg. In this city, which is situated upon one of the inlets of the Baltic Sea, there is an antique castle, very imposing in its structure, which overlooks and commands the city. In the chapel of this venerable edifice, the ceremony of coronation took place.

There was no enthusiasm on the occasion. The king, who had already attained the age of sixty-four, a bluff, stern man, fully conscious that he was hated by the populace, whom he despised, apparently made no efforts to secure popularity. He was far too proud to seek the applause of the *canaille*. An eye-witness thus graphically describes the scene at the coronation:—

"The first time I saw the king was when he rode in procession through the ancient city, some two or three days before the performance of the coronation. He seemed a fine, dignified, handsome, somewhat bluff old man, with gray hairs and gray mustache, and an expression, which, if it did not denote intellectual power, had much of cheerful strength and the charm of a certain kind of frank manhood about it. He rode well,—riding is one of the accomplishments in which kings almost always excel,—and his military costume became him.

"Certainly no one was just then disposed to be very enthusiastic about him: but every one was inclined to make the best of the sovereign and of the situation; to forget the past, and to look hopefully into the future. The manner in which the coronation ceremony was conducted, and the speech which the king delivered soon after it, produced a terrible shock of disappointment; for in each the king manifested that he understood the crown to be a gift, not from his people, but from Heaven.

"To me, the ceremonies in the chapel, splendid and picturesque as was the *mise en scène*, appeared absurd, and even ridiculous. The king, bedizened in a regal costume which suggested Drury Lane or Niblo's Garden, lifting a crown from off the altar, and, without intervention of human aid other than his own hands, placing it upon his head to signify that he had his crown from Heaven, not from man; then putting another crown upon the head of his wife to show that *she* derived her dignities from him; and then turning round, and brandishing a gigantic sword, as symbolical of his readiness to defend state and people, — all this seemed to me too suggestive of the *opéra comique* to suit the simple dignity of the handsome old soldier.

"Far better and nobler did he look in his military uniform, and with his spiked helmet, as he sat on his horse in the streets, than when, arrayed in crimson velvet cloak and other such stage paraphernalia of conventional royalty, he stood in the castle chapel, the central figure in a ceremonial of mediæval splendor, and worse than mediæval tediousness."[1]

The king is a man of unusually fine physique. He is of majestic and well-proportioned form; and his finely-chiselled features are expressive of that indomitable resolution which has characterized every act of his

[1] Mr. Justin McCarthy, in Galaxy for October, 1870.

life. There was present on this occasion Marshal McMahon, Duke of Magenta. He had just returned from the campaign in Italy against the Austrians, where he had won his title and European renown. At the coronation, he represented the empire of France.

"There was great curiosity among the Königsberg public to get a glimpse of the military hero; and, although even Prussians could hardly be supposed to take delight in a fame acquired at the expense of other Germans, I remember being much struck with the quiet, candid good humor with which people acknowledged that he had beaten their countrymen. There was, indeed, a little vexation and anger felt when some of the representatives of Posen, the Prussian Poland, cheered somewhat too significantly for McMahon as he drove in his carriage from the palace.

"The Prussians generally felt annoyed that the Poles should have thus publicly and ostentatiously demonstrated their sympathy with France, and their admiration of the French general who had defeated a German army. But except for this little ebullition of feeling, natural enough on both sides, McMahon was a popular figure at the king's coronation; and, before the ceremonies were over, the king himself had become any thing but popular.

"The foreigners liked him, for the most part, because his manners were plain, frank, hearty, and agreeable; and to foreigners it was matter of little consequence what he said or did in accepting his crown. But the Germans winced under his blunt repudiation of the principle of popular sovereignty; and, in the minds of some alarmists, painful and odious memories began to revive, and transform themselves into terrible omens for the future."[1]

William I. had but a bloody record to present. Every uprising of the people in behalf of liberty, whether in Prussia or in any other of the States, he had been eager to cut down with the sword. More than once, his dragoons had crimsoned the pavements of the streets of Berlin with the blood of its citizens; and when, in Hanover, in Saxony, in Baden, the people attempted by violence to effect that reform which they found themselves unable to attain by peaceful means, the helmeted squadrons of Prince William hewed them down, and trampled them in the dust.

"This pleasant, genial, gray-haired man," writes Mr. McCarthy, "whose smile had so much of honest frankness, and even a certain simple sweetness, about it, had a grim and blood-stained history behind him. The blood of the Berliners was purple on those hands which now gave so kindly and cheery a welcome to all comers. The revolutionists of Baden held in bitter hate the stern prince, who was so unscrupulous in his mode of crushing out agitation.

"From Cologne to Königsberg, from Hamburg to Trieste, all Germans had for years had reason, only too strong, to regard William, Prince of Prussia, as the most resolute and relentless foe of popular liberty. During the greater part of his life, the things he promised to do, and did, were not such as free men could approve. He set out in life with a general detestation of liberal principles and of any thing which suggested popular revolution."

[1] Mr. Justin McCarthy, Galaxy, October, 1870.

King William is not regarded by any who know him as a man of superior abilities, or of much intelligence. He has a dogged firmness of character, which his friends call decision, and his enemies stigmatize as obstinacy. His strongest mental development consists of a clinging to the despotism of the past, and a horror of reform. In the year 1815, he was one of the princes who entered Paris with the allies as they trampled beneath iron hoofs the first empire in France. Since then, he has seemed conscientiously to deem it his divinely-appointed mission to keep the people in subjection.

Frederick William IV. was one of the most vacillating of men. He was kind-hearted, and sought the happiness of the people, but had not sufficient force of character to mark out and pursue any clearly-defined policy. William I. is one of the most inflexible monarchs who ever sat upon a throne. The fundamental principle of his reign seems to be, that *there shall be no innovations.* The policy of the government is, not to bend to meet the exigencies of modern times, but to force those exigencies to frame and mould themselves in accordance with the existing government.

"William I.," writes Mr. McCarthy, "was for many years a downright, stupid, despotic old feudalist. At one of his brother's councils he flung his sword upon the table, and vowed that he would rather appeal to that weapon than consent to rule over a people who dared to claim the right of voting their own taxes."

Unattractive as appears the character of William I., he has secured a certain degree of respect by the unquestionable and almost religious sincerity with which he pursues his inflexible course. The simplicity of his mode of living and of his address invested the bluff, unpolished soldier with a certain charm over the minds of the people. The gray-haired old man could often be seen by the passers in the streets, sitting at one of the windows of his palace, reading or writing.

It is reported that domestic discord disturbs the repose of the palace. In the celebrated diary of Varnhagen von Ense, which seems to be authentic, and which very graphically describes life in the Prussian court, it is stated that the king and his wife Augusta do not live very lovingly together. Augusta has a vein of radicalism in her nature, and cannot conceal a certain degree of admiration for some of those popular leaders in Germany, and other parts of Europe, whom her husband detests and despises. King William is far too stubborn a man to be a yielding and agreeable companion.

Varnhagen represents the king as naturally kindhearted, but dull, brusque, and pig-headed in the extreme, — a man who will not do what he thinks is wrong; and who will do what he believes to be right, come what may. He is like those conscientious inquisitors who prayed God to strengthen them to break the bones of heretics on the rack, and to consign them to the flames.

From the revelations of Varnhagen, which have never been contradicted, it does not appear that the court in Berlin has been, in modern times, a model of purity. Humboldt was a constant inmate of that court. From his diary, it appears how thoroughly he despised most of those royal personages by whom he was patronized. His life at court must often have been almost loathsome to him. The following anecdote throws a flood of light upon the character, or at least the reputation, of the court: —

"The late King of Hanover was a coarse, rough, uncultivated man. His reputation for brutality was such, that he was accused, by the general voice of the people, of the murder of his valet.

"He once accosted Humboldt in the palace of the late King of Prussia, and, with his customary brusqueness, inquired why it was that the court was always full of philosophers and dissolute characters. Humboldt replied, 'Perhaps the king invites the philosophers to meet me, and the others to please your Majesty.'"[1]

After the coronation of the king, he grew, month after month, increasingly unpopular. He quarrelled constantly with his parliament, silenced the journals, and persecuted every one who ventured to speak in favor of reform. Count Bismarck, to whom we shall hereafter allude, was in entire sympathy with the king in his hostility to representative governments, and in his support of absolutism. He was called into the council of the king, and became the power behind the throne stronger than the throne itself.

"There was, probably," writes Mr. McCarthy, "no public man in Europe so generally unpopular as the King of Prussia, — except, perhaps, his minister, the Count von Bismarck. In England, it was something like an article of faith to believe that the king was a bloody old tyrant. The dislike felt towards the king was extended to the members of his family; and the popular conviction in England was, that the Princess Victoria, wife of the king's son, had a dull, coarse drunkard for a husband. It is perfectly wonderful how soon an absurdly erroneous idea, if there is any thing about it which jumps with the popular humor, takes hold of the public mind of England."

[1] Galaxy for November, 1870.

In the month of July, 1861, as the king was taking a walk, accompanied by one or two of his suite, along the fashionable avenue of Baden-Baden, a fanatic discharged at him two barrels of a pistol. Both balls, happily, missed the king. The event caused many deputations to wait upon him with congratulations for his providential escape.

An American gentleman who chanced to be in Baden at that time accompanied a delegation of Englishmen to present an address to the king. In the following terms he describes the interview: —

"At the appointed day and hour, we assembled, some fifteen or twenty of us, in the lower story of the hired house which the king occupied. It was known in Baden parlance as the *Mesmeric House*, from the name of its owner, Herr Mesmer.

"We were all in full evening-dress. The spokesman of the delegation, while mustering his forces, said to us, 'Gentlemen, please take off your gloves.' So I learned one bit of court etiquette, — that you take off your gloves to a king; at least, to the King of Prussia.

"The gloves being removed, we were conducted up stairs, and ushered into his Majesty's presence. The first impression his Majesty gave me was that of a very badly-dressed man. His dark cutaway and striped trousers looked as if they had been bought at a slop-shop, and a second-rate one at that.

"The next impression that his Majesty gave me was, that his manners were no better, that is, no more elegant or graceful, than his dress. He reminded one of a military puppet. All his actions were stiff and jerky. When he advanced, it was 'Forward, march!' When he turned, it was a manœuvre executed by pivoting on one heel. His massive features and powerful frame could not be devoid of a certain dignity; but it was a clumsy dignity at best, — like that of an Æschylean actor in mask and buskins.

"The king's reply to the address — probably the same speech which he had made to each successive deputation — was brief, and well worded. One expression some of us noted at the time, and had reason to remember afterwards: 'I am convinced,' said he, 'that Providence has preserved me for a special purpose.' But, when each individual was successively presented to him, his awkwardness came out again."[1]

With discriminating criticism Mr. McCarthy writes, "I do not believe that the character of the king is anywise changed. He was a dull, honest, fanatical martinet when he turned his cannon against the German liberals in 1848; he was a dull, honest, fanatical martinet when he unfurled the flag of Prussia against the Austrians in 1866, and against the French in 1870.

"The brave old man is only happy when doing what he thinks is right; but he wants alike the intellect and the susceptibilities which enable people to distinguish right from wrong, despotism from justice, necessary firmness from stolid obstinacy. But for the war, and the great national issues which rose to claim instant decision, King William would have gone on dissolving parliaments and punishing newspapers, levying taxes without the consent of representatives, and making the police-officer master of Berlin. The vigor which was so popular when employed in resisting the French, would assuredly, otherwise, have found occupation in

---

[1] Mr. Carl Benson, in Galaxy for November, 1870.

repressing the Prussians. I see nothing to admire in King William but his courage and his honesty.

"For all the service he has done to Germany, let him have full thanks; but I cannot bring myself to any warmth of personal admiration for him. It is, indeed, hard to look at him, without feeling, for the moment, some sentiment of genuine respect. The fine head and face, with its noble outlines, and its frank, pleasant smile; the stately, dignified form, which some seventy-five years have neither bowed nor enfeebled,—make the king look like some splendid old paladin of the court of Charlemagne. He is, despite his years, the finest physical specimen of a sovereign Europe just now can show.

"But I cannot make a hero out of stout King William, although he has bravery enough of the common military kind to suit any of the heroes of the Nibelungenlied. He never would, if he could, render any service to liberty. He cannot understand the elements and first principles of popular freedom. To him the people is always as a child,—to be kept in leading-strings, and guided, and, if at all boisterous or naughty, to be smartly birched, and put in a dark corner.

"There is nothing cruel about King William; that is to say, he would not willingly hurt any human creature, and is, indeed, rather kind-hearted and humane than otherwise. He is as utterly incapable of the mean spites and shabby cruelties of the great Frederick, whose statue stands so near his palace, as he is incapable of the savage brutalities and indecencies of Frederick's father.

"He is, in fact, simply a dull old disciplinarian, saturated through and through with the traditions of the feudal past of Germany; his highest merit being the fact, that he keeps his word; that he is a still, strong man, who cannot lie; his noblest fortune being the happy chance which called on him to lead his country's battles, instead of leaving him free to contend against, and perhaps, for the time, to crush, his country's aspirations for domestic freedom.

"Kind Heaven has allowed him to become the champion and the representative of German unity, — that unity which is Germany's immediate and supreme need, calling for the postponement of every other claim and desire. And this part he has played like a man, a soldier, and a king.

"But one can hardly be expected to forget all the past, — to forget what Humboldt and Varnhagen von Ense wrote; what Jacobi and Waldeck spoke; what King William did in 1848, and what he said in 1861. And unless we forget all this, and a great deal more to the same effect, we can hardly help acknowledging, that, but for the fortunate conditions which allowed him to prove himself the best friend of German unity, he would probably have proved himself the worst enemy of German liberty."

CHAPTER X.

THE CHIEF SUPPORTERS OF THE CROWN.

THE Crown Prince, Frederick William, the son of the king, is not considered a man of much ability, or of any marked integrity of character. He is now (1870) thirty-nine years of age; having been born in 1831. He has command of the central wing of the Prussian army invading France. Having seen considerable service, and not being wanting in energy or courage, he occupies a respectable rank as a military commander. Having married the eldest daughter of Queen Victoria, — who will thus, probably, soon become Queen of Prussia, — it is difficult for the British court to adopt any efficient measures to thwart the ambitious designs of the Prussian monarchy.

The most prominent military man is Prince Frederick Charles. He is forty-two years of age, and is commander-in-chief of the Prussian forces. Frederick Charles is the nephew of the king; being the son of the king's brother Frederick. At ten years of age, Frederick Charles entered the army. It was deemed essential that every prince of the House of Hohenzollern should be thoroughly instructed in military service, that, in case of necessity, he might be able efficiently to draw his sword in defence of his country.

Even in those early years, it is said that he was a passionate admirer of the heroic deeds of Frederick the Great. With great enthusiasm he studied the history of the Seven-Years' War, thoroughly familiarizing himself with all the strategic and tactical movements of that renowned struggle. His innate love of military affairs enabled him to make rapid progress in his studies; and his military genius soon became conspicuous to his teachers and his companions.

When but twenty years of age, in 1848, he was assigned to the staff of the commander-in-chief of the Prussian army, Gen. von Wrangel, in the first invasion of Schleswig-Holstein. His reckless courage greatly inspirited the troops, and contributed much to his renown.

When, in 1849, his uncle, now King William I., was sent to Baden to crush out with his dragoons a popular uprising there, Prince Frederick Charles accompanied him, and rendered signal service in the sanguinary conflicts which ensued. During the fifteen years of peace which followed, Prince Charles devoted himself with renewed assiduity to his military studies; making himself familiar with every branch of the service, and paying special attention to the organization and movements of large armies.

In the second invasion of Schleswig-Holstein, in 1863, — to which we shall hereafter refer, — Frederick Charles was intrusted with the command of the Prussian division. In the attack upon Düppel, one of the most formidable of the Danish strongholds, Frederick Charles, after two repulses, which were accompanied by terrible slaughter, grasped the flag of the Royal Guards, and personally led to a third attack, which was successful.

At the commencement of the war between Prussia and Austria, in 1866, Frederick Charles had command of the first division of the Prussian army. On the 23d of June he crossed the frontier, and, in ordering the attack of his troops upon the Austrians, addressed them in these singular words, characteristic of the blunt, uncultivated soldier: —

"May your hearts beat towards God, and your fists upon the enemy!" A series of almost unparalleled victories ensued. Triumphant as was this campaign, which was terminated by the utter defeat of the Austrians at Sadowa, it revealed to the eagle-eye of Prince Frederick Charles some serious defects in the organization of the Prussian army. He subsequently published a pamphlet upon the subject, which attracted great attention throughout all Germany.

Baron von Moltke is another Prussian whom the agitation of the times has brought prominently before the world. The baron was born in Mecklenburg on the 26th of October, 1800. In early life, he served in the Danish army. In the year 1822, he entered the Prussian army as second lieutenant. His superior military abilities soon rendered him conspicuous, and secured him rapid promotion.

In 1835 he went to Constantinople to organize the Turkish army. In the campaign which ensued against the Viceroy of Egypt, he greatly distinguished himself, and returned to Prussia crowned with new honors. In 1858 he was appointed chief of staff, and in 1864 took a very distinguished part in the war which wrested Schleswig-Holstein from Denmark. Soon after, he published several works on military science, which have been widely translated, and which have given him great celebrity in military circles.

"But the greatest field for the practical application of his genius was offered him during the campaign of 1866. It is said that not only was he in constant possession of information about every movement of the army, but that he never was at a loss, one single moment, how to counteract all his adversary's operations, and turn them to his own advantage.

"His character is as firm as a rock; and, when once engaged in the planning of a military movement, nothing can detain him from carrying it out, as long as he feels morally convinced that he is in the right, and that there is a chance of success. In spite of his advanced years (for he has reached his threescore years and ten), he is said to be still very robust; and has no fear of the fatigues of a campaign."[1]

But by far the most remarkable man whom these modern agitations have brought prominently to view is Count Otto Edward Leopold von Bismarck. He was born at Schönhausen on the 1st of April, 1815. His parents were opulent, and of an ancient family. Otto was the youngest of six children. When he was but a year old, his father removed to Pomerania, where he inherited some knightly estates at Kniephof, about five miles to the east of Naugard. Here Otto remained with his parents until he was six years of age.

The rural mansion at Kniephof was plain, but capacious. It was pleasantly situated. Its beautiful garden and surrounding woods and meadows gave it no incon-

---

[1] The Great European Conflict, by G. W. Bible. p. 55.

siderable celebrity. In 1821, when Otto was six years of age, he was sent to Berlin, and placed in the renowned school of Prof. Plamann. Here he remained for six years, until 1827; when he entered the Frederick William Gymnasium. His elder brother was in the class above him. Their parents were in the habit of spending their winter-months in Berlin. Thus the boys enjoyed much of home-life, as they resided with their parents.

The two boys were placed under the best of tutors; and Otto, in addition to becoming a good classical scholar, attained so familiar an acquaintance with English and French as to speak both languages with correctness and fluency. No expense was spared in the education of these children. Their mother was an accomplished lady, alike distinguished for her personal beauty and her mental endowments. She seems early to have appreciated the remarkable character and abilities of Otto; and she expressed a particular desire that he should devote himself to a diplomatic career. The father of Otto was a witty, kind-hearted, good-humored man, who took the world easily, and who was not remarkable for information or intellect.

In the year 1830, when Otto had attained his sixteenth birthday, he was confirmed in the Trinity Church at Berlin. Two years later, in 1832, he graduated at the gymnasium, and entered upon the study of the law. Dr. Bonnell, director of the gymnasium, speaks in the following terms of Otto when under his care:—

" My attention was drawn to Bismarck on the very day of his entry; on which occasion the new boys sat in the schoolroom on rows of benches, in order that the masters could overlook the new-comers with attention during the inauguration. Otto von Bismarck sat, as I still distinctly remember, with visible eagerness, a clear and pleasant boyish face and bright eyes, in a gay and lightsome mood, among his comrades: so that it caused me to think, 'That's a nice boy. I'll keep my eye on him.'

"He became an inmate of my house in 1831, where he behaved himself, in my modest household, in a friendly and confiding manner. In every respect, he was charming. He seldom quitted us of an evening. If I were sometimes absent, he conversed in a friendly and innocent manner with my wife, and evinced a strong inclination for domestic life. He won our hearts; and we met his advances with affection and care: so that his father, when he quitted us, declared that his son had never been so happy as with us." [1]

He is represented at this time as being quiet, retiring, formal, and quite punctilious in observing and exacting that courtesy which etiquette required. An admirable memory aided him in the study of languages. He was very fond of dogs and horses. Though not fond of athletic sports, he was a good fencer, an accomplished swimmer, and danced gracefully. He had grown rapidly; was tall, thin, with a pale face, though enjoying good health. At the university he became acquainted with Lothrop Motley, who has since become so distinguished.

Otto had wished to enter the University at Heidelberg. His mother objected, lest he should "contract the habit, detestable to her, of drinking beer." He therefore entered the University of Göttingen. Here he plunged into dissipation with great recklessness. His

---

[1] Life of Bismarck, by John George Louis Hesekiel, p. 115.

vigorous constitution enabled him to endure excesses under which others would have broken down. He fought a duel, in which he was slightly wounded. Soon after, he had four challenges at the same time upon his hands. In his "jolly life at Göttingen, he had no leisure to attend the classes."[1]

Upon going home in vacation, his dress and altered manners greatly grieved his mother. The months of so-called pleasure rolled on; and Bismarck became nominally a lawyer, opening his office in Berlin. He was a good-looking man, of majestic stature and courtly bearing.

During the winter succeeding the summer of 1835, young Bismarck attended a court-ball. Here he met, for the first time, Prince William, son of King Frederick William III. As Bismarck, with another lawyer of equally majestic stature, was introduced to the immediate heir to the throne, William, scrutinizing the two stately forms before him, said, "Well, Justice seeks her young advocates according to the standard of the guards." This was the first interview between the future monarch and his future illustrious prime-minister.

In the year 1836, Bismarck was sent as an *attaché* to the legation to the court at Aix la Chapelle. Here again he plunged into all the fashionable dissipation of the imperial city. He was thrown into convivial association with Englishmen and Frenchmen. Speaking fluently the two languages, he became a great favorite, and made several excursions to Belgium, France, and the Rhine province.

In the year 1837, he was transferred to the crown

---

[1] Life of Bismarck, by John George Louis Hesekiel, p. 127.

office at Potsdam. The next year, he entered the Jäger Guard to fulfil his military duties. He was a wild fellow. His improvident father had so managed the estate, that the family was threatened with pecuniary ruin.

The sons begged their father to grant them the administration of the Pomeranian property. The request was acceded to; and the parents retired to Schönhausen to spend the evening of their days. The mother, who was in feeble health, soon died, in November, 1839. It was in the summer of this year that Bismarck entered on the administration of the Pomeranian estates. He was then twenty-three years of age. He had been accustomed to extravagant expenditure. Now bitter want oppressed him. Thus impelled by necessity, he devoted himself, for a time, to the care of the wasted estates, with diligence and with wisdom.

But the change in his mode of life depressed him: he became subject to deep despondency. With returning prosperity came returning recklessness. His eulogistic biographer says of him, —

"Despite his wild life and actions, he felt a continually increasing sense of loneliness; and the same Bismarck who gave himself to jolly carouses among the officers of the neighboring garrisons, sank, when alone, into the bitterest and most desolate state of reflection. He suffered from that disgust of life common to the boldest officers at times, and which has been called 'first lieutenant's melancholy.' The less real pleasure he had in his wild career, the madder it became; and he earned himself a fearful reputation among the elder ladies and gentlemen, who predicted the moral and pecuniary ruin of 'Mad Bismarck.'"[1]

[1] Life of Bismarck, by John George Louis Hesekiel, p. 133.

The two brothers divided the estates in Pomerania, so that Kniephof and its surroundings fell to the share of Otto. "Strange scenes occurred at Kniephof when the youthful owner, tortured by dark thoughts, dashed recklessly, to kill time, through the fields, — sometimes in solitude, and sometimes in the company of gay companions and guests: so that Kniephof became renowned far and wide in the land.

"Strange stories were current about their nocturnal carouses, at which none could equal 'Mad Bismarck' in emptying the great beaker filled with porter and champagne. Tales of a wild character were whispered in the circles of shuddering ladies. At each mad adventure, each wild burst of humor, a dozen myths started up, sometimes of comical, sometimes of a terrible character, until the little mansion of Kniephof was looked upon as haunted. But the ghosts must have had tolerably strong nerves; for the guests, slumbering with nightcaps of porter or champagne, were often roused by pistol-shots, the bullets whistling over their heads, and the lime from the ceilings tumbling into their faces."[1]

Bismarck was of course, in his many hours of solitude, restless and unhappy. In vain he sought repose for his troubled spirit in reading. He tried travels, and visited France and England. His father died in 1845; and Bismarck received, as an addition to his property, the estate of Schönhausen. Here he took up his future residence. Some local offices of trivial importance were conferred upon him.

At the house of a friend Bismarck met a young lady, Johanna von Putkammer, and fell deeply in love with

---

[1] Life of Bismarck, p. 134.

her; but his reputation was such, that the friends of the young lady were horror-struck at the thought of her union with such a debauchee. Johanna, however, returned the affection of her ardent lover; and her parents, with great reluctance, at length gave their assent to the union. They were married in July, 1847. On his bridal tour, Bismarck visited Switzerland and Italy. At Venice he met King Frederick William IV., and was invited to dine with him. They conversed for a long time upon German politics. Bismarck had already imbibed a strong antipathy to democratic progress, and was strenuously in favor of preserving all the prerogatives of the crown. The views he expressed in this conversation were evidently very gratifying to the king. Here, probably, was laid the foundation of that royal favor with which the king ever after regarded his illustrious subject.

We are told by his eulogistic biographer that the first enemy Bismarck saw to the power of the throne was *liberalism;* and he showed a firm front to it. Then *democracy* ventured upon some of its utterances; and he met this foe with the most unhesitating conviction. " Liberalism, democracy, the inimical jealousy of Austria, the envy of foreign nations, — such are the enemies of the Prussian sovereignty; and Bismarck has, with equal courage and firmness, with as much insight as success, fought openly and honestly against these."

When, in 1847, Frederick William IV., constrained by the general popular uprising in his realms, consented to a constitution which granted many reforms, the old nobility were displeased. They adhered to the absolutism of their former sovereigns. In the debate upon this question, Bismarck, as deputy to the United Diet, first made his appearance as a public speaker. He entered his protest against the constitution, and against any concession to the spirit of liberalism. His remarks were so little relished, that his voice was drowned with hisses and outcries.

The whole liberal press now came down upon Bismarck with the utmost ferocity. With singular coolness, he had avowed himself the friend of feudal absolutism and the enemy of "popular rights." "Thus," says his biographer, "he found himself in full battle-array against liberalism. He gave utterance to his opinions in conformity with his natural fearless nature."

In a long speech in 1847, he said, "With whom does the right reside to issue an authentic declaration? In my opinion, in the king alone. The Prussian sovereigns are in possession of a crown, not by the grace of the people, but by God's grace, — an actually unconditional crown, some of the rights of which they have voluntarily conceded to the people."

Thus Bismarck took his stand, with ever-increasing boldness and ability, in support of the sovereignty of the crown, and in antagonism to popular rights. The summer of 1848 was terrible in its menaces to the absolutism of the Prussian throne. Bismarck was recognized as the boldest and ablest of the advocates of royalty. His courage never faltered. Consequently he was hated by the advocates of reform as much as he was cherished by the court.

One evening, he was in a beer-saloon which was frequented by those in political sympathy with him.

"He had just taken his seat, when a particularly offensive expression was used at the next table concerning a member of the royal family. Bismarck immediately rose to his full height, turned to the speaker, and thundered forth, —

"'Out of the house! If you are not off when I have drunk this beer, I will break this glass on your head!'

"At this there ensued a fierce commotion; and outcries resounded in all directions. Without the slightest notice, Bismarck finished his draught, and then brought down the mug upon the offender's pate with such effect, that the glass flew into fragments, and the man fell down howling with anguish. There was a deep silence, during which Bismarck's voice was heard to say in the quietest tone, as if nothing whatever had taken place, —

"'Waiter, what is to pay for this broken glass?'"[1]

In the spring of 1851, Bismarck was appointed by Frederick William IV. ambassador to the diet at Frankfort on the Main. The following anecdote is related of him, which, if not absolutely true, is certainly characteristic of the man: "He one day visited the presiding deputy, Count Thun. The count received him with a sort of brusque familiarity, and went on coolly smoking his cigar, without even asking him to take a chair. The latter simply took out his cigar-case, pulled out a cigar, and said in an easy tone, 'May I beg a light, Excellency?' Excellency, astonished to the greatest degree, supplied the desired light. Bismarck got a good blaze up, and then took the unoffered seat in the coolest way in the world, and led the way to a conversation."

In a letter from Bismarck to his wife, dated Frankfort, 3d July, 1851, we find the following sentiments: —

"I went, day before yesterday, to Wiesbaden, to ——; and, with a mixture of sadness and wisdom, we went to

---

[1] Life of Bismarck, p. 202.

see this scene of former folly. Would it might please God to fill this vessel with his clear and strong wine, in which formerly the champagne of twenty-one years of youth foamed uselessly, and left nothing but loathing behind! Where now are ——, and Miss ——? How many are buried with whom I then flirted, drank, and diced! How many transformations have taken place in my views of the world in these fourteen years! How little are some things to me now which then appeared to me great! How much is venerable to me which I then ridiculed!"

During the summer of 1855, Bismarck visited the Exposition at Paris. Here he was the guest of the Prussian ambassador, Count Hatzfeld; and was introduced, for the first time, to the Emperor of the French. Again, in the spring of 1857, he visited Paris, and had a special political conference with the emperor; after which he visited Denmark and Sweden. Sundry incidental remarks in his letters now begin to show how the idea of adding to the power of Prussia was daily more and more occupying his thoughts, and gaining strength in his mind. In an apparently official communication, dated May 12, 1859, we find the following expressions: —

"Perhaps I am going too far when I express it as my opinion, that we should seize every justifiable opportunity to obtain a revision, necessary to Prussia, of our relations to the smaller German States. I think that we should willingly take up the gauntlet, and regard it as no misfortune, but as real progress, if a majority at Frankfort should decide upon a vote which we could regard as an arbitrary change in the object of the confederation, a violation of its treaties. The more unmistakable this violation, the better. I see in our position in the diet a defeat of Prussia, which we shall have, sooner or later, to heal by fire and the sword."

The Italians were moving to escape from Austrian thraldom, and to establish Italian unity. Unaided, the divided States of Italy could by no means resist the powerful Austrian monarchy. France was the only nation to which the Italians could look for aid. Prussia had engaged to unite with Austria, should the French armies march to the aid of the Italians. In allusion to this subject, Bismarck wrote as follows, from St. Petersburg, on the 22d of August, 1860: —

"According to the journals, we have bound ourselves verbally to assist Austria, under all circumstances, should she be *attacked* by France in Italy. Should Austria find it necessary to act on the offensive, our consent would be requisite if our co-operation is to be anticipated. Austria having security that we should fight for Venice, she will know how to provoke the *attack* of France.

"Viennese politics, since the Garibaldian expedition, desire to make things in Italy as bad as they can be, in order that, if Napoleon himself should find it necessary to declare against the Italian revolution, movements should commence on all sides to restore the former state of things.

"Some kind of general rumors reach me that the press carries on a systematic war against me. I am said to have openly supported Russo-French pretensions respecting a session of the Rhine province, on condition of compensation nearer home. I will pay a thousand Frederick d'ors to the person who will prove to me that any such Russo-French propositions have ever been brought to my knowledge by any one."[1]

[1] Life of Bismarck, p. 292.

"The Edinburgh Review," in the following terms, expresses its estimate of the character of Bismarck: "His private life is pure. Nobody has accused him of having used his high position for his pecuniary advantage; but by the side of these virtues the darker shades are not wanting. He never forgets a slight, and persecutes people who have offended him with the most unworthy malice. His strong will degenerates frequently into absurd obstinacy. He is feared by his subordinates; but we never heard that anybody loved him. He can tell the very reverse of truth with an amazing coolness. He laughs at the fools who took his fine words for solid cash. His contempt of men is profound."[1]

Mr. Friedrich Kapp, in an article in "The New-York Nation" of October, 1870, upon the conversations of Count Bismarck, narrates the following incident: —

"To the Austrian minister, when this gentleman rather incredulously received one of Bismarck's assertions, he said, a few weeks before the outbreak of the war of 1866, 'I never make a false statement whenever I can avoid it. In your case it is not necessary. Therefore I have no earthly interest to deceive you, and you can believe my words.'"

[1] Edinburgh Review, vol. cxxx. p. 457.

CHAPTER XI.

SCHLESWIG AND HOLSTEIN.

EARLY in the spring of 1859, Bismarck was appointed ambassador to Russia. His labors were not arduous. Much of his time was devoted to the education of his three children, — one daughter and two sons. On the 2d of July, before his family had joined him in Petersburg, he wrote to his wife, —

"Half an hour ago, a courier awakened me with tidings of war and peace. Our politics are sliding more and more into the Austrian groove. If we fire one shot on the Rhine, the Italo-Austrian war is over: in place of it, we shall see a Prusso-French war, in which Austria, after we have taken the load from her shoulders, will assist, or assist so far as her own interests are concerned. That we should play a very victorious part, is scarcely to be conceded.

"Be it as God wills! It is, here below, always a question of time. Nations and men, folly and wisdom, war and peace, — they come like waves, and so depart; while the ocean remains. On this earth there is nothing but hypocrisy and jugglery; and whether this mass of flesh is to be torn off by fever, or by a cartridge, it must fall at last. Then the difference between a Prussian and an

Austrian, if of the same stature, will be so small, that it will be difficult to distinguish between them. Fools and wise men, as skeletons, look very much like one another. Specific patriotism we thus lose; but it would be desperate if we carried it into eternity."

That Bismarck possesses some warm human sympathies is evident from the following extracts from a letter of condolence to a friend who had lost a beloved child: —

"A greater sorrow could scarcely have befallen you, — to lose so charming and joyfully-growing a child, and with it to bury all the hopes which were to become the joys of your old age. Mourning cannot depart from you as long as you live in this world. This I feel with you in deeply painful sympathy. We are helpless in the mighty hand of God, and can do nothing but bow in humility under his behest.

"How do all the little cares and troubles which beset our daily lives vanish beside the iron advent of real misfortune! We should not depend on this world, or regard it as our home. Another twenty or thirty years, and we shall both have passed from the sorrows of this world. Our children will have arrived at our present position, and will find with astonishment that the life so freshly begun is going down hill."

On the 22d of May, 1862, Bismarck was appointed ambassador to Paris. Nothing of special interest seems to have occurred during his short mission there. He was now regarded by the liberals as the leader of the aristocratic, or Junker party as it was called. There was no one more bold and able than he in defence of the prerogatives of the nobility and of the crown. Greatly to the indignation of the democracy, the king, in the autumn of 1863, appointed Bismarck prime-minister. The biographer of his life, who was in entire sympathy with his political views, writes, —

"When Bismarck arrived in Berlin, about the middle of September, 1862, he found opposed to him the party of progress, almost sure of victory, clashing onward like a charger with heavy spurs and sword, trampling upon every thing in its path, setting up new scandals every day, and acting in such a manner that the wiser chiefs of that party shook their very heads. Beside that party of progress, and partially governed and towed along by it, was the liberal party, possessed, with the exception of a minority, of an almost still greater dislike for Bismarck than was entertained by the progressists."

Having declared himself in favor of Italian unity, which would weaken Austria, the hostility of that power was strongly excited against him. He therefore entered into more friendly relations with France. His great object seemed now to be to unite all parties (aristocratic and democratic), to wrest from Austria the leadership of Germany, and to confer that leadership upon Prussia. He was fully aware that this great feat could not be accomplished without war. Repeatedly he said, "The all-important questions of the day are not to be settled by speeches and by votes, but by iron and blood."[1]

Bismarck complained bitterly that most of the German States were in sympathy with Austria, and stood out offensively against Prussia. One of the first acts of his administration was to enter into an alliance with Russia to suppress the Polish insurrection.

Upon the accession of William I. to the throne, Prussia consisted of a territory of 24,464 square miles; being

[1] Life of Bismarck, p. 340.

but about half as large as the State of New York. It contained a population of but little more than eight millions. The kingdom was composed of eight provinces, two of which, Prussia and Posen, did not belong to the German Confederacy.[1]

Adjoining Prussia, on the north-west, there were two small duchies, — Schleswig and Holstein. Bounded on the north-west by the German Ocean, and on the north-east by the Baltic Sea, with the River Elbe at their base, they presented unusual facilities for commerce. Their united population was about a million.

These duchies were a part of the dominion of the King of Denmark, though under a different law of succession from that of the crown. For some time, both of the duchies had been under one ruler, — Duke Frederick. The title was hereditary. Upon the death of Frederick VII. of Denmark, his successor on the throne, Christian IX., claimed the dukedom of the two duchies. On the other hand, the reigning duke, Frederick, claimed it. Though the two duchies were inseparably connected, one of them, Schleswig, belonged to the Germanic Confederation; and the other, Holstein, did not: but, as one belonged to the confederation, the contested claim to the dukedom became a German question. The inhabitants of the duchies were, with great apparent unanimity, in favor of Duke Frederick, and opposed to the claims of Denmark. In view of this difficulty, the Danish government had secured a treaty, on the 2d of May, 1862, to which Austria, Prussia, France, Russia, and England were parties, guaranteeing the integrity of the Danish monarchy. Thus all Europe became involved in the controversy.

[1] American Annual Cyclopædia, 1867.

England was somewhat embarrassed in her action. Victoria's daughter had married the Crown Prince of Prussia, and thus was destined to be the queen of that kingdom. The eldest son of Victoria, the Prince of Wales, had married a daughter of the King of Denmark, thus this Danish princess was prospective Queen of England. This intimate family relationship between the British court and both Prussia and Denmark greatly embarrassed the court of St. James in its action.

Prussia and Austria, as members of the Germanic Confederation, espoused the claims of Frederick to the duchies. Notwithstanding their treaty obligations, they furnished military aid to wrest the duchies from the King of Denmark. England, embarrassed by her matrimonial connections, stood aloof. None of the other minor powers ventured to intervene. Thus, after a brief struggle, Schleswig and Holstein were wrested from Denmark, and were declared to be independent of the Danish crown.

This was Bismarck's first step in his very shrewd and successful intrigue. Immediately three new claimants appeared, demanding the duchies by the right of inheritance: these were the Grand Duke of Oldenburg, the Prince of Hesse, and, to the surprise of all Europe, William I., King of Prussia. Thus, including Duke Frederick and the King of Denmark, there were five claimants.

All Europe was at this time in a state of great agitation. Poland was in insurrection. There was, manifestly, a conflict arising between Prussia and Austria in reference to supremacy in Germany. Italy, triumphant (with the aid of France) at Solferino, and having thus attained almost entire unity, was gathering its forces for the conquest of the Papal States and for the liberation of Venetia; and France was clamorous for the possession of her ancient boundary of the Rhine.

Under these circumstances, the Emperor of the French adopted the extraordinary measure of addressing the following circular to all the crowned heads in Europe. It was dated

"Palace of the Tuileries, Nov. 4, 1863.

"In presence of events which every day arise, and become urgent, I deem it indispensable to express myself, without reserve, to the sovereigns to whom the destinies of peoples are confided.

"Whenever severe shocks have shaken the bases and displaced the limits of States, solemn transactions have taken place to arrange new elements, and to consecrate, by revision, the accomplished transformations. Such was the object of the Treaty of Westphalia in the seventeenth century, and of the negotiations of Vienna in 1815. It is on this latter foundation that now reposes the political edifice of Europe; and yet, you are aware, it is crumbling away on all sides.

"If the situation of the different countries be attentively considered, it is impossible not to admit that the treaties of Vienna, upon almost all points, are destroyed, modified, misunderstood, or menaced: hence duties without rule, rights without title, and pretensions without restraint. The danger is so much the more formidable, because the improvements brought about by civilization, which have bound nations together by the identity of material interests, would render war more destructive.

"This is a subject for serious reflection. Let us not wait, before deciding on our course, for sudden and irresistible events to disturb our judgment, and carry us away, despite ourselves, in opposite directions.

"I therefore propose to you to regulate the present, and secure the future, in a congress.

"Called to the throne by Providence and the will of the French people, but trained in the school of adversity, it is, perhaps, less permitted to me than to any other to ignore the rights of sovereigns and the legitimate aspirations of the people.

"Therefore I am ready, without any preconceived system, to bring to an international council the spirit of moderation and justice, — the usual portion of those who have endured so many various trials.

"If I take the initiative in such an overture, I do not yield to an impulse of vanity; but, as I am the sovereign to whom ambitious projects are most attributed, I have it at heart to prove by this frank and loyal step that my sole object is to arrive, without a shock, at the pacification of Europe. If this proposition be favorably received, I pray you to accept Paris as the place of meeting.

"In case the princes, allies, and friends of France, should think proper to heighten by their presence the authority of the deliberations, I shall be proud to offer them my cordial hospitality. Europe would see, perhaps, some advantage in the capital, from which the signal for subversion has so often been given, becoming the seat of the conferences destined to lay the basis of a general pacification.

"I seize this occasion, &c.,

"NAPOLEON."

In the speech which the emperor made the next day at the opening of the Legislative Corps, he said, —

"The treaties of 1815 have ceased to exist. The force of events has overthrown them, or tends to overthrow them, almost everywhere. They have been broken in Greece, in Belgium, in France, in Italy, and upon the Danube. Germany is in agitation to change them; England has generally modified them by the cession of the Ionian Islands; and Russia tramples them under foot at Warsaw.

"In the midst of these successive violations of the fundamental European pact, ardent passions are excited. In the south, as in the north, powerful interests demand a solution. What, then, can be more legitimate or more useful than to invite the powers of Europe to a congress, in which self-interest and resistance would disappear before a supreme arbitration? What can be more conformed to the ideas of the time, to the wishes of the greater number, than to speak to the conscience and the reason of the statesmen of every country, and say to them, —

"'Have not the prejudices and the rancor which divide us lasted long enough? Shall the jealous rivalry of the great powers unceasingly impede the progress of civilization? Are we still to maintain mutual distrust by exaggerated armaments? Must our most precious resources be indefinitely exhausted by a vain display of our forces? Must we eternally maintain a state of things which is neither peace with its security, nor war with its fortunate chances?

"'Let us no longer attach a fictitious importance to the subversive spirit of extreme parties, by opposing ourselves, on narrow calculations, to the legitimate aspirations of peoples. Let us have the courage to substitute for a state of things sickly and precarious a situation solid and regular, should it even cost us sacrifices. Let us meet without preconceived opinions, without exclusive ambition, animated by the single thought of establishing an order of things founded, for the future, on the well-understood interests of sovereigns and peoples.'

"This appeal, I am happy to believe, will be listened to by all. A refusal would suggest secret projects, which shun the light. But, even should the proposal not be unanimously agreed to, it would secure the immense advantage of having pointed out to Europe where the danger lies, and where is safety. Two paths are open: the one conducts to progress by conciliation and peace; the other, sooner or later, leads fatally to war, from obstinacy in maintaining a course which sinks beneath us.

"Such is the language, gentlemen, which I propose to address to Europe. Approved by you, sanctioned by public assent, it cannot fail to be listened to, since I speak in the name of France."

The address of the Emperor of the French was sent to all the crowned heads in Europe, — fifteen in number. England declined the proposal. In a letter from Earl Russell, dated Nov. 28, 1863, it was stated, —

"Not being able to discern the likelihood of those beneficial consequences which the Emperor of the French promised himself when proposing a congress, her Majesty's government, following their own strong convictions, after mature deliberation, feel themselves unable to accept his imperial Majesty's invitation." [1]

Austria, following the lead of England, without positively declining, did not accept, the proposal. The em-

---

[1] "The reception of the proposal of the emperor, in England, was generally unfavorable. England could not expect any territorial aggrandizement from the congress, but only the loss of her European dependencies, and, in particular, Gibraltar. The press, almost unanimously, discouraged a participation in the congress." — *American Annual Cyclopædia*, 1863, p. 390.

peror stated that the treaties of 1815 were still regarded by Austria as the public law of Europe, and asked several questions, strangely assuming that it depended upon France, and not upon the congress, to decide what measures should be discussed.

Alexander of Russia cordially acceded to the proposal. In his reply, he said, " My most ardent desire is to spare my people sacrifices which their patriotism accepts, but from which their prosperity suffers. Nothing could better hasten this moment than a general settlement of the questions which agitate Europe. A loyal understanding between the sovereigns has always appeared desirable to me. I should be happy if the proposition emitted by your Majesty were to lead to it."

All the other crowned heads accepted the proposal with much cordiality. Victor Emanuel of Italy wrote, " I adhere with pleasure to the proposal of your Majesty. My concurrence, and that of my people, are assured to the realization of this project, which will mark a great progress in the history of mankind." Louis I., King of Portugal, who had married one of the daughters of Victor Emanuel, wrote, " A congress before war, with the view of averting war, is, in my opinion, a noble thought of progress. Whatever may be the issue, to France will always belong the glory of having laid the foundation of this new and highly philosophical principle."

The youthful King of Greece, George I., who was the second son of the King of Denmark, and consequently brother to the wife of the Prince of Wales, wrote, " This appeal to conciliation, which your Majesty has just made in the interests of European order, has been inspired by views too generous and too elevated not to find in me the most sympathetic reception. The noble thought which predominates therein could not be better enhanced than by the frank language and the judicious considerations with which your Majesty has accompanied your proposition."

In a similar strain, the kings of Belgium, of the Netherlands, of Denmark, of Bavaria, Saxony, Wurtemberg, and Hanover, expressed their approval of the congress. The Pope was prompt in his acceptance. Even the Sultan of Turkey gave in his adhesion to the plan, saying that he should be glad to attend the congress in person, if the other sovereigns would do the same. The Swiss Confederation replied, " We can only, therefore, accept with eagerness the overture your Majesty has deigned to make."

It was regarded as essential to the plan, that there should be a *general* congress; that *all* the leading powers should unite. If any should refuse to join, they would also refuse to be bound by the decisions of the congress: thus the refusal of two such leading powers as England and Austria thwarted the measure.

After all the replies were received, the French minister, M. Drouyn de Lhuys, in the name of the French Government, issued another circular to the European courts, with a summary of the responses, and giving the following as the result: —

" The refusal of England has, unfortunately, rendered impossible the first result we had hoped for from the appeal of the emperor to Europe. There now remains the second hypothesis, — the *limited* congress. Its realization depends upon the will of the sovereigns. After the refusal of the British cabinet, we might consider our duty accomplished, and henceforth, in the events which may arise, only take into account our own convenience and our own particular interests; but we prefer to recognize the favorable dispositions which have been displayed toward us, and to remind the sovereigns who have associated themselves with our intentions that we are ready to enter frankly with them upon the path of a common understanding."

The Emperor of the French was much disappointed at this result. In a letter written soon after to the Archbishop of Rouen, dated Jan. 14, 1864, he wrote, —

"You are right in saying that the honors of the world are heavy burdens which Providence imposes upon us. Thus I often ask myself if good fortune has not as many tribulations as adversity. But, in both cases, our guide and support is faith, — religious faith and political faith; that is to say, confidence in God, and the consciousness of a mission to accomplish."

In the mean time, Count Bismarck had submitted to the syndics of the crown of Prussia at Berlin the question of the legal title to the sovereignty of the duchies of Schleswig and Holstein. After several conferences, these legal gentlemen decided that the King of Denmark *had been* the legitimate heir, but that the duchies *now* belonged, by right of conquest, to Austria and Prussia.

This curious decision, it is said, was brought about by the diplomatic skill of Count Bismarck. Until this time, Austria had never laid any claim whatever to the duchies. Francis Joseph was as much surprised as he was gratified to learn that one-half of the sovereignty of the duchies enured to him. As, however, the duchies were at a great distance from Austria, and consequently of but little value to that kingdom, Count Bismarck supposed that Francis Joseph would sell, for a consideration, his share of the sovereignty. Prussia, accordingly, offered Austria sixty millions of dollars for the relinquishment of her title.

Austria refused: she would only consent that Prussia should, for the present, hold Schleswig, while Austria should hold Holstein. This agreement was entered into at what was called the Convention of Gastein, which was held in August, 1869. Both France and England announced in diplomatic notes their dissatisfaction with this arrangement. Austria appointed Marshal von Gablenz governor of her newly-acquired province of Holstein. Prussia appointed Gen. von Manteuffel governor of Schleswig. The duchies were quite dissatisfied with this arrangement. A large majority of the people in both duchies sent memorials to the federal diet, protesting against the division of the duchies, and demanding the recognition of Duke Frederick. These remonstrances of the people were of no avail.

Count Bismarck, having thus annexed Schleswig to the Prussian crown, now turned his attention to the acquisition of Holstein. The agitations in other parts of Europe greatly favored his plans. The Prussian army was placed on a war-footing. Negotiations were opened with Victor Emanuel in Italy, stating, that if, while Prussia should attack Austria upon the north, Italy should assail Austria from the south, Venetia could be wrested from her grasp, and re-annexed to Italy. "If you will help us gain Holstein," said Prussia, "we will help you gain Venetia."

Having thus made all his arrangements, Count Bismarck demanded the surrender of Holstein. The reason assigned for this demand was as follows: —

"King William I. is grievously affected to see developed under the ægis of Austria tendencies revolutionary, and hostile to all the thrones. He therefore declares that friendly relations no longer exist between Prussia and Austria."

This astonishing declaration, that Austria was allowing too much popular freedom in Holstein, was soon followed by another, in which it was declared that the repose of Prussia rendered it necessary that the government should pursue with firmness the annexation of both of the duchies, so desirable in all points of view.

Still this was not a positive declaration of war. Austria inquired of Prussia if she intended to break the treaties of the Convention of Gastein.

"No!" was the characteristic response; "but, if we had that intention, we should tell you we had not."

It seems to have been an avowed principle in European diplomacy, that sincerity was a virtue not to be expected in the intercourse of cabinets. In one of Bismarck's letters, dated Frankfort, May 18, 1851, he writes, —

"I am making enormous progress in the art of saying nothing in a great many words. I write reports of many sheets, which read as tersely and roundly as leading articles; and if Manteuffel can say what there is in them, after he has read them, he can do more than I can."[1]

[1] Life of Bismarck, p. 228.

CHAPTER XII.

THE LIBERATION OF ITALY.

TO understand those intrigues of cabinets and those majestic military movements which have recently arrested the attention of the whole civilized world, it is necessary that there should be brief allusion to the liberation of Italy from Austrian domination by the combined armies of France and Sardinia.

By the treaties of 1815, the constitutional kingdoms of Italy, which, by the aid of the French Empire, had been established upon the foundation of equal rights for all men, were overthrown. Italy was cut up into petty States, over which the old despotic *régimes* were inaugurated. Thus parcelled out, most of these States were merely provinces of Austria; and the vast armies of Austria watched with an eagle-eye, ready instantly to quell any popular uprising in any part of the Italian Peninsula. The kings, dukes, and princes whom the allies had placed over these petty States, were the guardians of Austrian despotism.

Upon the re-establishment of the empire in France in 1852, the popular masses all over Italy were greatly excited with the desire of regaining their former liberties. Victor Emanuel was King of Sardinia; Count Cavour, his prime-minister. They applied to the newly-elected French emperor to learn if France would support Sardinia against Austria, should Sardinia commence the work of popular reform within her own kingdom. The pledge was promptly given.

Sardinia entered upon enactments of liberty. Schools were established, aristocratic privileges were abolished, freedom of worship was proclaimed, and freedom of the press restrained only by laws of libel. Austria vigorously remonstrated, and gathered an army of two hundred and fifty thousand troops upon the Sardinian frontier. These reforms in Sardinia would excite discontent in despotic Austria.

The French minister in Austria informed the court in Vienna, in very significant diplomatic phrase, "that France could not look with indifference upon the invasion of Sardinia by the Austrian troops."

The latter part of April, 1859, the Austrian troops crossed the Ticino, and commenced a rapid march upon Turin, the capital of Sardinia. The Emperor of France immediately issued a proclamation, dated Tuileries, May 3, 1859, containing the following words: —

"Austria, in causing her army to enter the territory of the King of Sardinia, our ally, declares war against us. She thus violates treaties, justice, and menaces our frontiers. We are led to inquire what can be the reason for this sudden invasion. Is it that Austria has brought matters to this extremity, — that she must either rule up to the Alps, or Italy must be free to the shores of the Adriatic?

"The natural allies of France have been always those who seek the amelioration of humanity. When she draws the sword, it is not to subjugate, but to liberate. The object of this war is, then, to restore Italy to herself, and not to impose upon her a change of masters."

Two hundred thousand French troops were immediately transported to the plains of Sardinia. The French nation, with great unanimity, approved of the measure. M. Thiers, leading the opposition in the Legislative Corps, severely condemned it. He declared that enlightened statesmanship demanded that Italy should be kept divided into fragmentary States, and not that a strong kingdom of twenty-five millions of people should be organized on the frontiers of France. He urged that France should aid in maintaining the treaties of 1815. But the voice of the French nation was almost unanimously with the government.

After a series of sanguinary conflicts, the Austrians were driven out of Sardinia. Upon the plains of Magenta and Solferino, they encountered another terrible defeat, which liberated Lombardy. All Italy now rose in insurrection against its Austrian oppressors. The duchies of Tuscany, Parma, Modena, chased the Austrian rulers out of their domains. From all parts of Italy, the young men crowded to the liberating banners of France and Sardinia.

All dynastic Europe was alarmed. The spirit of the old French Revolution of 1789 seemed to have burst from its long burial, and to be again menacing every feudal throne. Hungarians were grasping their arms. Polanders were shouting the battle-cry of freedom. Ireland was clamoring for deliverance from that English throne by which it had been so terribly oppressed.

In hot haste, a coalition was formed against France and regenerated Italy. It was not only the wish but the intention of France and Sardinia to liberate Venetia. Thus all Italy, delivered from the despotism of the Austrians, would be the master of its own destinies, and could organize such institutions as it might see fit to adopt.

England has always chosen alliance with despots, rather than with the advocates of popular liberty. If the twenty-five millions of Italy, emancipated by the aid of French armies, were to be consolidated into one kingdom or one confederacy, under the banner of the abolition of aristocratic privilege and the establishment of equal rights for all, Italy and France would be in sympathy. The two kingdoms, renouncing feudalism, would support each other. This would add amazingly to the strength of the principles of reform throughout Europe.

Under these circumstances, England and Prussia entered into an alliance, and informed Sardinia and France, that, if they made any attempt whatever to liberate Venetia, all the military power of England and of Prussia should be combined with that of Austria to repel the movement.

This was a fearful threat. There were indications that other leading northern dynasties would also co-operate with England and Prussia. This would surely lead to an invasion of France from the Rhine. All Europe would thus be plunged into one of the most desolating wars earth ever witnessed.

Thus the liberating army of Sardinia and France was arrested in its march. The poor Venetians, to their unutterable disappointment, were left bound more firmly than ever, hand and foot, in Austrian chains. The peace of Villafranca, which liberated all of Italy except Venetia from Austrian rule, sounded the death-knell of those peoples, who, not in Venetia only, but in Hungary, in Poland, and in various other parts of Europe, were rising to break their chains.

There is something very affecting in the tones in which the noble Kossuth pleaded, and pleaded in vain, with the British cabinet, not to intervene against Venetia, and in favor of Austria. The sympathies of the British *people* were cordially with Kossuth. In his celebrated speech in the London Tavern on the 20th of May, 1859, the lord-mayor being in the chair, the eloquent Hungarian said, —

"Now, my lord, I do not remember to have heard one single official or semi-official declaration, that, if her Majesty's government were not to remain neutral, they would side with Sardinia and France against Austria; but I have heard many declarations forcibly leading to the inference that the alternative was either neutrality, or the support of Austria. We are told, that, if a French fleet should enter the Adriatic, it might be for the interest of England to oppose it; that, if Trieste were attacked, it might be for the interest of England to defend it; that it might be for the interest of England to defend Venice. From what? Of course, from the great misfortune of being emancipated from Austria.

"I love my fatherland more than myself, — more than any thing on earth. Inspired by this love, I ask one boon, one only boon, from England; and that is, that she shall not support Austria. England has not interfered for liberty: let her not interfere for the worst of despotisms, — Austria."

To this imploring cry the cabinet of St. James paid no heed. England united with Prussia to help Austria hold Venetia. Thus Venetians and Hungarians were left to groan in their chains. England, as well as all the other feudal monarchies, has ever been in great dread of any republican movement. A large part of the republicans hoped, that by a compromise, in which monarchical forms should be retained, this hostility might be in some degree disarmed, and that under these forms the spirit of republican equality might be established without provoking the armed hostility of Europe.

Father Gavazzi, one of the most renowned champions of Italian liberation, in a letter written to influence the British cabinet, dated Aug. 4, 1860, says, —

"We fight for the sole purpose of uniting all Italy under the constitutional sceptre of Victor Emanuel. Let Englishmen repudiate the idea that there is any thing republican in the present movement; since the most ardent advocates of republicanism have sacrificed their views to the great cause of our independence, unity, and constitutional liberties. Be sure, that, if there is no intervention in our fightings, we shall arrive to crown in the capital our dear Victor Emanuel king of Italy."

Such was the state of affairs, when Bismarck, who had aided England in preventing the liberation of Venetia, suddenly changed his policy. He had for years been maturing his plans to consolidate Germany in one great empire, with the King of Prussia at its head. In that enterprise, Austria was Prussia's only rival. Bismarck had made the most extraordinary preparation for war with Austria by raising an immense army, giving it the most perfect organization and discipline, and arming it with the most deadly weapons.

Still Austria was a very formidable military power.

With her supremacy in Germany, she could bring a much larger force into the field than Prussia, though that energetic little kingdom had arrayed every able-bodied man under her banners. Bismarck, therefore, sent a confidential envoy to Victor Emanuel to inform him that Prussia was about to attack Austria from the north to obtain possession of both of the Elbe duchies; that this would furnish Italy with an admirable opportunity, by co-operating in an attack upon the south, to wrest Venetia from Austria.

Italy eagerly availed herself of the opportunity, though perfectly aware that she owed no thanks to Prussia, who was consulting only her own interests in the alliance. Thus the great Germanic war, so fatal to Austria, was ushered in.

"The London Times" of Dec. 12, 1866, contained the following very just tribute to the efforts of the Emperor of the French for the liberation of Italy: —

"The Italians must acknowledge in the Emperor of the French their greatest, most unwearied, most generous benefactor. To the Italians, the emperor has always been, at heart, that Louis Napoleon who took up arms for Italy, and against the temporal power, five and thirty years ago. It seems as if some vow made by the bedside of his brother, dying in his arms at Forli, swayed Napoleon's mind through life, and bade him go firmly, however slowly, to his goal. In all other measures, in any other home or foreign policy, the emperor had friends and opponents; but the Italian game was played by him single-handed, and the game is won."

M. Thiers, as we have mentioned, was bitterly opposed to the aid which the imperial government lent Italy in escaping from Austrian domination, and becoming a consolidated kingdom. In his celebrated speech before the Legislative Corps on the 18th of March, 1867, he said, —

"As for me, when distinguished Italians have spoken to me of unity, I have said to them, 'No, no, never! For my part, I will never consent to it.' And if, at the time when that question came up, I had had the honor to hold in my hands the affairs of France, I would not have consented to it. I would say to you even, that, upon that question, the friendship, very ardent and sincere, which existed between Monsieur Cavour and me, has been interrupted." [1]

The imperial government has been consistent and unwavering in its approval of Italian unity and German unity. But for the aid of France, Italy could by no possibility have shaken off the yoke of Austria, and have become consolidated; and nothing would have been easier than for France to have united her armies with those of Austria, and, thus driving back the invading Prussians to their native Brandenburg, to have prevented the unification of Germany. Truly does M. Thiers say, that France *created* the unification of Italy, and *permitted* that of Germany.

[1] "Je vous dirais même, sur cette question, l'amitié très sincère et très vive, qui existe entre M. Cavour et moi, a été interrompue." — *Moniteur*, March 16, 1867.

CHAPTER XIII.

THE GERMAN WAR.

AUSTRIA, which had just emerged from a disastrous war with Italy aided by France, and now menaced with war by Prussia aided by newly-united Italy, had a standing army at her disposal of nine hundred thousand men. Prussia, having mobilized her whole force, could bring six hundred thousand into the field. Under the Italian banners, four hundred and fifty thousand troops were marshalled. Thus Prussia and Italy united could bring over a million of men to assail Austria in front and rear.

It was necessary for Austria to divide her forces to meet this double assault. Strong garrisons were also requisite to hold the Hungarians in subjection, who seemed upon the eve of rising. An outbreak in Hungary would surely lead to an insurrection in Poland. This would bring the armies of Russia into the arena. Thus all Europe was menaced with war.

In view of this awful conflagration which now threatened Europe, and to avert which the Emperor of the French had proposed a congress, England manifested regret in not having acceded to that pacific overture.

Lord Cowley was sent in haste with a despatch from

Lord Clarendon to the Emperor of the French, containing the announcement that England would withdraw her declinature to the proposal of a congress, and was now prepared to unite with France in that measure. The reply which the Emperor of the French made, as reported to the British cabinet by Lord Cowley, was as follows: —

"In 1859, England refused to assist me in the liberation of Italy, and, by her coalition with Germany, compelled me to stop short, leaving the work undone.

"When in 1864 I proposed a congress for the purpose of removing the endless complications which I foresaw would result from the Danish war, it was still England that opposed my project, and did her utmost to make it abortive.

"Now she wants peace, even at the price of the congress which she then rejected. I will, however, assure her Majesty that I am ready to do all I can to prevent war; but, as the most favorable opportunity for doing so has passed, I can no longer take upon myself the responsibility for any event that may occur."

M. Thiers, in his very eloquent speech in the Legislative Corps against the liberation of Italy, had said, —

"No sovereign should create voluntarily, on his own frontier, a state of twenty-five millions of inhabitants. By committing such a fault, we have not promoted the welfare of France, of Italy, or of Europe."

The ambitious desires of Prussia to unite all Germany under one empire, either roused M. Thiers' apprehensions anew, or presented him another favorable opportunity to attack the imperial government. He united with the democrats in this opposition, hoping to reconstruct upon the ruins of the empire the Orleans throne. On the other hand, the democrats hoped upon those ruins to rear a republic.

With terrible energies of denunciation, M. Thiers condemned the government of being "guilty of the greatest of all possible blunders" in allowing the formation of a united Germany. With great powers of eloquence, he called upon France to rouse all her military strength to resist the ambitious encroachments of Prussia.

It is clear, that, had France then pursued the policy urged by Thiers, Prussia could have been overwhelmed. Comparatively weak as Prussia then was, France, aided by Austria, could, with all ease, have driven the Prussians across the Rhine, and have regained her ancient boundary. Thus the terrible humiliation which now overwhelms France would have been averted; and the empire, protected by the Rhine, could bid defiance to German invasion.

But, in pursuing this course, France must have proved false to her most sacredly-avowed principle of allowing the people of each nationality to unite in a consolidated government. She would also have been compelled to send her soldiers, fresh from the fields of Magenta and Solferino, to fight against the unification of Italy, by aiding Austria to retain her hold upon Venetia. The empire refused thus to ignore its principles, and embrace in their stead the doctrine of political expediency.

Therefore, in opposition to the forcible arguments of M. Thiers, the imperial government emphatically reavowed its adhesion to the doctrine of "nationalities."

This doctrine had been unfolded in the following terms by the Emperor Napoleon I. at St. Helena: —

"One of my great plans," said Napoleon to Las Casas

on the 11th of November, 1816, " was the rejoining, the concentration, of those same geographical nations which have been disunited and parcelled out by revolution and policy. There are dispersed in Europe upwards of thirty millions of French, fifteen millions of Spaniards, fifteen millions of Italians, and thirty millions of Germans; and it was my intention to incorporate these several people each into one nation. It would have been a noble thing to have advanced into posterity with such a train, and attended by the blessings of future ages. I felt myself worthy of this glory.

" In this state of things, there would have been some chance of establishing in every country a unity of codes, of principles, of opinions, of sentiments, views, and interests; then perhaps, by the help of the universal diffusion of knowledge, one might have thought of attempting in the great European family the application of the American Congress, or of the Amphictyons of Greece. What a perspective of power, grandeur, happiness, and prosperity, would thus have appeared!

" The concentration of thirty or forty millions of Frenchmen was completed and perfected; that of fifteen millions of Spaniards was nearly accomplished. Three or four years would have restored the Spaniards to profound peace and brilliant prosperity. They would have become a compact nation, and I should have well deserved their gratitude; for I should have saved them from the tyranny with which they are now oppressed, and from the terrible agitations that await them.

" With regard to the fifteen millions of Italians, their concentration was already far advanced: it only wanted maturity. The people were daily becoming more established in the unity of principles and legislation, and also in the unity of thought and feeling, — that certain and infallible cement of human concentration. The union of Piedmont to France, and the junction of Parma, Tuscany, and Rome, were, in my mind, only temporary measures, intended merely to guarantee and promote the national education of the Italians.

"All the south of Europe would soon have been rendered compact in point of locality, views, opinions, sentiments, and interests. The concentration of the Germans must have been effected more gradually; and therefore I had done no more than simplify their monstrous complication. How happens it that no German prince has yet formed a just notion of the spirit of his nation, and turned it to good account? Certainly, if Heaven had made me a prince of Germany, I should infallibly have governed the thirty millions of Germans combined.

"At all events, this concentration will certainly be brought about, sooner or later, by the very force of events. The impulse is given; and I think, that since my fall, and the destruction of my system, no grand equilibrium can possibly be established in Europe, except by the concentration and confederation of the principal nationalities. The sovereign who, in the first great conflict, shall sincerely embrace the cause of the people, will find himself at the head of all Europe, and may attempt whatever he pleases." [1]

In advocacy of these views, France had assisted in liberating the Italians from the thraldom of Austria, and in promoting the unification of Italy. The emperor had also stated, in an address to the Corps Législatif, that

---

[1] Abbott's Napoleon at St. Helena, pp. 272-274.

France had neither the right nor the disposition to interfere with the attempts which might be made for the unification of Germany. These views were very violently assailed by the opposition, consisting of united legitimists and republicans.

In the German war, France remained neutral. The hostile armies were soon upon the move. Two millions of men, along lines hundreds of leagues in extent, armed with the most formidable weapons of modern warfare, were rushing against each other. Europe looked on, appalled by the spectacle. The genius of Bismarck was conspicuous on this occasion. For years he had been preparing for the struggle which he knew that the measures he was introducing would inaugurate. The Prussian army was in the highest state of discipline; all the material of war abundant, and in the right position; and the infantry were provided with arms capable of such rapidity of fire, that, in effective service, one Prussian could throw as many bullets as three Austrians.

War was declared on the 18th of June, 1866, with the usual appeal to God, on both sides, for his aid, and the usual declaration that each party had drawn the sword only in defence of justice and liberty. At a given signal, the Prussian armies from the north plunged simultaneously and impetuously into the Austrian provinces. At the same time, the Italians from the south, in divisions whose united strength amounted to four hundred thousand men, rushed into Venetia.

The reader would be weary with the details of the battles, — the charges and the repulses, the awful scenes of carnage, conflagration, and misery, which ensued. For forty days, this tempest of war raged with scarcely a moment's intermission. The spectacle was such as had seldom been witnessed on earth before. The discipline of the armies, their numbers, and the murderous engines of war which they wielded, secured results which had never before been accomplished in so short a period.

The advance of the Prussian armies was almost as resistless as the sweep of the tornado or of the avalanche. Their path was over smouldering ruins, and through pools of blood, as they drove before them their foes, ever desperately fighting. With perfect organization, and armed with the terrible needle-gun, they overran kingdoms, dukedoms, and principalities almost as fast as armies could march.

Francis Joseph, in terror, was compelled to withdraw his troops from Venetia, to repel, if possible, the Prussian advance upon his capital. Too proud to surrender the province to the Italians, he transferred it to France. It was probably his hope that France, in possession of so magnificent a pledge, would be able, by some friendly intervention, to arrest those devastations of war which the imperial government had, before hostilities commenced, endeavored to avert by means of a congress; but Prussia, now flushed with victory, would listen to no terms but such as she herself might dictate.

France immediately surrendered Venetia to Italy. Kossuth was in Italy, shouting the war-cry, and calling upon the Hungarians to rush into the Italian ranks.

"Hungarians!" he exclaimed, "flock to the standard of Victor Emanuel: here is your place of honor. Austria is our enemy. Italy gave shelter, bread, and kindness to the exiled Hungarians.

"Italy is for Italians: Hungary is for the Hungarians. Out with Austria from Italy! Out with Austria from Hungary! Come here, my braves! I await you; and I

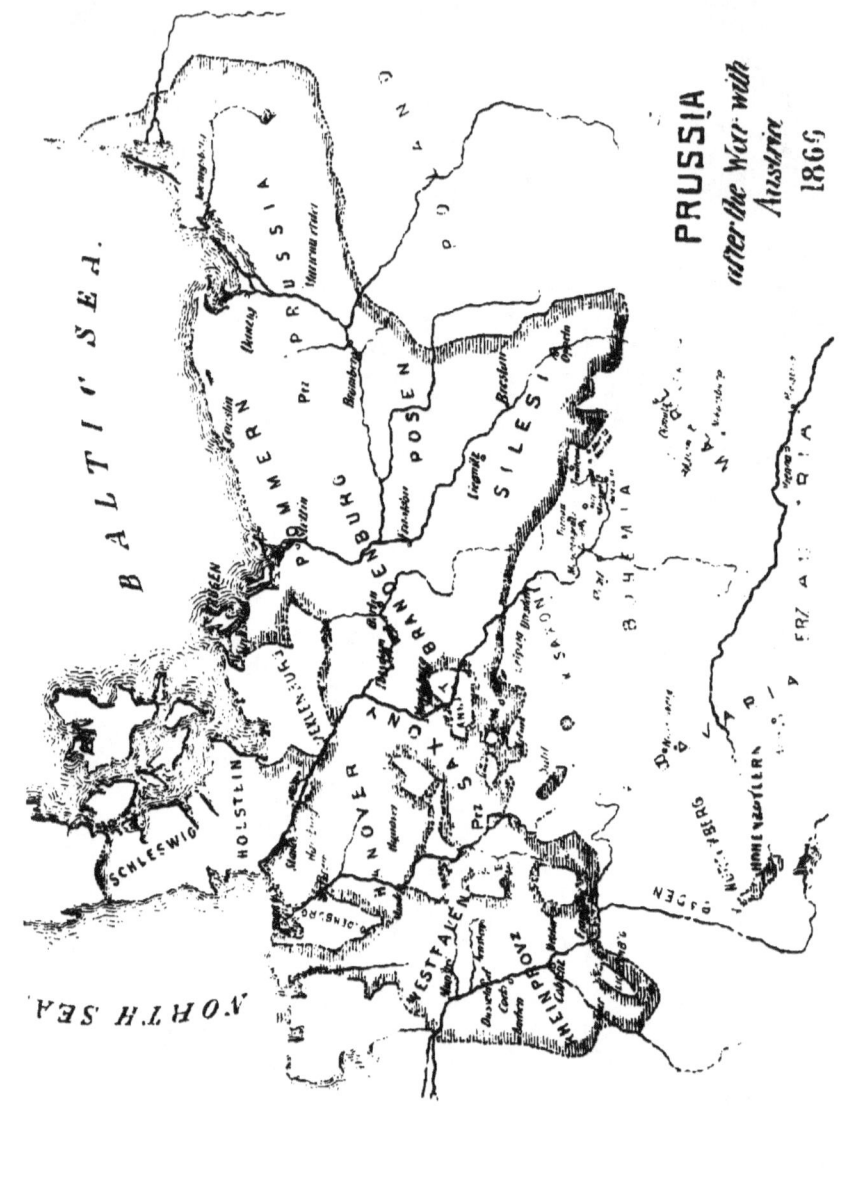

call upon you also in the name of Garibaldi, who is ready to draw his glorious sword in behalf of Hungary, which will rise and break her chains."

In the terrible battle of Sadowa, which was fought near a small village of that name, about five miles from Königgratz, the military power of Austria was, for the time being, broken down. In that conflict there were two hundred and fifty thousand men engaged on each side. The very hills trembled beneath the concussion of fifteen hundred pieces of artillery. The Austrians were utterly routed, and with dreadful slaughter. In a campaign of seven weeks, Austria had lost nearly one hundred thousand men.

The banners of the victorious Prussians were now visible from the steeples of Vienna. Further resistance was hopeless. Humiliated Austria, prostrate and bleeding, was compelled to accede to whatever terms the conqueror proposed. Prussia demanded the sovereignty over all the provinces she had overrun. Thus she obtained both Schleswig and Holstein, the kingdom of Hanover, the kingdom of Saxony, the magnificent dukedom of Saxony, large parts of Bohemia, Austrian Silesia, and Bavaria, with minor dukedoms and principalities too numerous to mention.

Though there was, at first, a slight disposition manifested by Prussia to veil these conquests behind the verbiage of diplomatic phrases and pious utterances, it was soon evident that all these realms were virtually annexed to the Prussian kingdom. In a campaign of about forty days, Count Bismarck had doubled the territory, and doubled the population, of Prussia. Thus suddenly, Prussia, from a second-rate kingdom, had risen to an equality in rank with the most powerful monarchies in Europe. In population and in military strength, she was fully equal to France. In addition to this, she held both banks of the Rhine. Prussia could thus, from her strong fortresses on the Rhine, invade France at her pleasure. Should she meet with any reverse, her armies could retire behind that broad and rapid river, both banks frowning with Prussian fortresses, and bid defiance to pursuit.

The door from Prussia into France was wide open: the door from France into Prussia was hermetically sealed.

CHAPTER XIV.

FRANCE DEMANDS HER ANCIENT BOUNDARY.

IN consequence of the immense conquests made by Prussia, France found herself without any natural boundary to protect herself from one of the most formidable of European powers. By the treaties of 1815, the allies had placed in the hands of Prussia both banks of the Rhine and the Valley of the Moselle.

The avowed object of this cession to Prussia of those provinces south of the Rhine which had belonged to France was to deprive France of any available northern boundary; so that, should there be another popular uprising in France, an avenue would be opened, lined with Prussian fortresses, through which the allied troops might march into the heart of the kingdom.

All France now became agitated with the new peril with which the empire was menaced. A rival nation, with institutions in many respects hostile to those of France, and, in all the elements of national power, the equal of France; a nation ambitious, encroaching, and with apparently boundless designs of enlargement, — had the command of the portals of the empire from the north. And this government, adhering to feudal absolutism, was bitterly hostile to the republican principles which the empire advocated.

In a speech which M. Thiers addressed the Legislative Corps on the 3d of December, 1867, he said, —

"The Germanic Confederation, which, for fifty years, has been the principal authority for maintaining the peace of the world, has disappeared, and has been replaced by a military monarchy, which disposes of forty millions of men. You are placed between two unities, — one of which, Italy, you made; and the other, Prussia, you permitted. They are joining hands over the Alps. They only consent to preserve peace on condition that you will allow the one to complete itself by seizing upon the States of the pope, and the other to swallow up the German governments of the south. Such is the situation; and I defy any one to deny it."

In the course of this exciting debate, the French minister, M. Drouyn de Lhuys, read a letter from the Emperor of the French in reference to the proposed congress, containing the following sentiments: —

"Had the conference assembled, my government would have declared that France repudiated all idea of territorial aggrandizement so long as the European equilibrium remained undisturbed.

"We should have desired for the German confederacy a position more worthy of its importance, — for Prussia, better geographical boundaries; for Austria, the maintenance of her distinguished position in Europe after the cession of Venetia to Italy in exchange for territorial compensation.

"France could only think of *an extension of her frontiers in the event of the map of Europe being altered to the profit of a great power, and of the bordering provinces expressing by a formal and free vote their desire for annexation."* [1]

Alluding to the severe attacks upon the government for refusing to oppose the unification of Germany, the emperor had said in his discourse at the opening of the session of the Legislative Corps, on the 15th of February, 1865, —

" In reference to the conflict which has risen upon the Baltic, my government, cherishing sympathies for Denmark, and kind wishes for Germany, has observed the strictest neutrality. Summoned in a conference to express its opinion, it has limited itself to the avowal of the principle of nationalities, and of the right of the populations to be consulted respecting their destiny. Our language, corresponding with the attitude which we wish to preserve, has been moderate, and friendly towards both parties." [2]

It is a little remarkable, that while the illustrious French statesman, M. Thiers, so severely censures the emperor for befriending German unity, the illustrious American senator, Mr. Sumner, with equal severity condemns him for opposing that unity.

" Early in life," says Mr. Sumner, " a ' charcoal' conspirator against kings, he now became a crowned conspirator against republics. The name of a republic was to him a reproof; while its glory was a menace. Against the Roman republic he conspired early; and, when the rebellion waged by slavery seemed to afford opportunity, he conspired against our republic, promoting as far as he

---

[1] Moniteur, June 13, 1866.

[2] La Politique Impériale, Exposée par les Discours et Proclamations de l'Empereur Napoléon III., depuis le 10 Décembre, 1848, jusqu'en Juillet, 1865, p. 423.

dared the independence of the slave States, and at the same time, on the ruins of the Mexican republic, setting up a mock empire. *In similar spirit has he conspired against German unity, whose just strength promised to be a wall against his unprincipled ambition.*"[1]

France had been terribly humiliated by the march of the allies to Paris, and by those treaties of 1815, which, wresting from her the natural boundary of the Rhine, had left the kingdom defenceless from invasion from the north. Even the Bourbons, who had taken part in those treaties, felt keenly the national humiliation; but they submitted to it from fear that the people might again rise in defence of popular rights, and that again the presence of the allied armies might be needed to maintain the Bourbon throne.

The years rolled on, — the sad years of disquiet and suffering which have imbittered all the centuries. At last, even the Bourbons could endure the shame no longer of having the northern provinces of France in the hands of a foreign nation, and those very fortresses which had been constructed to guard France from invasion garrisoned by foreign troops.

But these Rhine provinces had been assigned to Prussia by treaties which all the governments assembled at Vienna were pledged to maintain. Even the Bourbons themselves had agreed to hold them sacred. They could not be regained without war and also perfidy on the part of the Bourbon government.

The discontent, however, of the people was so great, in view of this degradation, that the Bourbons thought it would be a popular measure, and would strengthen

---

[1] Senator Sumner on the war, New-York Herald, Oct. 29.

them on the throne, should they make an attempt to regain these provinces, even at the expense of their plighted word and of a war.

Viscount Chateaubriand was one of the ministers of Charles X. He testifies in his memoirs that the government of Charles X. had entered into a secret treaty with Russia to aid her in her designs upon Constantinople; and, in return, Russia was to aid France in regaining her lost Rhenish provinces.

Just before there was time to execute this treaty, there was, in the year 1820, a new revolution, in which the French people a third time drove the Bourbons from the throne. By the adroit management of a few opulent and influential men in Paris, the crown was placed upon the brow of Louis Philippe, without submitting the question to the vote of the people.

Louis Philippe, who could claim the throne neither by right of the popular vote nor by the doctrine of legitimacy, fearing that the allies might again combine in defence of the "divine right" of sovereigns, and reinstate the Bourbons, endeavored to secure the support of the surrounding dynasties by pledging himself to the maintenance of their policy. He therefore wrote to each of the leading sovereigns, promising that, in case his government was recognized by them, he would respect the treaties of 1815; which was equivalent to saying that he would make no effort to regain the Rhine provinces.

Alison writes in reference to the secret negotiations to which we have alluded between the *Bourbon cabinets* and Russia, "The result was a secret agreement that Russia should support France in the eventual extension of its frontier to the Rhine, and that France should countenance Russia in the advancing its standards to Constantinople. Prussia was to be indemnified for the loss of its Rhenish provinces by the half of Hanover; Holland, for the sacrifice of Belgium, by the other half. But this agreement, how carefully soever veiled in secrecy, came to the knowledge of the British Government; and it was the information which they had gained in regard to it which led to the immediate recognition of the government of Louis Philippe."[1]

"The treaties of 1815," writes Louis Blanc, "had left burning traces in the hearts of Frenchmen. These, it was hoped, would be effaced by the recovery of the Rhine as the frontier of France."

Again he writes, speaking of the government of Louis Philippe, "The first thought of the new government had been to obtain recognition. It therefore resolved to base its policy upon the maintenance of the treaties of 1815. Louis Philippe promised to shield from every blow the European system established in 1815. His accession was therefore hailed with joy by the sovereigns who had in 1815 divided the spoils of France between them."[2]

This subserviency of Louis Philippe to the policy of the allies, rendered him, in France, by far the most unpopular monarch who had ever sat upon that throne. Still, sustained by the sympathies of all the surrounding monarchies, who regarded him as their agent in arresting the progress of liberal opinions, he retained the throne for about eighteen years.

The downfall of Louis Philippe in 1848 was followed

---

[1] Alison's History of Europe, vol. vi. p. 165; also France under Louis Philippe, vol. i. p. 88.

[2] Louis Blanc, vol. i. p. 290.

by the brief republic, and that by the re-establishment of the empire in 1851. Upon the establishment of the republic, it was feared by monarchical Europe that French armies would immediately be pushed forward to seize the ancient boundary of the Rhine. To allay these fears, and thus to prevent an armed alliance against the republic, the leaders of that party, Ledru Rollin and Louis Blanc, issued a circular to the governments of Europe, in which they said, —

"The treaties of 1815 do not exist in right in the eyes of the French Republic. But war does not necessarily follow from that declaration. The territorial limits fixed by those treaties are the bases which the republic is willing to take as the *point of departure* in its external relations with other nations."

They hoped by this declaration, that, *for the present*, they would make no attempt to push their boundaries to the Rhine to allay the fears of those who were pledged to maintain the treaties of Vienna.

When Louis Napoleon was chosen *president*, the allies were much alarmed. It was quite manifest that this election would prove but a stepping-stone to the re-establishment of the empire; and it was very certain that the empire, once consolidated in any thing like its former splendor, would insist, eventually, upon its ancient and only natural boundary on the Rhine. "The London Morning Post" of 1852 said, —

"The allies are willing to tolerate the *temporary presidency* of the nephew of Napoleon; but they will not tolerate the transformation of the presidency into an empire."

The French people do not appear to have been intimidated by this threat. They were not disposed to inquire of the British cabinet what government France might adopt. In six months after the utterance of this threat, the French people, by majorities which astounded Europe, re-established the empire, and chose the heir of Napoleon as emperor.

The two extreme parties, the legitimists and the republicans, were united in the Corps Législatif in opposition to the imperial government. As we have mentioned, the government was severely censured by this opposition for aiding in the unification of Italy, and for permitting Prussia to create a great German nation of forty millions of population. In an address at the opening of the chambers on the 18th of November, 1866, the emperor said, in allusion to these censures, —

"Notwithstanding the declaration of my government, which has never varied in its pacific attitude, the belief has been spread that any modification in the internal system of Germany must become a cause of conflict. It is necessary to accept frankly the changes which have taken place on the other side of the Rhine; to proclaim, that, so long as our interests and our dignity shall not be threatened, we will not interfere in the transformations effected by the wish of the populations." [1]

On the 14th of February, 1867, the emperor, after the astounding conquests of Prussia, still more explicitly expressed his views upon the subject in the following words: —

"Since your last session, serious events have arisen in Europe. Although they may have astonished the world by their rapidity and by the importance of their results, it appears, that, according to the anticipation of the first

---

[1] La Politique Impériale.

emperor, there was a fatality in their fulfilment. Napoleon said at St. Helena, —

"'One of my great ideas has been the agglomeration and concentration of the same nations, geographically considered, who have been scattered piecemeal by revolutions and policy. This agglomeration will take place sooner or later by force of circumstances. The impulse is given; and I do not think, that, after my fall and the disappearance of my system, there will be any other great equilibrium possible than the agglomeration and confederation of great nations.'

"The transformations," continues Napoleon III., "which have taken place in Italy and Germany, pave the way for the realization of this vast programme of the union of the European States in one sole confederation. The spectacle of the efforts made by the neighboring nations to assemble their members, scattered abroad for so many centuries, cannot cause disquiet in such a country as ours, all the parts of which are irrevocably bound up with each other, and form a homogeneous and indestructible body.

"We have been impartial witnesses of the struggle which has been waged on the other side of the Rhine. In presence of these conflicts, the country strongly manifested its wish to keep aloof from it. Not only did I defer to this wish, but I used every effort to hasten the conclusion of peace." [1]

[1] Speech at the opening of the French Chambers, Feb. 14, 1867.

CHAPTER XV.

THE POLICY OF COUNT BISMARCK.

FRANCE had felt very uneasy in having her northern provinces and fortresses in the hands of Prussia, even when that kingdom was a feeble power, numbering but eighteen millions. But France could not move to recover those provinces without bringing against her all of monarchical Europe, pledged to maintain the treaties of 1815.

But now Prussia, in entire disregard of those treaties, had engaged in as stupendous a system of conquests as Europe had ever witnessed. She had suddenly risen to the position of a first-class power. The Prussian kingdom had become an organized camp. Every man was a soldier. The armies of Austria had been scattered by her military bands like sheep by wolves. In population, in resources, in the number and appointment of her armies, she had become at least fully the equal of France. And yet she held both banks of the Rhine. She held the Valley of the Moselle. There was neither mountain-range nor river to present any barrier to the impetuous rush of her legions into the heart of France.

On the other hand, should an invading Prussian army be repelled, and find it necessary to retreat, it need only retire behind the broad and rapid Rhine, with all the bridges at its command, and the most formidable fortresses fringing both its banks; and there it could rest in security.

It is said that ambition grows with what it feeds upon. Prussia, instead of being satiated with the enormous acquisitions which she had made, was supposed to be looking around for new conquests. The French "Journal Officiel" says, —

"No one can ignore the ambitious designs of Prussia against Holland. Bismarck wishes that little nation to submit, as the Danish duchies were forced to submit. He wished to render Holland a naval State of the North German Confederation. But for the stand taken by France, Prussian policy would have proved fatal to the independence of the Netherlands."

Under these changed circumstances, every man, of all parties, in France, became alarmed. It was deemed fearful to leave the key of entrance into France in the hands of so majestic and menacing a power. Bourbonists, Orleanists, Imperialists, and Republicans, all alike were agitated. And yet the hands of France seemed tied. Prussia made no attack upon France: she was simply gaining gigantic strength, which would soon enable her to dictate laws to the French Empire, and to be the controlling power in Europe.

Such was the state of affairs when the sagacious Bismarck endeavored to place Leopold of Hohenzollern upon the throne of Spain. Leopold was a prince of one of the most important principalities of Prussia, a near relative of the royal family, and a colonel in the Prussian army. The successful accomplishment of this feat would indeed have been the revival of the empire of Charlemagne; Spain would have been but a province of the great German Empire, submissive to the crown of Prussia; France would have been quite at the mercy of this gigantic power. And yet it was very adroitly done.

"You Frenchmen," said Bismarck through all his organs, "profess that the people have a right to choose their own sovereigns. Has not Spain, then, a right to choose her monarch? And, if Spain choose Leopold of Hohenzollern, is it not intolerable insolence in France to pretend to object to this free choice of a free people? and can Prussia submit to the insult of being commanded by France to forbid Leopold to accept the crown offered him by the suffrages of an independent nation?"

In reply, the French journal, "Le Gaulois," very forcibly puts the other side of the question:—

"Let us look back a little. Prussia seized Schleswig and Holstein: we said nothing. Prussia accomplished Sadowa: we were silent. Prussia made fresh annexations: we held our peace. Prussia occasioned the serious difficulty about Luxemburg: we were conciliatory. Prussia enthroned a Hohenzollern in Roumania: we said nothing. Prussia violated her engagements at the treaty of Prague: we do not resent it.

"Bismarck has now prepared for us a candidate for the throne of Spain to cut our hamstrings, and to crush us between him and the Spaniards as he crushed Austria between Germany and Italy. If we had submitted to this last affront, there is not a woman in the world who would have accepted the arm of a Frenchman."

A writer in "The New-York Herald," commenting upon this subject, writes, "No statement touching the war is more flagrantly impudent and unjust than that accredited to 'The London Times,'—that France, without a shadow of excuse or justification, plunges Europe into war.

"On the contrary, regarding the situation from an impartial standpoint, it does not appear that France is without justification. So far from it, it appears that France could not, without humiliation, stand in any other position than that which she now assumes.

"It was not merely the candidacy of Hohenzollern France objected to: it was the appearance of Prussia beyond the Pyrenees; it was the assumption of Prussia to take possession of Spain as if it were a German duchy. France was fully justified in making an indignant protest against this."

A very interesting article upon the war recently appeared in "The New-York Observer," from the pen of Mr. J. T. Headley, who probably is as familiar with the politics of Europe as any other American. In this article, Mr. Headley says, —

"That Bismarck anticipated, nay, desired war, there can be little doubt. His object was twofold: first, to consolidate Germany; second, to secure a safe frontier against France. Most people may have forgotten that this question of placing a German prince on the throne of Spain was raised a year ago, and demanded an explanation. Bismarck ridiculed the whole thing as a fable.

"From that moment, at least, he knew that an attempt to bring about such an event would result in war. Then why did he allow such a firebrand to be thrown into France? He knew, from the conduct of the French minister a year before, that war would follow; and, if he did not desire war, he could easily have prevented Prim's proposition from being offered or made public. Moreover, Prim had no authority or power to make it; showing, conclusively, that the whole thing was concocted between him and Bismarck to bring about just what happened.

"To make this still more apparent, note, that from the time, a year before, when the manner in which the rumored proposition was received foretold the result, he commenced putting Germany on a war-footing. Cars for the express purpose of transporting troops were built, and lay in trains along the various railroads of the State. More than this, the result proved, that, before the shell that had been prepared exploded, he had called out and concentrated his troops so near the frontier, that while Bonaparte, by his sudden declaration of war, and advance to the Rhine, expected to be eight or ten days ahead of his adversary, he was more than that time behind him.

"Such an accumulation of circumstantial evidence furnishes incontestable proof of a deep, well-laid plot, on the part of Bismarck, to provoke a war."[1]

A nation of forty millions of people, as intelligent, as enlightened and liberty-loving, as any people on the globe, does not unanimously rush into war without truly believing that there is some provocation.[2]

In France, this is not a war of the government, but of the people; not a war to aggrandize a dynasty, but to rectify a frontier. It can, with more propriety, be

---

[1] New-York Observer, Oct. 27, 1870.

[2] "Bismarck, who had played with Austria before 1866 till he knew that he had a force in hand strong enough to crush her, gained time by fooling the French diplomatists till every thing was in so perfect a state of preparation, that, within a fortnight after war had been declared, half a million of trained soldiers were ready to enter France." — *Manchester (England) Guardian*, Aug. 25, 1870

said that the people impelled the government to the war, than that the government dragged the people into it. It is the general admission, that the people, instinctively alarmed by the enormous growth of Prussia, and less informed of the relative strength of the two powers than the government, demanded war with a degree of unanimity which no government could have withstood, even if disposed to do so.

It has been the general impression in the United States, that the imperial government had sedulously fostered the war-spirit in France; that the whole empire was converted into a military camp, and that thus all Europe was compelled to keep up enormous armaments. The startling events which have occurred show how erroneous was this opinion. Just before the breaking-out of the war, the French minister, the Duke de Grammont, said, in a circular published in the "Journal Officiel," —

"If Europe remains armed, if a million of men are on the eve of the shock of battle, it cannot be denied that the responsibility is Prussia's, *as she repulsed all idea of disarmament when we caused the proposal to be made and began by giving the example.* The conscience of Europe and history will say that Prussia sought this war by inflicting upon France, pre-occupied with the development of her political institutions, an outrage no nation could accept without incurring contempt."

The deputies of the Corps Législatif, chosen by universal suffrage, and consequently representing all parties, sustained the war by a vote of 246 to 10. In the Senate, composed of two hundred and fifty of the most illustrious men in France, it is not reported that there was a single dissentient voice. Immediately after the decisive vote in the Corps Législatif, the Senate, in a body, on the 17th of July, repaired to St. Cloud to pledge to the emperor their cordial support in the conduct of the war. In a very emphatic speech which M. Rouher made upon the occasion, he said, "Your Majesty draws the sword, and the whole country goes with you."

"The right is on our side," exclaims the "Courrier des États-Unis:" "the world cannot refuse to see it. At this hour, the hearts of all Frenchmen beat in unison. '*To the Rhine*' is the cry of the whole nation."

One hundred million dollars were in a few hours subscribed to the war-fund. A hundred thousand volunteers came forward, almost in a day, to join the army.

In Germany, the people followed, they did not lead, the government; but they followed with the enthusiasm, and all the deep conviction, that they were in the right, which inspired the French. How deplorable is this spectacle! what a comment upon the frailty of human nature! Here are forty millions of people on either side of the Rhine. They are rushing against each other with the utmost conceivable fury, crimsoning the battle-fields with blood, and filling the two kingdoms with widowhood, orphanage, and misery; and each party, through thousands of churches, appeals to God in attestation of the righteousness of its cause. There can be no doubt that there are, on both sides, thousands of sincere Christians, who conscientiously invoke the assistance of Heaven.

France assumes that she is fighting to regain her original and legitimate boundaries, — boundaries which she deems essential to her independent existence under the changed state of affairs in Europe. Prussia assumes that she is fighting to resist a wanton and unprovoked attack from France, who is endeavoring to wrest from her important portions of her territory, — territory which she has held, without dispute, for half a century.

Throughout Christendom, intelligent, conscientious religious communities are divided. Millions are in warm sympathy with Prussia: other millions are no less ardent in their prayers for the success of the arms of France. Surely such facts should teach a lesson of charity.

CHAPTER XVI.

THE DECLARATION OF WAR.

AND now events of the most momentous nature succeeded each other with marvellous rapidity. The ex-queen, Isabella of Spain, an exile in Paris, on Sunday, the 26th of June, 1870, formally abdicated the throne in favor of her eldest son, Prince Alphonso. On Tuesday, the 6th of July, the intelligence was made public in the streets of Paris that the Prussian court was secretly intriguing to place Prince Leopold of Hohenzollern on the vacant throne of Spain. The abdication of Isabella in favor of Alphonso had but little force, since neither the ex-queen nor her son dared to cross the Pyrenees to enter the kingdom from which insurrection had expelled them.

It will be remembered, that, once before, the rumor had been circulated, that Prussia was intriguing to place one of her princes on the Spanish throne, and that Bismarck had declared that there was no foundation for the rumor. The tidings which now reached the French court, that a Prussian prince was again a candidate for the crown once worn by Charles V., caused agitation throughout the whole of Paris. It gave immediate rise to a very exciting debate in the Legislative Corps. All parties seemed to be united in the conviction, that this renewed measure of Count Bismarck was a direct menace to the independence of France. Almost the universal press gave utterance to the popular feeling, that the proposed encroachment must be resisted, even at the peril of war.

The question was one in which imperialists, monarchists, and republicans were alike interested. If Prussia, with forty millions of inhabitants, in compact military organization, and already in possession of both banks of the Rhine, were virtually to annex Spain to her domain, France would be quite at her disposal. The republicans had more to fear from this movement than either the imperialists or the monarchists; for there could be no question respecting the deadly hostility of Prussia to a republic. France had already advanced, in the line of popular rights, from the old feudal monarchy to the republican empire, founded, not upon "legitimacy," but upon universal suffrage. Even this reform excited the hatred and the dread of Prussia. Should France still take another step, and advance to a republic, no one could question that Prussia would summon all her energies to crush out those institutions which would be threatening Europe with revolution.

Influenced by such considerations, after mature deliberation, the French minister (the Duke of Grammont) gave official notice to the Prussian court, on Monday, the 11th of July, that France could not permit a German prince to ascend the throne of Charles V. In the mean time, agitation was rapidly increasing all over France. The discussion clearly revealed the peril in which France was placed in having both banks of the Rhine in the possession of a power which had suddenly assumed such gigantic proportions. The conviction became apparently universal, that France must immediately, and at all hazards, reclaim her ancient boundary of the Rhine. She did not demand both banks, but only the southern bank, as essential to the protection of France; leaving the northern bank with Prussia for the protection of Germany. The war-cry resounded through France; but that cry was not, "On to Berlin!" but "On to the Rhine!" All that France demanded was that ancient boundary which she deemed essential to her defence from Germanic invasion.

The next day, July 12, it was announced that Leopold was withdrawn from the candidature; but the agitation had become so great and extended, that something more than this was needed to allay it.

"To-morrow," it was said, "some new intrigue may place some other German prince upon that throne. It is not to Leopold *personally* that we object. We demand of Prussia the pledge that she will not place any of her princes on the Spanish throne. One Prussian prince is just as dangerous as another; and, moreover, these encroachments of Prussia show the peril of France. Since Prussia has trampled the treaties of 1815 beneath her feet in her enormous encroachments, a regard to our own safety imperatively demands that we should have surrendered back to us the provinces which Prussia holds on the south bank of the Rhine."

On the 14th of July, the King of Prussia refused to receive Count Benedetti, the French ambassador, under circumstances which increased the exasperation then rapidly rising between the two nations. King William accused the count of presenting his demands at an unseemly time and in an insolent manner. The French court accused the king of insulting France in the person of her ambassador, and of rudely refusing to receive propositions intended to avert war. Each nation told its own story. Forty millions of Germans believed that their king had been impudently approached by the French ambassador: forty millions of Frenchmen believed that imperial France had been designedly insulted by the Prussian monarch.

On the 15th of July, the French Government, sustained by the Legislative Corps, by the Senate, and apparently by the enthusiastic acclaim of the French people, declared war against Prussia. Though there were individual remonstrants, it seems to be the undisputed testimony of the French press, and of all the American and English correspondents in France at that time, that the general voice of the nation was for war. It is said that the emperor, better acquainted than others with the military preparation of the two nations, was almost the only man in Paris opposed to the immediate declaration of hostilities; but the popular current was so strong, that even he could not resist it. A very intelligent American gentleman who was in Paris at the time, and who had resided in Paris so much of his time as to be quite at home in Parisian society, wrote me, —

"In respect to this war, it seems hardly fair to hold Napoleon responsible for it; since he said, so it is stated, that he was opposed to it at the outset, but that the French people '*slipped away from him*,' and that he was obliged to go with them, or lose hold of them entirely. This seems, I must acknowledge, rather against my theory of government by the will of the people; but so, they say, it was. At any rate, all of whom we inquired in Paris told us that the war was generally popular."

In a brief speech which the emperor made to the Senate on the occasion, he said, " War is legitimate when it is made with the assent of the country and the approbation of its representatives. You are right in recalling the words of Montesquieu, ' *The true author of a war is not he who declares, but he who renders, it necessary.*' "

In an address to the French people, issued on the 23d of July, the emperor said, " There are in the life of peoples solemn moments, when the national honor, violently excited, presses itself irresistibly, rises above all other interests, and applies itself to the single purpose of directing the destinies of the nation. One of these decisive hours has now arrived for France.

" Prussia, to whom we have given evidence, during and since the war of 1866, of the most conciliatory disposition, has held our good will of no account, and has returned our forbearance by encroachments. She has aroused distrust in all quarters, in all quarters necessitating exaggerated armaments; and has made of Europe a camp, where reign disquiet, and fear of the morrow.

" A final moment has disclosed the instability of the international understanding, and shown the gravity of the situation. In the presence of her new pretensions, Prussia was made to understand our claims. They were evaded, and followed with contemptuous treatment. Our country manifested profound displeasure at this action; and quickly a war-cry resounded from one end of France to the other.

" There remains for us nothing but to confide our destinies to the chance of arms. We do not make war upon Germany, whose independence we respect. We pledge ourselves that the people composing the great

Germanic nationality shall dispose freely of their destinies. As for us, we demand the establishment of a state of things guaranteeing our security, and assuring the future. We wish to conquer a durable peace based on the true interests of the people, and to assist in abolishing that precarious condition of things when all nations are forced to employ their resources in arming against each other."

King William of Prussia, in accepting the gage of battle thus thrown down by France, addressed in the following terms the North German Parliament on the 20th of July: —

"The King of Prussia had no interest in the selection of the Prince of Hohenzollern for the Spanish throne, except that it might bring peace to a friendly people. It had, nevertheless, furnished the Emperor of the French with a pretext for war unknown to diplomacy; and, scorning peace, he has indulged in language to Germany which could only have been prompted by a miscalculation of her strength.

"Germany is powerful enough to resent such language and repel such violence. I say so in all reverence, knowing that the event is in God's hands. I have fully weighed the responsibility which rests on the man who drives into war and havoc two great and tranquil nations yearning for peace and the enjoyment of the common blessings of Christian civilization and prosperity, and for contests more salutary than those of blood."

In the declaration of war issued by the French Government, it was stated that the French were obliged to consider the proposal to elevate a Prussian prince to the throne of Spain as menacing the independence of France; that, consequently, France had requested Prussia to *disavow that scheme;* that Prussia refused to do so; that this refusal imperilled France and the European equilibrium. The declaration concludes with the following words: —

"The French Government, therefore, in taking steps for the defence of its honor and injured interests, and having adopted all measures which the circumstances render necessary, considers itself at war with Prussia."

The enthusiasm with which this declaration was greeted in France was equalled by the enthusiasm with which all Prussia sprung to arms. The whole population rose in support of the king. Somewhat to the surprise, and greatly to the disappointment, of France, the *South* German States declared their intention to support Prussia. Thus both North and South Germany became a unit in the prosecution of the war.

It was found that Prussia was thoroughly prepared for the conflict, as though she had anticipated it, and had made secret arrangements accordingly. France, on the other hand, was found singularly unprepared, indicating that her government was taken by surprise.

"The Moscow Gazette" declared, that, though France commenced the conflict, it was originated by Prussia. "A war with France," it said, "was absolutely necessary for the unification of Germany. Prussia had felt this fatal necessity hanging over her for more than three years, and at last had seized the opportunity when it was ripe. The war was prepared by the astute policy of Berlin, not only at home, but also in the enemy's camp; and when all was ready, and when France was quite incapable of entering on a great war, she was goaded into fighting, in such a manner that it seemed as if the provocation came from France herself."

One of the largest armies of which history gives any record was immediately on the march from Prussia for the invasion of France, — an army, in the aggregate, estimated at over seven hundred thousand men. These troops were in the highest state of discipline, abundantly supplied, and armed with the most powerful weapons of destruction which modern art could create. Another German army, equal in numbers, was held in reserve, to be pushed forward in detachments as occasion might require.

The Southern German States co-operating with Prussia enabled Bismarck, from the Prussian fortresses upon the Rhine, to commence his march upon Paris with troops three or four times as numerous as France had in the field to repel them.

CHAPTER XVII.

THE EASTERN QUESTION.

BEFORE proceeding any farther, let us turn aside for a moment to contemplate what is called "The Eastern Question," which has become inextricably involved in the complications of European diplomacy. It is confidently affirmed by the partisans of France, that Bismarck, anxious to extend along both sides of the Rhine the territory of the great German empire he was seeking to construct, goaded France into the war (for which Prussia was all prepared), and purchased the neutrality of Russia by a secret treaty, in which he agreed to co-operate with the czar in his designs upon Constantinople.

It has long been the great object of Russian ambition to drive the Turks back into Asia, and, seizing upon Constantinople, to make it the southern capital of the Russian Empire. A brief reference to the geography of those regions will show the vast importance of this measure to Russia.

The Mediterranean Sea is connected with the Sea of Marmora by a serpentine strait, usually called the Hellespont, which is from half a mile to a mile and a half in width. At the mouth of this strait there are four strong Turkish forts, called the Dardanelles: consequently the strait itself frequently takes the same name. Nothing can be easier than to crown the crags and bluffs which line these waters with fortresses that no fleet can pass.

Having threaded the Strait of the Dardanelles, you pass into the Sea of Marmora, — a hundred and eighty miles in length, and sixty in breadth. Crossing this sea to its northern shore, you enter the Bosphorus. This strait, which is about fifteen miles long, and of an average width of half a mile, conducts you to the Black Sea, in itself an ocean, — seven hundred miles long, and three hundred broad. The Strait of the Bosphorus is considered the most attractive sheet of water upon the globe. But a short distance up the strait, on the European side, the imperial city of Constantine is reared. It seems to be the uncontradicted testimony of all observers, that earth presents no other site so favorable for a great metropolis.

The Black Sea receives into its immense reservoir not only the Danube, but nearly all the majestic rivers of Russia, — the Dnieper, the Dniester, and the Don.

The great empire of Russia, with a territory three times as large as that of the United States, and with more than twice its population, has no access to the ocean for purposes of commerce but by a few seaports on the Baltic, far away in the north, which, for a large portion of the year, are blocked by the ice. It seems essential to the prosperity of Russia, to the development of her resources, to her emergence from comparative barbarism, that she should have free commercial intercourse with the outside world. It is only through the Bosphorus and the Dardanelles that Russia can find avenues to this commerce. But the Turks can at any time close this door, and refuse to allow any Russian ship to enter or depart. In case of war, Turkey can thus almost annihilate Russian commerce.

For about a hundred years it has been the constant object of Russian ambition to obtain Constantinople as her southern capital, and the Dardanelles and the Bosphorus as her commercial avenues. This has been the constant effort of her diplomacy; and it has led to many sanguinary conflicts.

When, in 1827, the Greeks emancipated themselves from the Turkish yoke, they were encouraged to the effort, and aided in the struggle, by Russia. As the result of that conflict, the czar took a long stride towards the possession of Constantinople; but all the European monarchies seem united in their determination that Russia shall not obtain Constantinople. They say that Russia, in possession of the imperial city and of the straits which lead to it, would be invulnerable, and could bid defiance to combined Europe: the Black Sea would become an impregnable harbor; its shores a navy-yard, which no fleet or army could penetrate.

The anxiety which England feels upon this subject may be inferred from the following extract from "The London Quarterly Review:"—

"The possession of the Dardanelles would give to Russia the means of creating and organizing an almost unlimited marine. It would enable her to prepare in the Black Sea an armament of any extent, without its being possible for any power in Europe to interrupt her proceedings, or even to watch or discover her designs. It is obvious, that, in the event of war, it would be in the power of Russia to throw the whole weight of her disposable forces on any point in the Mediterranean, without any probability of our being able to prevent it. Her whole southern empire would be defended by a single impregnable fortress. The road to India would be open to her, with all Asia at her back. The finest materials in the world for an army destined to serve in the East would be at her disposal. Our power to overawe her in Europe would be gone; and, by even a demonstration against India, she could augment our national expenditure by millions annually, and render the government of the country difficult beyond all calculation."

M. Meneval, the private secretary of Napoleon I., testifies, that, in one of the interviews of the emperor with Alexander I., the czar offered to co-operate with the Emperor of France in all his plans of aggrandizement, if Napoleon would consent that Russia should take possession of Constantinople. The emperor, after a moment's reflection, replied, "Constantinople, never! It is the empire of the world."[1]

On the 6th of November, 1816, Napoleon, at St. Helena, conversing with Las Casas, said, "Russia has a vast superiority over the rest of Europe in regard to the immense powers she can call up for the purpose of invasion, together with the physical advantages of her situation under the pole, and backed by eternal bulwarks of ice, which, in case of need, will render her inaccessible. Who can avoid shuddering at the thought of such a vast mass, unassailable on the flanks or in the rear, descending upon us with impunity; if triumphant, overwhelming every thing in its course; or, if defeated, retiring amidst

---

[1] Meneval, Vie Privée de Napoléon.

the cold and desolation which may be called its forces of reserve, and possessing every facility of issuing forth again at every opportunity? Constantinople is, from its situation, calculated to be the seat and centre of universal dominion." [1]

Again: on the 14th of February, 1817, Dr. O'Meara inquired of the emperor if it were true that Alexander of Russia intended to seize Constantinople. The emperor replied, —

"All his thoughts are directed to the conquest of Turkey. We have had many discussions about it. At first I was pleased with his proposals, because I thought it would enlighten the world to drive those brutes, the Turks, out of Europe; but when I reflected upon the consequences, and saw what a tremendous weight of power it would give to Russia on account of the number of Greeks in the Turkish dominions who would naturally join the Russians, I refused to consent to it, especially as Alexander wanted to get Constantinople, which I would not allow; for it would destroy the equilibrium of power in Europe." [2]

A few months after this, on the 27th of May, 1817, the conversation again turned on this all-important subject, in the humble apartment of the exile at St. Helena. Speaking to Dr. O'Meara, the emperor said, —

"In the course of a few years, Russia will have Constantinople, the greatest part of Turkey, and all Greece. Almost all the cajoling and flattery which Alexander practised towards me was to gain my consent to effect this object. In the natural course of things, in a few years Turkey must fall to Russia. The powers it could

---

[1] Napoleon at St. Helena, p. 451. [2] Idem, p. 534.

injure, who could oppose it, are England, France, Prussia, and Austria. Now, as to Austria, it will be very easy for Russia to engage her assistance by giving her Servia, and other provinces bordering on the Austrian dominions. *The only hypothesis that France and England may ever be allied with sincerity will be in order to prevent this.* But even this alliance will not avail. France, England, and Prussia, united, cannot prevent it: Russia and Austria can at any time effect it." [1]

In the month of June, 1844, the Czar Nicholas of Russia visited the court of Queen Victoria. He was received in a blaze of splendor at Windsor Castle. All the honors which the court of St. James could confer were lavished upon him. It was subsequently made known to the world through the memorandum of the Russian minister, Count Nesselrode, that the object of the czar in this imperial visit was to induce England to lend her countenance and co-operation in driving the Turks out of Europe, and in dividing the conquered territory between them. It was indeed a princely estate which it was proposed thus to seize. Turkey in Europe covers a territory twice as large as the Island of Great Britain, and embraces a population of fourteen millions, only three millions of whom are Mohammedans.

The following, according to Count Nesselrode, was the proposition which the czar made to the British cabinet: Russia was to incorporate into her dominions the three splendid Danubian provinces of Moldavia, Wallachia, and Bulgaria. This would give her the entire command of the mouths of the Danube. The czar was also to be permitted to establish nominally a Greek

---

[1] Napoleon at St. Helena, p. 502.

power in Roumalia, but under Russian protection, with Constantinople as its capital. This was, of course, surrendering Constantinople to Russia.

Austria was to receive as her share in the division the fertile and beautiful provinces of Servia and Bothnia. These provinces, situated on the south side of the Danube, adjoined the Austrian possessions, and presented a territory of great fertility, which enjoyed the lovely clime of Italy. The provinces embraced over forty thousand square miles, being a little larger than the State of Kentucky, and contained about two million inhabitants. Austria was also to be permitted to extend her southern frontier so as to embrace nearly the whole of the eastern coast of the Adriatic Sea.

The lovely Island of Cyprus, the gem of the Eastern Mediterranean, a hundred and forty-six miles long and sixty miles broad, was to be transferred to England. With this island as a naval dépôt, England was also to take possession of the whole of Egypt. This would give her the command of the canal between the Mediterranean and the Red Sea, and would greatly facilitate her intercourse with India.[1]

And why did not England and Austria embrace this magnificent and perfectly feasible plan? That there was no moral principle to restrain them from any measure of national aggrandizement, the past history of the two kingdoms amply proves.

And, moreover, what claim, it might be asked, can the Turk show to his European possessions? He crossed the Hellespont a blood-stained robber. With dripping

---

[1] Alison, vol. viii. p. 40.

cimeter he hewed his path through the quivering nerves of the vanquished Christians. Smouldering ruins and gory corpses marked every step of his progress.

Why, then, did not England and Austria consent to this division of European Turkey? It was because this arrangement would make Russia so powerful, that she would be the undisputed monarch of the Eastern world. The balance of power in Europe would be destroyed, and Russia would attain a supremacy before which all other European powers would tremble.

And yet nothing in the future seems more certain than that Russia will advance to Constantinople. The late Crimean War did but postpone the event for a few years. On this side of the Atlantic, where questions of European balances of power disturb us not, the popular sympathies are almost unanimously in favor of Russia. There would be no mourning here should the crescent fall, and should the Greek cross be raised over the dome of St. Sophia, and over all the fortresses which frown along the heights of the Bosphorus and the Dardanelles.

Such is the general aspect of the "Eastern Question." In all the diplomacy which now agitates Europe, this question invariably comes up as one of the most essential elements. There are many rumors that a secret understanding now exists between Russia and Prussia, by which Russia consents that Prussia shall organize an immense German empire in the heart of Europe, which shall overshadow the surrounding monarchies; and Prussia, in return, is to support Russia in her march to Constantinople. If this be the fact, Russia and Germany henceforth hold Europe in their grasp. All the other monarchies will be virtually tributary to these two gigantic powers. Russia enthroned at Constantinople, and Prussia the head of imperial Germany, occupying the whole Valley of the Rhine, from the sea to the Alps, can bid defiance to Europe in arms.

France is now powerless. Prussia is acting in cooperation with Russia. England, without the aid of France, can accomplish but little. Any alliance between England and *democratic* France is impossible. The British Government has even more to fear from democracy across the Channel than from Russia on the Bosphorus and the Dardanelles.

The last phase of this all-exciting and ever-changing question is, that England, Russia, and Prussia enter into a virtual alliance; that Prussia be permitted to work her will upon France, now prostrate before her; that Russia be permitted to do as she pleases with the Ottoman Empire; and that England seize upon the Suez Canal, thus appropriating to herself this new and magnificent avenue of East-Indian commerce, which France devised, engineered, and constructed. To this arrangement, France, without a government, without an army, impoverished, exhausted, bleeding, can present no opposition.[1]

[1] Telegram from London, Dec. 1, 1870.

CHAPTER XVIII.

FRANCE INVADED.

ON Friday, the 22d of July, but one week after the declaration of war, immense divisions of the Prussian army were gathered on the French or left side of the Rhine. These vast military bands, numbering several hundred thousands, were marshalled between the two massive and almost impregnable fortresses of Coblentz and Mayence. Braver troops than these German soldiers, or troops better disciplined, armed, and officered, never marched to the sound of the drum. They were inspired, not only by patriotic fervor, but by the full conviction that their cause was just in the sight of God.

The next day, July 23, a division of this army, advancing from Saar-Louis, on the southern frontier of the Prussian-Rhine provinces, crossed the boundary, and, invading France, marched directly south, some ten or twelve miles, towards St. Avold. There was nothing to oppose them. The frontier was there but an imaginary line, unprotected by river, mountain, or fortress.

In these modern days there is great power in public opinion. Both France and Prussia were alike anxious to obtain the moral support of other nations. As the

Prussian troops commenced their march, Count Bismarck caused a communication to be inserted in "The London Times" of the 25th of July, in which he accused M. Benedetti, the French minister at Berlin, of proposing that Prussia should allow France to seize and annex Belgium in compensation for the conquests Prussia was making. This statement caused intense exasperation in England against the imperial government.

To this M. Benedetti replied in an official communication to the Duke of Grammont, the French minister in Paris. This document, which attracted the attention of all Europe, was published in the "Journal Officiel" of July 29. In this paper, M. Benedetti declares, that, instead of making that proposal to Prussia, Count Bismarck himself had made it to the French minister; and that, upon its being transmitted to the French emperor, he had immediately rejected it.

"It is matter of public notoriety," writes M. Benedetti, "that Count Bismarck offered to us, before and during the last war, to assist in re-uniting Belgium to France in compensation for the aggrandizement he aimed at, and which he has obtained for Prussia. I might on this point invoke the whole diplomacy of Europe. The French Government constantly declined these overtures. M. Drouyn de Lhuys is in a position to give, on this point, explanations which would not leave any doubt subsisting."

Count Bismarck had stated that he had this communication in the handwriting of M. Benedetti. To this the French minister replied, —

"In one of these conversations, and in order to form a thorough comprehension of his intentions, I consented to transcribe them in some sort *under his dictation.* The form, no less than the substance, clearly demonstrates that I confined myself to reproducing a project conceived and developed by him. Count Bismarck kept the paper, desiring to submit it to the king. On my side, I reported to the imperial government the communications which had been made to me. The emperor rejected them as soon as they were brought to his knowledge.

"If the initiative of such a treaty had been taken by the emperor's government, the draft would have been prepared at the ministry, and I should not have had to produce a copy in my own handwriting: besides, it would have been differently worded, and negotiations would have been carried on simultaneously in Paris and Berlin."

These contradictory statements agitated the press of England and America. Probably each reader came to a decision in accordance with his predilections, whether they were in favor of Prussia or France. There seemed to be no room for misunderstanding. The contradiction was positive and unqualified. Either Count Bismarck or Count Benedetti must have uttered a deliberate falsehood.

We ought, in justice to the French minister, to state that Lord Lyons, the British minister at Berlin, wrote a letter to Lord Granville, in which he fully confirmed the statements of the French ambassador. This letter was dated "Foreign Office, July 29, 1870," and was published in "The London Daily News" of Aug. 2.

"Those who have watched," he writes, "the course of European affairs since the accession to office of M. Bismarck, are aware from which side have come those suggestions which are now attributed to France. Ever since the year 1865, M. Bismarck has constantly endeavored to carry out his own plans by endeavoring to turn the attention of the French Government to territorial aggrandizement. He told M. Lefebore de Behaine that Prussia would willingly recognize the rights of France to extend her borders wherever the French language is spoken, thereby indicating certain Swiss cantons, besides Belgium. These overtures the government of the emperor declined to entertain.

"After the battle of Sadowa, Count Bismarck told the French ambassador that the course of France was clear: The French Government should go to the King of Belgium, and explain that the inevitable increase to Prussian territory and influence was most disquieting to their security, and that the sole means of avoiding these dangerous issues would be to unite the destinies of Belgium and France by bonds so close, that Belgium, whose autonomy would, however, be respected, would become in the north a real bulwark of safety for France. The French Government declined to listen to these proposals. These suggestions were again made at the time of the Luxemburg affair. They were categorically rejected by the emperor."

Lord Lyons closes his long letter by the statement, "that the document under the handwriting of M. Benedetti was written under the dictation of Count Bismarck, who wished to entangle the French Government in a conspiracy against the liberties of Belgium."

On the 26th of July, at half-past six o'clock in the evening, King William left Berlin for the seat of war. The queen accompanied him to the railroad-station, which was decorated for the occasion with flowers. The king was greeted with the cheers of an

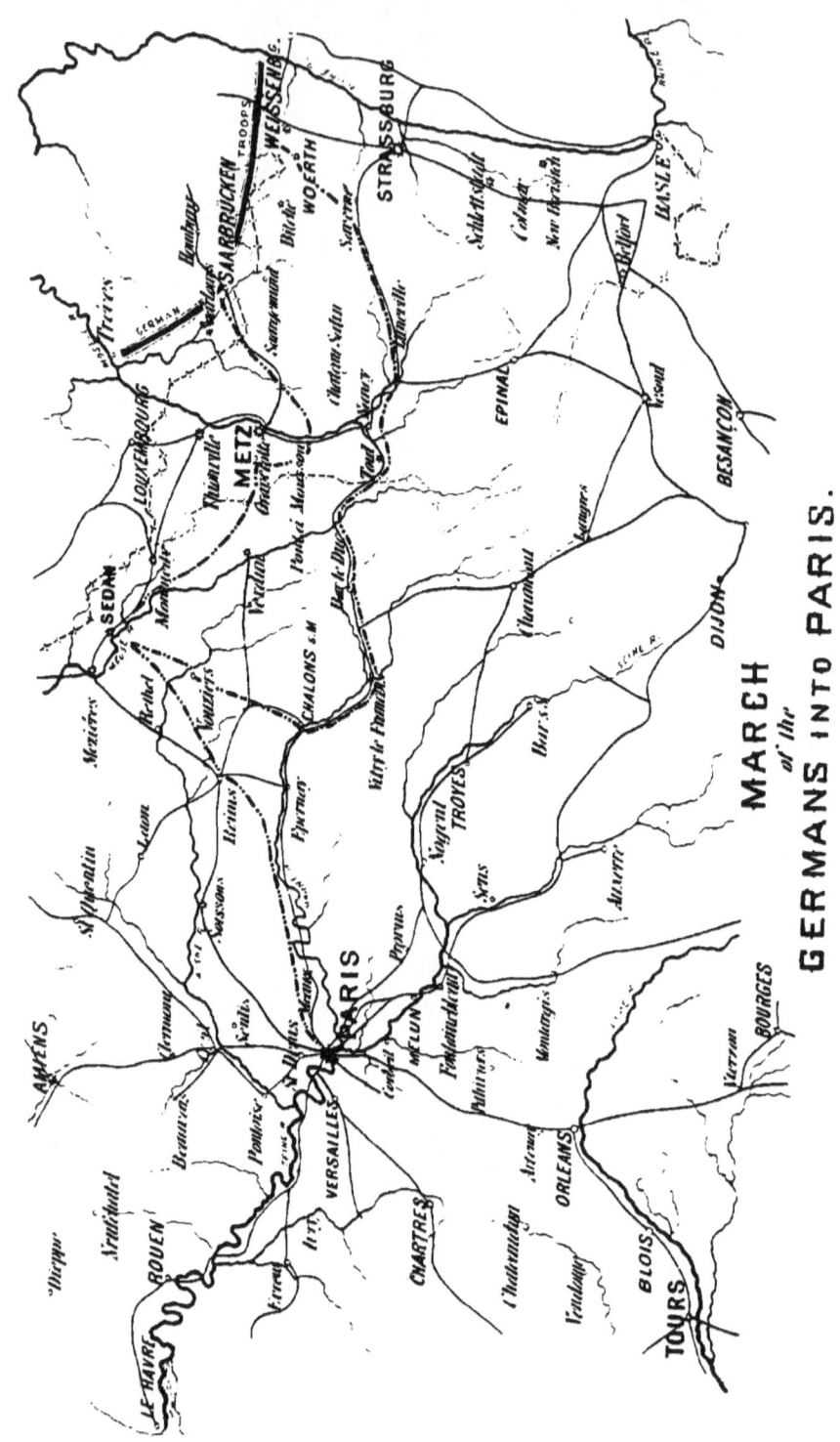

immense multitude. He issued the following proclamation: —

"On my departure to-day for the army, to fight with it for Germany's honor and the preservation of our most precious possessions, I wish to grant an amnesty for all political crimes and offences, in recognition of the unanimous uprising of my people at this crisis. My people know, with me, that the rupture of the peace, and the provocation to war, did not emanate from our side; but, being challenged, we are resolved, placing full trust in God, to accept the battle for the defence of Fatherland."

Two days after, on the 28th, the French emperor, taking with him his son, fifteen years of age, left St. Cloud for the frontier. The empress was left as regent.

As the emperor took his departure for a conflict into which he had been so reluctantly drawn, he said, in a brief and by no means exultant address to the Legislative Corps, "We have done all in our power to avoid war; and I can say that it is the entire nation which has, in its irresistible impulse, prompted our resolution."

In his proclamation to the army, he said in despondent tones, which, at the time, were severely censured, "The war which now commences will be long, and hardly contested; for its theatre will be places hedged with obstacles, and thick with fortresses."

On Sunday, July 31, there was skirmishing between the advance-posts of the French and Prussians near St. Avold. The French were repulsed; but, as larger French forces were in the vicinity, the Prussians recrossed the boundary, and retired upon Saarbruck. On Tuesday, the 2d of August, the French troops crossed the frontier, marched upon Saarbruck, and in a short conflict, which lasted from eleven o'clock, A. M., to one o'clock, P. M., stormed the heights. The emperor and the Prince Imperial were present. It was an affair of but little moment, rendered memorable only by the private despatch which the emperor, proud of his son's heroism, sent to the mother of the boy. The telegram from the battle-field was as follows: —

"Louis has just received his baptism of fire: he behaved with admirable coolness. A division of Gen. Frossard took the heights which overlook the left bank of Saarbruck. The Prussians made a short resistance. We were in the first line: the balls and bullets fell at our feet. Louis has kept a bullet which fell near him. Some of the soldiers wept on seeing him so calm."

There were many who ridiculed this despatch as absurd. "The London Echo" of Aug. 4, quoting from "The London Standard," says, —

"The stern ordeal with which the Prince Imperial was confronted was a state necessity. The baptism of war is a sacrament which the French nation regards with peculiar devotion. When we are told that many soldiers wept at seeing him so calm, we perceive that the incident may have its theatrical side to English eyes; but to Frenchmen it is an episode not easily forgotten: and it may be, that, in after-years, the memory of the baptism of fire at Saarbruck will serve the prince better than all the traditions of his house."

CHAPTER XIX.

PRUSSIAN VICTORIES AND FRENCH DEFEATS.

GEN. DOUAY'S division of Marshal MacMahon's corps was stationed at Weissenbourg, which was the extreme northeastern post of France. The pretty little town, on the south bank of the Lauter, contained about five thousand inhabitants. The country around, rough and broken, was covered with dense masses of forest.

There were about thirty thousand French troops at Weissenbourg. Considerably over a hundred thousand Prussians, advancing from the strong fortresses of Landau, Manheim, and Mayence, emerged unexpectedly from the forests, and fell upon the French with great fury. The battle was long and bloody. The Prussians, marching recklessly upon the ramparts of their foe, were cut down with awful carnage by the accuracy and rapidity of the French fire. The mitrailleuses annihilated whole regiments; but the French were overpowered, routed, and put to flight.

The Crown Prince of Prussia led the German troops in this brilliant and successful assault. MacMahon retreated in a westerly direction to Bitche and Woerth. The Prussians pursued vigorously. The French, having received slight re-enforcements, made another stand, with about thirty-five thousand men, near Woerth. The Prussians, a hundred and forty thousand strong, again fell upon them.[1] Notwithstanding the disparity of force, the battle was fought with equal desperation on both sides. The slaughter was dreadful. The Prussians, advancing in dense masses against the artillery, the mitrailleuses, and the musketry of their foes, suffered more severely than the French. King William's exultant telegram to Queen Augusta was as follows:—

"Wonderful luck!—this new, great victory won by Fritz. Thank God for his mercy! We have taken thirty cannon, two eagles, six mitrailleuses, four thousand prisoners. A victorious salute of a hundred and one guns was fired upon the field of battle."

Napoleon was at Metz. He sent the following telegram to Paris: "Marshal MacMahon has lost a battle. Gen. Frossard, on the Saar, has been compelled to fall back. The retreat is being effected in good order. All may be regained."

As the French retreated, the immense German army, estimated at from five to eight hundred thousand men, came pouring across the frontier into France. Their impregnable fortresses upon the Rhine afforded them a perfect base of operations.

The German cavalry, in pursuit, came upon many thousand fugitives who had thrown away their arms. All the villages were crowded with wounded from the battle of Woerth.

---

[1] "It is positively ascertained at the ministry of war in Paris that Marshal MacMahon had only thirty-five thousand men at the battle of Woerth, and that the Prussians numbered a hundred and forty thousand."—*Correspondent of the London Times*, Aug. 9, 1870.

The Prussians testify to the valor of their foes on this occasion. Eleven times the French charged the Prussian lines, each time breaking through only to find a mass of fresh troops behind. Nearly all of MacMahon's staff were killed. The marshal himself, after having been fifteen hours in the saddle, was unhorsed, and fell fainting into a ditch. Nothing can be imagined more horrible than this flight, as thirty thousand fugitives rushed pell-mell, pursued by four times their number, hurling upon them a murderous storm of shot and shell.

The correspondent of "The London Times," then with the Prussian army, writes, "The fighting of the French was grand. The Prussian generals say they never witnessed any thing more brilliant. But the Prussians were not to be denied. With tenacity as great, and a fierce resolution, they pressed on up the heights, where the vineyards dripped with blood, and, though checked again and again, still pressed on with a furious intrepidity which the enemy could not withstand in that long fight of six hours, during which the battle raged in full vehemence. It lasted, indeed, for thirteen hours."[1]

It is a wild and sad glimpse we catch of Marshal MacMahon at the close of this disastrous battle. Accompanied by a melancholy procession of the wounded, he entered Nancy in search of food for his routed and starving army. He was covered with mud; his clothes were torn with bullets; one of his epaulets had been shot away; and his face and hands were blackened with powder. It was almost impossible to recognize him. At the hotel he asked for some cold meat. For twenty-

---

[1] London Times, Aug. 9.

eight hours he had tasted no food. Some one asked him of the cuirassiers. "There are none of them left," he replied sadly. The Crown Prince was in hot pursuit. The marshal, with his broken and dispirited ranks, hurried on.[1]

The French retreated in two bands, — one, under Gen. Frossard, towards Metz; the other, under Gen. MacMahon, by a more southerly route, towards Nancy. It was manifest, to the surprise of France and all Europe, that Prussia had brought into the field forces so overwhelming in numbers, that the French troops would be compelled to take refuge in their fortresses until the nation could be roused to arms. France had not more than three hundred and fifty thousand troops in all her northern departments. A gentleman in Berlin wrote, — and subsequent facts sustain his declaration, —

"There are now in France over seven hundred thousand effective German troops. Besides these, three new armies are forming; and in less than a fortnight they will be where they are most needed. The rapidity with which the present army was equipped and sent to the frontier was one of the most stupendous achievements of war. These new armies will raise the effective German force to something over a million. There are, besides, enough trained and experienced soldiers here to double that number, if there should be even a suspicion of their necessity.

"The first principle the government adopted for carrying on the war was, not to see with how few soldiers they could get on, but rather how many could in any way be employed to hasten its successful termination.

---

[1] London Daily News, Aug. 20, 1870.

If one million of men could make final success reasonably certain, and two millions would hasten that success, two millions were to be called without a moment's hesitation."

There was now apparently a constant battle. The roar of artillery, the crackle of musketry, and the tramp of charging squadrons, were heard almost every hour of every day. Wherever the French made a stand, they were assailed. No matter how strong their position, no matter with what desperation of valor they might face their foes, they were invariably overwhelmed and routed. Even if they succeeded for a time in repelling at any point the Prussian assault, and literally covered the field with the Prussian dead, new forces of the foe soon came rushing forward; and the French shouts of victory were hushed in the silence of defeat, flight, and death.

The Prussian officers seemed quite reckless of human life. The German soldiers fought as though life to them was of no value. Not three weeks had passed from the commencement of hostilities ere it was announced that two hundred thousand Prussian soldiers had fallen, or had been captured, in a constant series of Prussian *victories*.

While Gen. MacMahon was on his flight towards Nancy, pursued by numbers which he could not resist, another immense German army was advancing in rapid strides for the investment of the French fortress of Metz. This was by far the strongest military post which France had in her north-eastern provinces. At the same time, another German army marched to lay siege to the French city and fortress of Strasburg on the Rhine.

The alarm in Paris was great. The government had

no force sufficient even to retard the advance of the victorious foe to the walls of the metropolis. Vigorous measures were immediately adopted for the defence of the city. Laws were passed summoning all unmarried Frenchmen between the ages of twenty-five and thirty-five to the defence of the country.

On the 7th of August, the Empress Eugénie, who had been intrusted with the regency during the absence of the emperor to the front, issued the following proclamation from the Tuileries: —

"Frenchmen, the opening of the war has not been in our favor. Our arms have suffered a check. Let us be firm under this reverse, and let us hasten to repair it. Let there be among us but a single party, — that of France; but a single flag, — the flag of our national honor.

"Faithful to my mission and my duty, you will see me first where danger threatens, to defend the flag of France. I call upon all good citizens to preserve order: to disturb it would be to conspire with our enemies.   "EUGÉNIE."

Marshal Bazaine at Metz was appointed commander-in-chief of the French armies on the Rhine. He had a disposable force, could he concentrate it, of about two hundred and thirty thousand men with which to repel three times that number of Germans. Gen. MacMahon, with thirty-five thousand troops, was effectually cut off from him at Nancy, about thirty miles on the south.

The generalship of the French officers in these conflicts has been very severely, and perhaps justly, condemned. Still it is obvious that no skill of generalship could counteract such a vast disproportion in numbers. The Prussian troops were as brave, as well armed, and as ably officered, as any troops that ever entered a battlefield.

A correspondent, writing to "The London Standard" from Berlin, Aug. 13, says, "Great credit is given the French emperor, in Berlin, for the straightforward way in which he has acknowledged his disasters. 'MacMahon has lost a battle' is a direct style of speaking not usual among the French when there is any thing unpleasant to relate."

Just after the battle of Woerth, a French officer, who was taken prisoner, reported in the "Gaulois," "His Royal Highness the Crown Prince of Prussia talked to us about the war, which he said he detested. He was inexhaustible in his praises of the bravery of the French. 'Two regiments of cuirassiers,' he said, 'were sent against the Prussian batteries. Our infantry was decimating them; and yet they formed again as if on parade, and charged again, sword in hand, with wonderful *ensemble.*

"'I was at Paris,' he continued, 'about the end of December, and saw the emperor, who always showed great kindness to my wife and me.'"[1]

These reverses caused intense excitement in Paris, and inspired the opponents of the government with new energies. Jules Favre, the eloquent leader of the democratic opposition in the Legislative Corps, in an impassioned speech, attributed the reverses of the army to the absolute incapacity of the emperor. He demanded that the emperor should relinquish the command, and that the

[1] Le Gaulois, Aug. 12, 1870.

legislative body should take in hand the direction of the affairs of the country.

Indescribable agitation followed this speech. The deputies in opposition to the government applauded; but the majority protested. Gen. Cassagnac declared that such a movement was the commencement of revolution. Gesticulating frantically, he exclaimed, "If the ministry did their duty, you would be tried by court-martial, and shot!"

There was a great uproar. The members rushed from their seats. It is said that there were some personal rencounters. The president, after in vain attempting to restore order by ringing his bell, put on his hat, thus announcing that the sitting was suspended. The commotion in the streets of Paris was still more exciting.[1]

The shattered fragments of the French army, no longer able to cope with the foe, were on the retrograde movement for the defence of Paris. The Germans vigorously pursued, spreading in all directions, foraging freely, capturing small towns, and levying heavy contributions upon the people. The vilest of men always rush into the ranks of an army. There is no power of discipline which can prevent awful scenes of outrage wherever armies move. Stories are told of atrocities committed by both French and Germans, too revolting to be repeated.

It was about sixty miles from Woerth to Metz and to Nancy. An army, with its artillery-train, can seldom move more than fifteen miles a day. The Prussians were in such amazing force, that they occupied all the passes of the Vosges Mountains. One strong body of

---

[1] Lloyd's Weekly London Newspaper, Aug. 14, 1870.

troops was sent to lay siege to Strasburg; another surrounded the fortress of Bitche; while the cavalry from the army of the Crown Prince, Frederick William, approached Metz. The cavalry of the army of the Prince Royal, which was on the advance to Paris by parallel roads about thirty miles south, moved upon Luneville.

Marshal Bazaine, with about a hundred and eighty thousand men, was compelled to take refuge beneath the walls of Metz. Beyond Metz, the road to the capital was open. The Prussian army, pushing on between Metz and Nancy, prevented any union of MacMahon's division with that of Bazaine. MacMahon continued his retreat towards Paris; and, on the morning of the 12th of August, the Prussians took possession of the city of Nancy. The Prussians were now within two hundred and twenty miles of Paris.

Metz, which was to be the scene of so much heroism and suffering, was a fine city of fifty-six thousand inhabitants. It was situated at the confluence of the Seille and the Moselle, and contained one of the largest arsenals in France, with founderies and machinery of all kinds for the manufacture of arms and military equipments. Its defences were considered almost impregnable; the fortifications having been constructed by Vauban. In the year 1552, the emperor, Charles V., besieged the place for ten months. Though the garrison was small, it held the works firmly; and the emperor, after the unavailing efforts of nearly a year, was compelled to raise the siege, having lost ten thousand men.

Into this fortress Bazaine was driven, with not less than a hundred and eighty thousand troops under his command. He was a man of great military renown. It was supposed that such a fortress, so garrisoned, could hold out against any odds for many months. Bazaine had risen to his proud eminence as a marshal of France through his own energies. In 1831 he had enlisted as a private in the army, and had started for Africa with his knapsack on his back. In four years he rose to a sub-lieutenancy. He accompanied the army sent by Louis Philippe to Spain to assist Isabella against the Carlists. In 1839 he returned to Algiers with the rank of captain. In 1850 he obtained a colonelcy. During the Italian war, his bravery and military ability were brilliantly displayed. In Mexico he won his marshal's *bâton*. He is the youngest of the French marshals, being now fifty-nine years of age. He has ever been an ardent supporter of the imperial government in France.

On the 14th of August, the emperor was at Verdun, about thirty miles west of Metz. MacMahon had retreated from Nancy to Toul, moving towards Verdun. Bazaine, leaving a garrison in the fortress of Metz, endeavored with the main body of his army to effect a junction with MacMahon at Verdun. He had transported about half his force across the Moselle, to the left bank, when the Prussians fell suddenly upon him. The battle was fierce even to desperation. The slaughter on both sides was dreadful. The French were driven back to Metz.

For days and weeks almost, an incessant battle raged around this fortress. Marshal Bazaine had about a hundred and fifty thousand men whom he could bring into the field. Prince Frederick Charles, in command of the Prussian force, had two hundred and thirty thousand. With great military sagacity, he had so posted his troops as to cut off all the avenues of escape. It has generally been thought that Bazaine ought to have cut his way through his foes. It is easy, seated by one's fireside, to form such a judgment. No one can doubt the ability, bravery, or patriotism, of Bazaine. The bloody battles which were fought day after day testify to the energy of his attempts. It must not be forgotten that Prince Charles was one of the most able and experienced of military commanders; that he had an army outnumbering the French by eighty thousand men; that he had thrown up intrenchments across every avenue of escape, which intrenchments were bristling with artillery, mitrailleuses, and the needle-gun. Never before were battles so bloody. The slain were counted by tens of thousands. The hospitals were crowded with the mutilated victims of this awful strife.

CHAPTER XX.

THE CAPTURE OF SEDAN.

THE "London Globe" of Aug. 15 contains a letter from an intelligent gentleman in Berlin, containing the following statement: "A very reliable informant states, that, within one week, Germany will have an effective army of 1,200,000 men. I should feel great caution in giving currency to these figures, were it not that I am certain that my informant is in a position to know."

The movements of the Prussians were as cautious as they were impetuous. It was their evident design that the whole country behind the German armies, as far back as the Rhine, should be cleared of every military obstruction. They therefore seized upon all the barriers of the Vosges; and their numbers were so immense, that, while a victorious army was advancing upon Paris, they had all the forces they needed to conduct the sieges of Metz, Strasburg, Bitche, and every other fortress they found upon their way. The annals of war scarcely present an example of so triumphant a march. The dismay and distress occasioned in the homes of the peasantry, and in the villages, as these apparently countless thousands of Prussians swept triumphantly along, cannot be imagined. Vast numbers (men, women, and children) fled from their homes, abandoning every thing, and in utter destitution sought refuge in the walled towns. God alone can comprehend the amount of misery inflicted; and as, on the field of battle, the missiles of war strewed the ground with the mangled, far away, amid the vineyards of Germany and the cottages of France, the woe was reduplicated as mothers and wives and loving maidens in despair surrendered themselves to life-long woe.

A French officer who was taken prisoner gives the following pleasing accounts of an interview with his victor: —

"Prince Frederick William, heir to the crown of Prussia, is a tall, thin man, with a tranquil and placid physiognomy; to which, however, the curve of his aquiline nose and the vivacity of his eye lend a stamp of decision. He speaks the French language with great purity. 'We all,' said he, 'admired, yesterday, the tenacity and courage evinced by the very meanest of your soldiers. I do not like war: if I ever reign, I will never make it. But, in spite of my love of peace, this is the third campaign I have been obliged to make. I went yesterday over the field of battle: it is frightful to look at. If it only depended on me, this war would be terminated on the spot. It is, indeed, a terrible war. I shall never offer battle to your soldiers without being superior in number: without that, I should prefer to withdraw.'"[1]

All alike seem to combine in testifying to the heroism of the French soldiers. A writer in "The London Times" of Aug. 16 says, "It may be questioned

[1] London Daily News, Aug. 15, 1870.

whether the French have not gathered more real glory from their defeats than the Prussians from their victories. Greater devotion was probably never witnessed in any war than that of certain French regiments, which rushed, at the voice of their general, upon inevitable destruction. The Prussians have fought where they liked and when they liked, and always with treble forces."

While Bazaine was in vain endeavoring to cut his way from Metz over the ramparts of his foe, MacMahon, with about thirty thousand men, was retreating upon Chalons, pursued by the Crown Prince at the head of a hundred and twenty thousand troops flushed with victory. On the 16th of August, the remnants of MacMahon's corps, numbering but fifteen thousand men, reached Chalons, where re-enforcements were met which raised their number to eighty thousand.

"MacMahon," says "The London Times," "in this retreat, has inflicted awful loss on the German army. There will be mourning in many thousand households, from the Rhine to the Vistula, and from the shores of the Baltic to the frontiers of Southern Bavaria. But then the Duke of Magenta has been utterly routed, and his defeat must have carried terror to the gates of Paris."[1]

In these hours of disaster, Gen. Trochu, who had already attained celebrity as a brilliant officer, was appointed, by the emperor, Governor of Paris, and commander-in-chief of all the forces assembled for its defence. Gen. Trochu was an imperialist; believing, with the overwhelming majority of his countrymen, that the

[1] London Times, Aug. 11, 1870.

empire was a better government for France than the old monarchy under a Bourbon or an Orléans prince, or the republic under such men as Favre and Hugo and Rochefort.

Strasburg on the Rhine contained eighty-four thousand inhabitants. "The Alsatians," says "The London Times," "are more loyal Frenchmen, almost, than the Parisians." A large force surrounded the city, and soon opened upon it a terrible bombardment from the siege-guns which they gathered from their fortresses near at hand. MacMahon had retreated to Chalons, fifty miles west of Metz. The Crown Prince, with a hundred and fifty thousand troops, was on the triumphant march towards Paris. Bazaine was hopelessly shut up in Metz, with his ammunition and provisions rapidly disappearing. Bands of Prussian cavalry were riding in all directions, emptying the granaries and the barn-yards of the peasants, and imposing enormous contributions on the towns which were captured. Desolation and misery were everywhere. The fields were covered with the unburied dead. Vionville, Flavigny, Rézonville, and Gravelotte were mostly in ashes. Families were wandering in the fields in terror and starvation.

The emperor was at Chalons, striving to assemble there a new army to arrest the advance of the Prussians upon Paris. There was no longer any French army in the field. Such a sudden collapse of one of the strongest military powers in the world was never before witnessed. A war of a fortnight had laid France prostrate; and this was done by a nation which but about a century ago could count but five million inhabitants. It was supposed that the Prussians would march irresistibly over the fortifications of Paris, and speedily encamp their hosts in the Garden of the Tuileries and in the Elysian Fields. Sorrows never come singly. Disaster followed disaster. The scenes described by eye-witnesses appall the imagination. In the silence of night, all the wooded gorges of the Ardennes resounded with the moan of the mutilated and the dying, rising in one continuous wail. The houses and the barns were filled with the sufferers. In one short battle, the French alone lost fifteen thousand in killed and wounded; and the Prussians, who marched recklessly up to their batteries of artillery and mitrailleuses, lost twice as many. The few surgeons could do comparatively nothing in the midst of such an accumulated mass of misery. Thousands groaned and died in the open fields, with none to give them even a cup of cold water.

The great object of Prussia in this war, as expressed by Bismarck after having entered upon it, and by all the leading Prussian journals, was to wrest from France so much additional territory, and so to weaken her, that she could never again make an attempt to recover her lost Rhine provinces. The panic in Paris was great; and frantic efforts were made to prepare for a siege.

The emperor remained with MacMahon's army, hoping to effect a junction of his troops with those of Bazaine. The plains of Chalons are as level as a floor, and thus poorly adapted for a defensive battle. On the 21st of August the French camp at Chalons was broken up, and the army retired about thirty miles to the north-east, — to the more broken ground of Rheims. As these armies of retreat and pursuit rushed along, scenes of heart-rending woe were witnessed among the inhabitants of the region thus swept by the devastating tempests of war. The Belgian frontier was overrun with thousands of families seeking refuge there in utter impoverishment.

The Crown Prince of Prussia was now within a hundred miles of Paris. There was no force before him to oppose his march. An advance force of cavalry had been pushed forward to within sixty-five miles of the capital. The zeal of the French people in the war, notwithstanding their disasters, is manifest from the fact, that a new war loan of a thousand million francs was taken up in forty-eight hours. Strasburg was holding out firmly against a terrible bombardment. The whole populace of Paris was roused to prepare the city for the approaching siege. Though the Prussians had encountered enormous losses, the railroad-trains from the Rhine were crowded with their re-enforcements hurrying forward to fill the places of those who had fallen.

Never was the march of an invading army more resolute. On Sunday, the 25th of August, the Prussian scouts had reached Mieux, within twenty-five miles of Paris. It was a distance of three hundred miles from Sierca, the nearest point on the Prussian frontier, to the city; and yet this long line, through French territory, Prussia guarded perfectly against a warlike nation of forty millions inhabitants. The French, unable to meet their foes in the field, did what they could to harass their march by blowing up bridges, cutting railways, and blocking roads.

A constant stream of French prisoners and of captured guns and flags was entering the streets of Berlin, causing the frequent blaze of illuminations and the most enthusiastic demonstrations of joy. The French, acting on the defensive, fought from behind their ramparts and in their fortresses. Though invariably in the end defeated, they as invariably inflicted upon their assailants a heavier loss in killed and wounded than they encountered. The shouts of joy which resounded through the streets of Berlin were answered by deeper wails of woe emerging from thousands of German cottages, whose inmates were plunged into life-long woe. It seems to be authentically stated that Prussia had then 1,124,000 well-trained and disciplined men under arms. Seven hundred and twenty thousand of these were in France. The condition of France was apparently hopeless. The exultant Prussians were marching wherever they pleased, filling their camps with abundance, exacting enormous contributions, and compelling France to drain the cup of humiliation to its dregs.

We have space for but one illustration of these exactions. It is given by a correspondent of "The London Times;" which journal was in cordial sympathy with the Prussians. The little town of Saverne contained 5,331 inhabitants. As the Prussian troops approached, the more wealthy portion of the inhabitants fled. The contributions demanded of the town were ten thousand loaves of three pounds each; sixteen thousand pounds of rice; two hundred and fifty pounds of roasted coffee; fifteen hundred pounds of salt; one thousand pounds of tobacco; seventy-five thousand cigars of superior quality; fifteen thousand quarts of wine; two hundred pounds of sugar; fifty pounds of extract of meat; a hundred and twenty thousand pounds of oats; fifty thousand pounds of hay; fifty thousand pounds of straw. These were all to be delivered before six o'clock the next morning in warehouses appointed for the purpose. A hundred wagons were to be furnished to enable the victors to carry away this food and forage. The penalty of non-compliance was the general plunder of the town by the soldiers.

Scarcely any thing conceivable is more awful than the march through a country of half a million of hostile troops. A garden may bloom before them: a desert will be left behind. Famine and pestilence inevitably follow in the train.

On Tuesday, the 30th of August, the army of the Crown Prince overtook MacMahon's corps a short distance north of Rheims; and after a fierce battle, of enormous slaughter on each side, the Prussians drove the shattered army of the French in utter rout towards Sedan. During all the hours of the 31st, the battle raged in an incessant series of bloody skirmishes, as the French troops, about a hundred thousand in number, pressed on every side, fell back, bleeding, exhausted, despairing, into Sedan.

From the commencement of the war, the Prince Imperial, notwithstanding his youth, had accompanied his father, sharing all the fatigues of the campaign. At the commencement of these hours of terrible disaster, Marshal MacMahon, foreseeing that he was to be surrounded by overwhelming numbers, urged the emperor, with his son, to withdraw. The emperor resolved to remain with the army, and share its fate. He sent his son, however, to Mézières, and thence into Belgium.

The dawn of the morning of the 1st of September found the French so surrounded as to be cut off from all possibility of retreat. They were crowded together in a narrow space, while five hundred pieces of artillery were opening fire upon them. At five o'clock in the morning, the terrific storm of battle opened its thunders. It was an awful day. In the first hour of the battle, Gen. MacMahon was struck by the splinter of a shell, and was carried back, severely wounded, into Sedan. The command passed to Gen. Wimpffen. Nearly three hundred thousand men were now hurling a storm of bullets, shot, and shell, into the crowded ranks of the French. It was an indescribable scene of tumult and carnage. A correspondent of one of the London papers writes, —

"All describe the conduct of the emperor as that of one who either cared not for death, or actually threw himself in its way. In the midst of the scene of confusion which ensued upon the irruption of the panic-stricken French into Sedan, the emperor, riding slowly through a wide street swept by the German artillery and choked by the disordered soldiery, paused a moment to address a question to a colonel of his staff.

"At the same instant a shell exploded a few feet in front of Napoleon, leaving him unharmed; though it was evident to all around that he had escaped by a miracle. The emperor continued on his way without manifesting the slightest emotion, greeted by the enthusiastic *vivats* of the troops. Later, while sitting at a window inditing his celebrated letter to the King of Prussia, a shell struck the wall just outside, and burst only a few feet from the emperor's chair, again leaving him unscathed and unmoved."

For five hours the emperor had been exposed to a fire which filled the air with bullets, ploughed up the ground at his feet, and covered the field with the mutilated and the dead. At half-past three o'clock in the afternoon, Gen. Wimpffen sent an officer to propose that the emperor should place himself in the middle of a column of men who should endeavor to cut their way through the enemy. The emperor replied, that he could not consent to save himself at the sacrifice of so many men; that he had determined to share the fate of the army. Though a large portion of the army was still fighting valiantly upon the heights around the walls, the streets of Sedan were choked with the *débris* of all the corps, and were fiercely bombarded from all sides.

After twelve hours of so unequal a conflict, the commanders of the *corps d'armée* reported to the emperor that they could no longer offer any serious resistance. The emperor ordered the white flag to be raised upon the citadel, and sent the following letter to his Prussian Majesty, who was with the conquering army:—

"Sire, my brother, not having been able to die in the midst of my troops, it only remains for me to place my sword in the hands of your Majesty.

"I am of your Majesty the good brother,
"Napoleon."

William immediately replied, "Sire, my brother, regretting the circumstances under which we meet, I accept the sword of your Majesty; and I pray you to name one of your officers provided with full powers to treat for the capitulation of the army which has so bravely fought under your command. On my side, I have named Gen. Moltke for this purpose.

"I am of your Majesty the good brother,
"William."

Gen. Wimpffen was sent to the Prussian headquarters. "Your army," said Gen. Moltke, "does not number more than eighty thousand men. We have two hundred and thirty thousand, who completely surround you. Our artillery is everywhere in position, and can destroy the place in two hours. You have provisions for only one day, and scarcely any more ammunition. The prolongation of your defence would be only a useless massacre."[1]

Gen. Wimpffen returned to Sedan. A council of thirty-two general officers was called. With but two dissentient voices, it was decided to be useless to sacrifice any more lives. The capitulation was signed.

Our distinguished countryman, Dr. J. Marion Sims, was present at the battle of Sedan as surgeon-in-chief of the Anglo-American ambulance-corps. He testifies as follows to the necessity of the surrender: —

"It was impossible for the French to do otherwise than surrender. The emperor was not to be blamed. It was simply an act of humanity to have surrendered. On the morning of the 1st of September, MacMahon left his hotel at six o'clock. The battle had been progressing for some time. At half-past six he received his wound in the thigh, and was carried back to his hotel. The command then devolved upon Gen. Wimpffen, who had arrived only the day before. At five o'clock in the evening, white flags were raised; and, at six o'clock, the firing ceased entirely.

"On the next day, when the emperor had an interview with the king and talked of capitulation, Gen. Wimpffen said he could not sign the articles; but Bismarck showed him how the forces were situated, the French hemmed in, and without ammunition or provision, and no way of escape. Then Gen. Wimpffen, seeing he was surrounded by three times his own

---

[1] Campagne de 1870. Des Causes qui ont amené la Capitulation de Sedan, par un Officier attaché à l'État Major-Général.

strength and was powerless, had to sign the articles, after being but a few hours in command.

"The newspaper reports of the cruelty of the Prussians are not in the least exaggerated. The particulars are not fit for publication. Some eighty thousand French marched from Sedan before the Prussian lines to the little peninsula formed by the river, where they were halted after the capitulation. It was the saddest day in my life when I followed the poor French prisoners; and, if I lived a hundred years, I could never forget what I saw them endure. They were several days there on that piece of land, dying of sickness and starvation.

"The Bavarians utterly destroyed Bazeilles, a town of three thousand inhabitants. They say they were fired upon from the windows of the houses. In their rage they fastened up the doors, and set fire to each house, burning a great number of women and children. The smell of charred human flesh, for several days afterwards, was sickening. The Bavarians also shot a priest there, and some nuns and school-girls, besides a great number of citizens.

"I think the emperor never looked better than on the day of his surrender. It is a great mistake to suppose he is a decrepit old man. His intellect was never more vigorous; and his physical health is perfect, with the exception of some mere infirmities. He is occasionally subject to sciatica, but to no disease that threatens life.

"It is said that the Prince Imperial is a scrofulous boy. That is another great mistake. He is strong and rosy, in perfect health, and very intelligent, — a splendid boy, take him all in all. When he was ill a few years ago, and was reported scrofulous, he simply had an abscess, the result of pressure in taking horse-riding lessons, — nothing connected in the least with disease of the bones or joints.

"They say the emperor has millions. I sincerely hope it may be so; but I have it, on the highest authority, that he is poor. The empress has property; and the Prince Imperial has property, left him two years ago by an Italian lady who died in Paris; but the emperor is not a rich man."[1]

[1] Testimony of Dr. Sims in the New-York Times, Nov. 4, 1870.

CHAPTER XXI.

THE OVERTHROW OF THE EMPIRE.

KING WILLIAM, in a letter which he wrote to Queen Augusta, speaks as follows of his fallen foe : —

"You already know, through my three telegrams, the extent of the great historical event which has just happened. It is like a dream, though one has seen it unroll itself hour after hour. On the morning of the 2d I drove to the battle-field, and met Moltke, who was coming to obtain my consent to the capitulation. He told me that the emperor had left Sedan at five o'clock, and had come to Donchery. As he wished to speak to me, and there was a château in the neighborhood, I chose this for our meeting. At one o'clock I started with Fritz, escorted by the cavalry staff. I alighted before the château, where the emperor came to meet me. We were both much moved at meeting again under such circumstances. What my feelings were, considering that I had seen Napoleon only three years before at the summit of his power, is more than I can describe."

"At this conference," writes one of the officers of the imperial staff, "the king showed the lofty feelings which animated him by exhibiting to the emperor all the consideration which his misfortunes demanded; and the emperor preserved an attitude of the utmost dignity."

The illustrious captive was assigned to the Castle of Wilhelmshöhe, near Cassel, one of the most attractive castles in Germany. Accompanied by his friends, supplied with every comfort, and surrounded by a guard of honor, the chains which held the prisoner of war were invisible.[1]

The tidings of this great calamity soon reached Paris, and created intense excitement. The democratic party, which numbered in its ranks many of the lower orders of the Parisian populace, deemed it a favorable opportunity to overthrow the empire and to grasp the reins of power. An American gentleman then in Paris writes, under date of Sept. 4, —

"Paris is in a state of riotous excitement. Crowds are tearing down the imperial arms, and destroying the golden eagles of the empire. Fears are entertained that the city will soon be at the mercy of mobs."

The mob shouted, "Down with the empire!" "Live the republic!" Gen. Trochu, Governor of Paris, was called for. He told the mob, that, having taken the oath of allegiance to the empire, he could not thus renounce it. The crowd at length became so menacing,

---

[1] Wilhelmshöhe is one of the finest mansions in Europe. It is said to have cost about ten million dollars, and was built from the money which the Elector William received from England for the Hessian troops loaned her to fight the North-American colonies. The castle is situated but a short distance from Cassel, which was the capital of the kingdom of Westphalia. It is erected upon a hill commanding a magnificent view of the adjacent country. It is approached by a grand avenue, and is surrounded by one of the finest parks in Europe. The palace, which is built of white sandstone resembling marble, consists of a massive central tower, flanked by spacious wings. The garden, spreading out from the foot of the tower, is renowned for its picturesque beauty.

that the police dispersed it with fire-arms. At one o'clock, P.M., a crowd of a hundred thousand armed men surrounded the building of the Legislative Corps, and crowded all its avenues, rending the air with frenzied shouts. From all parts of the city, the agitated masses were converging towards the Legislative Hall. The friends of the government found it necessary to secrete themselves, or to keep silent. The Place de la Concorde presented a compact mass of human beings. A strong military force guarded the Tuileries. Shouts of "Vive république!" rose on all sides. The police were overpowered by the populace, and their arms thrown into the Seine. Paris was in the hands of the mob. The populace began to shout for the abdication of the empress-regent. Her life was menaced by brawny men and women.

There are few things on earth more to be dreaded than a Paris mob. The men were armed with muskets and revolvers. The tumults, the shouts, the surgings to and fro, and the menaces, were horrible. Terror had commenced its reign; and the friends of order, utterly helpless, fled. The mob burst open the doors of the Legislative Hall. The president trembled in his chair as the *blouses*, with oaths and execrations, took possession of the room. Some of the radical speakers tried in vain to appease them. The friends of the government, composing the very large majority of the deputies, escaped as they could.

"What the minister of war would have said, what M. Thiers, and even Jules Favre, would have said, remains to be imagined; for the people would not hear, but yelled '*Déchéance!*' so savagely, that nothing else was heard. The crowd kissed the jubilant leaders of the left, and hurrahed until the hall rang. The president, putting on his cap to announce that such proceedings could not be tolerated, received such a blow on the head from a club, that he fell covered with blood, and was led away moaning, while other infuriated workmen were striving to hit him again. Enthusiastic blouses at once set off up the boulevard, bearing huge placards announcing that the republic was proclaimed by 185 votes against 113. But there really was no voting at all, and no one to vote against it."[1]

In these hours of tumult and terror, the deputies being all dispersed by the vast riot, the Empress Eugénie was at the Tuileries. All were bewildered by the sudden outbreak of lawlessness and violence. Worn down with care and sorrow, she listened appalled to the clamor which was surging through all the streets. Tidings came that the mob was advancing to sack the Tuileries. Her woman's heart shrank from ordering the body-guard to shoot them down. The conflict between the small body-guard and the mob would be bloody, and almost certainly unavailing. The only safety for the empress was in immediate flight, with as few attendants as possible, that she might avoid observation.

The empress had but just retired by a private door, when the mob came surging through the gravelled alleys of the garden, burst open the doors of the palace, and rioted unrestrained through all its apartments. The flag of the French Empire was hauled down, and insulting sentences were scribbled upon the statues and the walls. Hundreds of degraded women, foul and drunken, ransacked the apartments of Eugénie, — that empress

---

[1] Paris correspondence of the Boston Journal, Sept. 5, 1870.

who for twenty years had proved that the children of sorrow could never appeal to her in vain. They broke into the private cabinet of the emperor. The Babel of their songs and cries resounded far and wide through the streets.

While these scenes were transpiring, a few of the leaders of the democratic party in Paris met in the Hôtel de Ville, and organized themselves into a provisional government. Gambetta, one of the most prominent of these men, repaired to the office of the minister of the interior, and, with but two men to support him, demanded the books. The imperial officers, aware that the mob of Paris was at the command of Gambetta, withdrew from the office, leaving him in full possession.

It was thus that the empire in France was overthrown by a few hundred men in Paris. The empire, in an appeal to universal suffrage, in every city and village in France, in the army, in the navy, and in Algiers, had been established by a vote of nearly eight millions. There were but about three hundred thousand in the negative. The republic was established by the democratic portion of the populace in Paris. The opponents were overawed, and dared not express an opinion. Outside of the walls of Paris, there were thirty-eight millions of French people. Their voice was not listened to at all. The ecclesiastics, almost without an exception, were in favor of the empire. The peasantry composing the millions of the rural districts were supporters of the empire with scarcely a dissenting voice.

The democratic party in the leading cities — Lyons, Marseilles, &c. — followed the lead of the democrats in Paris in renouncing the empire and in proclaiming a republic; but they refused to give in their adhesion to the self-constituted provisional government in Paris, and established governments of their own. Thus immediately there sprang up four distinct governments in France, each claiming to be "the French republic." First, there was the self-constituted "committee of national defence" in Paris. The second was a sort of delegated government in Tours. The third was a committee of public safety at Marseilles, under the dictator Alphose Esquiros. The fourth was the red republican committee at Lyons. And there was still another attempt to grasp the reins of power by the democrats of Grenoble.

During the progress of the French revolution of 1789, the people of France were divided in opinion respecting the best form of government to be adopted. The aristocracy, and all under their control, demanded the old monarchy. They were sustained by wealth, by the immense influence of ancestral rank, and by all the courts and nobles of Europe. On the other hand were the republicans, mainly composed of the energetic populace of the cities and the more intelligent of the inhabitants of the rural districts. In some portions of France, nearly all the peasantry were in favor of the old monarchy. Never was there a more dreadful war waged on earth than that between the French monarchists and republicans in La Vendée.

The empire was an attempt at a compromise between the old *régime* and the modern republic. It maintained monarchical forms; while it rejected all aristocratic privilege, rearing the whole fabric of the government upon the principle of *equal rights for all men*. It rejected the principle of the *divine right* of kings, and proclaimed the *divine right* of the *people*. The re-established empire which the democratic party in the great cities was now endeavoring to overthrow had been adopted by the voice of universal suffrage. Every man in France, who was not a felon or a pauper, voted. The historic facts, beyond all dispute, were as follows: —

In 1848, the French people overthrew the monarchical throne of Louis Philippe, established a republic, and chose Louis Napoleon Bonaparte president by 5,562,834 votes. The fairness of the vote cannot be questioned, since the polls were in the hands of Gen. Cavaignac, a rival candidate, *who was then dictator*.

A conspiracy was formed by the leaders of the Legitimist, Orléans, and Jacobin parties, to overthrow this republic. The monarchists deemed it too democratic in its character, and the red republicans deemed it not democratic enough. Thus the monarchist Thiers and the radical Louis Blanc clasped hands for its overthrow. Each hoped upon its ruins to rear his own favorite governmental fabric.[1]

By the *coup d'état*, on the morning of Dec. 2, 1851, the president thwarted this conspiracy, and rescued the republic from the destruction with which it was menaced. An immediate appeal to universal suffrage, on the 20th of December, sustained the president in the *coup d'état*. Thus France made the act her own, and rewarded Napoleon by re-electing him president of the republic, which he had saved, for an additional period of ten years. The vote was taken throughout the eighty-six departments of France. There were 7,439,216 votes in favor of the president, and but 640,737 against him.

---

[1] See Alison's History of Europe, vol. vii. p. 535.

And now the people of France resolved to re-establish the empire, — the old republican empire of Napoleon I. Petitions were sent in from all parts signed by millions. "It became every day more evident that Paris, all entire, associated itself heart and soul in the wish universally and spontaneously uttered by the departments. From all parts of the territory, addresses soliciting this change, covered by thousands of signatures, flooded the Senate, which alone, in accordance with the constitution, could effect amendments of this nature. Thus it was the totality of France which demanded the re-establishment of the empire."[1]

The polls, to decide upon the question whether the empire should be re-established, were opened on the 21st and 22d of November, 1852. This was eleven months after the *coup d'état*, by which the president had saved the republic. There were 7,864,180 votes in favor of the empire, and but 253,145 cast against it.

Thus the empire was re-established with a degree of unanimity quite unparalleled in the history of nations.[2] It is said that Napoleon, having taken an oath to be true to the republic, could not, under these changed circumstances, lend his aid to the establishment of the empire

[1] MM. Gallix et Guy, p. 594.

[2] It is generally estimated, that, where suffrage is universal with all males over twenty-one years of age, there is one voter to about five of the population. The empire was established by a vote of 7,864,180. This represents a population of 39,320,900. Surely such unanimity was never before manifested in the establishment of a government. For twenty years, this government conferred upon France prosperity never enjoyed before, and was repeatedly sanctioned by the votes of the people. The opposition was confined to the great cities. It is easy to say that the vote was fraudulent; but the cordial support of the empire for twenty years proves that it was in harmony with the popular sentiment.

without perjury. Such is Senator Sumner's opinion. He says, —

"Promise, pledge, honor, oath, were all violated in this monster treason. Never in history was greater turpitude. As I am a republican, and believe in republican institutions, I cannot forgive the traitor."[1]

The re-establishment of the empire made but a slight change in the republican constitution, which still remained in force. The government consisted of the supreme executive called Emperor, his Ministers, a Council of State, a Senate, and a House of Representatives called the Corps Législatif.

The emperor, chosen by universal suffrage, transmitted his crown to his natural heirs. He appointed his ministers.

The Senate was composed of the cardinals, the marshals, and the admirals of France, with enough others, appointed by the crown from citizens most distinguished for their services, to bring the number up to a hundred and fifty. The senators held their seats for life. After being appointed, they were entirely independent of the crown.

The members of the Corps Législatif were chosen by the people; one deputy for every thirty-five thousand electors. Every Frenchman over twenty-one years of age was a voter; and the deputies were chosen for a term of six years.

The councillors of state were from forty to fifty in number, were appointed by the emperor, and were removable by him. No law could be established, or tax imposed, without receiving the sanction of the Council

---

[1] Senator Sumner on the war, — New-York Herald, Oct. 29, 1870.

of State, the Senate, the Legislative Corps, and the signature of the emperor. The executive, legislative, and judicial functions were clearly defined, and carefully separated. This constitution could at any time be amended by the votes of the people, without rendering it necessary to resort to revolutionary violence.

While this constitution was less popular in its provisions than that of the United States, it was an immense advance from the spirit of the old Bourbon *régimes*, and was decidedly more republican in its character than the constitution of Great Britain.

Such, in brief, was the government which the democratic leaders in the great cities, in the midst of the terrible disasters by which France was overwhelmed, had overthrown, and replaced by several self-constituted committees of public safety.[1]

Gen. Dix, who was for several years the American ambassador to the French Empire, in his parting speech to the American residents in Paris said, —

"It speaks strongly in favor of the illustrious sovereign who for the last twenty years has held the destinies of France in his hands, that the condition of the people, materially and intellectually, has been constantly improving; and that the aggregate prosperity of the

---

[1] "It was not from the necessity of circumstances that France chose Louis Napoleon. It was because France preferred him above all others, without exception. It is because he is the only man truly popular; the only name to which attach souvenirs of grand achievements accomplished for the country. What can any one say respecting the achievements of our *legitimate* kings? Who, in cottage or shop, knows any thing of them? Nobody. But all the world knows of the man who raised France to grandeur unheard of before; who subdued anarchy, and brought Europe to our feet; the man who knew how to recompense services rendered, and to discover merit wherever it existed; the man who took the son of the citizen to make him a marshal, and the son of a workman to make him a king." — *MM. Gallix et Guy,* p. 9.

country is greater, perhaps, at the present moment, than at any former period.

"As you know, debates in the Corps Législatif, on questions of public policy, are unrestricted. They are reported with great accuracy, and promptly published in the official journal and other newspaper presses. Thus the people of France are constantly advised of all that is said for or against the administrative measures which concern their interests. In liberal views, in that comprehensive forecast which shapes the policy of the present to meet the exigencies of the future, the emperor seems to me decidedly in advance of his ministers, and even of the popular body chosen by universal suffrage to aid him in his legislative labors."

Bismarck scornfully called the new governments which had usurped the place of the empire the "gutter democracy," and refused to recognize them. M. Thiers, the Orléanist, would not acknowledge their authority, though terribly embarrassed in consequence in his endeavors to obtain a treaty of peace. The monarchies of Continental Europe, almost with one accord, refused to recognize any of these *governments*, which were founded neither upon legitimacy nor upon popular suffrage.

For twenty years the empire had been the acknowledged government of France, recognized by all the nations of Europe and America. Nearly every civil, ecclesiastical, and military office was in the hands of the friends of the empire. The marshals and generals and the rank and file of the army were, with scarcely an exception, ardent imperialists. Fearful as was the pressure upon them to drive back that Germanic invasion which was perilling the very life of France, their energies were in a degree paralyzed by the rebellion against

17

the government which had so suddenly sprung up in the great cities. Marshal Bazaine, at Metz, scornfully refused any recognition of the self-constituted committee in Paris, — a committee co-operating with the Prussian armies in overthrowing the established government. But for the presence of nearly a million of armed Prussians in France, the empire would have remained firm.

The democratic leaders in Europe are generally infidels, bitter foes of the Church. The peasantry, almost to a man, were friends of the empire, which respected their religion. The priesthood had immense influence in all the rural districts; and the whole priesthood, as a body, were opposed to the democracy. Thus, when Favre and Rochefort called upon France to rise *en masse* to repel the invaders, there was no cordial response. The priests and the peasants scarcely knew which to dread the most, — the Prussians, or the democrats; and when Garibaldi, who, by his assaults upon the Church, had rendered himself extremely obnoxious to all the Catholic priesthood, hastened to the aid of the democratic government in France, thousands of the Catholic soldiers refused to serve under such a leader.

Thus France was apparently doomed to destruction. With no acknowledged government, with democrats reviling imperialists in the most unmeasured terms of abuse, and imperialists treating the democrats as the enemies of religion and order, while at the same time the empire was overrun by as terrible an invasion as ever afflicted a people, and with but few words reaching French ears from England or America but words of scorn, the cup of misery the nation was doomed to drain seemed to be full to the brim. There was a latent Orléans element in the community, which did not develop itself in these disastrous hours.

Bismarck seemed appalled. He had expected that the overthrow of the republican empire would re-introduce the old monarchy under a Bourbon or an Orléans king. Instead of this, the democrats leaped upon the vacant throne, and grasped the sceptre. Bismarck, in consternation, would gladly have wrenched the sceptre from them, and restored it to the emperor. Democracy he feared above all things else.

"A republic," says Mr. Headley, "stares him in the face. He knows, from the effect of the last French republic on Germany, that another one established to-day will threaten the stability of his government more than Strasburg or Metz ever did or can; that a republic surging up to the borders of Germany is a more fearful menace than a hundred thousand French troops stationed along the Rhine. This very fact may furnish the key to his conduct in insisting on the overthrow of Paris. He knows that Paris is not France; and though the *city* may vote for a republic, the *entire country* has just cast an overwhelming vote in favor of an empire.

"Therefore, could he once occupy the capital, — so that, on the one hand, it could not overawe the provinces, and, on the other, give free scope to the monarchists to electioneer among the people, — a similar result would follow, and thus France become an empire. With this he could accomplish a double object, — secure Europe from the dreaded effect of a vast republic rising in its midst, and obtain also such a frontier as he desires. Such a plan would be worthy of this prince of diplomatists."

CHAPTER XXII.

THE PRISONER AND THE EXILE.

NEVER was the adage respecting one going down hill more strikingly verified than in the case of the emperor in his hours of misfortune. Even his buried mother Hortense and the Empress Eugénie had to take their share of the merciless vituperation. They were held up to the scorn of the world as women whose very touch was pollution. It was feared by the foes of the empire that popular suffrage might re-establish the imperial throne. Resort was therefore had to all the poisoned weapons of calumny to prevent this result. Accusations were fabricated, and documents, letters, and private papers, forged to prove that the Palace of the Tuileries, where for twenty years the most pure and illustrious of the gentlemen and ladies of England and America had found hospitable welcome, had been but a warehouse of infamy, seething with pollutions scarcely equalled by those of Sodom and Gomorrah. Must it be forever so that political antagonism shall extinguish every sentiment of magnanimity and honor?

Probably never before in the history of the world was a man assailed so fiercely and unscrupulously as was the Emperor of the French in his hours of misfortune. A writer in "The London Sunday Times" of Aug. 14 raised a feeble voice of remonstrance.

"I feel constrained," he wrote, "to lift up my voice in humble but earnest protest against the splenetic, malevolent, and contemptuous tone adopted by too many of your contemporaries in their allusions to the present monarch of the great French nation.

"Even had the emperor no claim whatever on the esteem and courtesy of Englishmen, there would still be something exceedingly repulsive and ignoble in the zest with which the writers referred to have seized upon the moment of his supreme anxiety to heap upon him abuse which could only be merited by a monster in whom the knave and the fool were equally dominant.

"The culmination of adversity should at least impose some restraint upon scorn and resentment, even though it fail to awaken compassion and sympathy. The Emperor of the French may have been at fault in permitting his ministers to hurry him into a causeless and awful war. It is not of legitimate comment and criticism that I now venture to complain. I protest against violent, scornful, unjust, and vulgar abuse ; against irritating sneers and vindictive insolence ; against lying vituperation and swaggering impertinence. Let it not be said that I exaggerate."

After quoting sundry of these assaults from "The Daily News," "The Pall-Mall Gazette," and "The London Times," which abundantly sustained his statement, he continues : —

"Now, of whom is all this written ? Of a man, who, during the whole period of his ascendency, has been the self-sacrificing friend and the faithful ally of this country. For years after he assumed the chief direction of affairs in France, he was treated every day and every week, by nearly the whole English press, to foul and scornful reprobation; yet, under provocations which would have goaded almost anybody else to madness, he sustained those onslaughts with marvellous patience. He never once resented them.

"In great enterprises he has co-operated with us, maintaining a candor, a courtesy, a consideration, and delicacy of respect, which all who have had directly to deal with him have gratefully acknowledged. In evil report and in good report, he has been fast and frank in his friendship with England. We owe vast expansions of our trade to his sagacity in framing and instituting the commercial treaty.

"Say what we will, under his auspices the material interests of France have undergone a marvellous development. The prosperity has been accompanied by some of the higher forms of popular progress. Have we any reasons for hunting down a monarch who never did us harm, and who has established the most venerable claims on our respect and gratitude?"

On the 18th of October, an English gentleman had an interview with the emperor at Wilhelmshöhe. In a communication he made to "The London Telegraph," he writes, —

"Napoleon III. was seated before a desk encumbered with documents, books, and newspapers. The apartment he uses as a study is a small square room not unlike the cabinet he used at the Tuileries. The emperor looked in every respect as well as when I last saw him at St. Cloud in July last. I reminded him that he had then spoken to me of the Hohenzollern incident, which he had regarded as *finished*.

"'Yes,' said the emperor with a sigh. '*L'homme propose, mais Dieu dispose*. I had no wish to make war; but fatality willed that it should be so. Public opinion was aroused in its favor; and I was obliged to acquiesce in the popular wish.'

"The emperor confidently relies upon the verdict of history to exonerate him from all the charges heaped upon his head. He alluded, but without bitterness, to the numberless calumnies of which he is the object in many parts of France. He spoke in despondent terms of the present distracted condition of France, — a prey to a foreign foe without, and anarchy within.

"When I ventured to ask him if the time would not soon come when he would be authorized to make some movement by his own initiative to retrieve his fortunes, he at once replied, that the sole aim of France must now be to drive out the invader of her soil; and he would never, by word or deed, throw any obstacles in the way of accomplishing that task." [1]

On the 9th of November, a correspondent of "The New-York Herald" was favored with an interview with the emperor at the Castle of Wilhelmshöhe. He found his Majesty perfectly free in his daily movements, and treated with profound respect. Traversing a number of stately halls and apartments, he was presented to the emperor in a room so small, that a writing-desk before the fire took up nearly the whole floor.

In the course of the conversation, the emperor is reported to have expressed the following sentiments: —

"All must admit that the press is a powerful institution. In France it has worked much good, and also

---

[1] London Telegraph, October, 1870.

much injury. When I consented to its being freed entirely from censorship, it was seized by demagogues and unscrupulous politicians, who openly preached disobedience to the laws; and they were but too successful in perverting the minds of the people.

"The same intelligence does not prevail in France that is found in the United States. The seditious arguments advanced by the press, when in the hands of pretended reformers, easily inflamed the untutored minds of the people.

"I suppose that Americans would naturally sympathize with republican institutions; but all the conditions requisite to a true republican form of government are absolutely wanting in France. Those who boldly grasped the reins of power have already discovered their utter inability to establish such a government. That for which they blamed me most, they have been compelled to do themselves, and in a form still more obnoxious.

"The restraint imposed upon the press, for instance, was the constant theme of the most violent attacks upon my government. But while I made but moderate use of this law, while fines and punishments were rare, and were preceded by a mild system of *avertissements*, they have suppressed a number of journals because they did not chime in with their fantastic ideas of republican sentiments.

"The republic of America and the republic of France are as different as white is from black. Your country submits to law. Public sentiment and public spirit, based upon general intelligence and morality, dictate the control of society. In New York and Boston, the theatres are allowed to perform such plays as they deem fit. Suppose they should treat the public to impure and offensive pieces: the press would denounce them; nobody would go to see them; they would be condemned by the verdict of the public.

"But, in France, the greater the departure from morality and decorum, the greater will be the crowd flocking to delight in it. It is no easy work to curb such an extravagant and depraved spirit in a country so often unhappily shaken by revolution. It requires the utmost energy to build up any thing, — any form of state government.

"I know the American people to be a frank-hearted, generous nation; and I cannot believe they approve of the slanderous accusations now preferred against me. Have you read the vile statement, published in the 'Indépendance Belge' and in other journals, that I had appropriated the public funds, and conjured up war to conceal such illegal transactions? I wish to state emphatically that such a breach of trust under my government in France is an utter impossibility. Not a single franc is expended without severe checks on the part of the administration. This fact is well known to every intelligent person in France. I could hardly attempt to contradict all these vile calumnies, though I have denied a few of them."

In reference to the war the emperor remarked, "We deceived ourselves as to the strength of our own army as well as that of the Prussians. I have often cautioned my ministers against erroneous statements. It was probably no fault of their hearts, but of their heads, that they would not listen to me when I told them that we could not compete with Prussia's military establishment; that our effective strength as compared to hers was insufficient. This was the deception, the fault of which must be shared more or less by all of us, which has led to the most disastrous results. We were to have ready for service, at a moment's notice, two hundred thousand reserves. When they were needed, however, not more than one-half the number was at hand. Thus the Prussians got 'ahead' of us, as you would say. Notwithstanding all this, the bravery of our troops obliged them to use double numbers of men to gain easy victories.

"France needs peace; but the conditions imposed by Count Bismarck are too exacting. What government in France could accept them, and at the same time maintain itself against the outraged people? France cannot endure so deep a humiliation."

"Will your Majesty," the correspondent inquired, "have the goodness to explain why the provisional government so obstinately refuses to hold an election for representatives in the constituent assembly?"

"In my opinion," the emperor replied, "it is because it is afraid of the reds."

"May they not," it was asked, "have as much reason to apprehend that a large number of Bonapartists may be returned?"

"I do not think so," said the emperor. "The discordant elements of socialism, communism, and anarchy, have spread terror throughout the country, and gotten the upper hand; and it is very difficult to contend with such Utopian and seductive influences."

In reference to the restoration of the empire, and the recall of the emperor by the popular voice, Napoleon said, —

"When I consider the uncertainty lurking on the road

to such an aim, when I consider the vast impediments to be removed, I really feel but little ambition. I would rather be independent. I would rather be as I now am, — a prisoner, — and never step again on French soil."

"But with regard to your Majesty's interest as a father," it was said, "you must be naturally desirous of bequeathing your throne to your promising son, and thus upholding the dynasty."

"No," the emperor replied with much manifest emotion: "not even for him could I wish it. I love him too much to desire for him chances of such dread uncertainty. If these cannot be avoided, he would be far happier in private life, without the overwhelming responsibilities attaching to such a station, and that, too, in France, which can never forget a humiliation."

Some journals have expressed doubts respecting the authenticity of the above narrative; but the sentiments expressed are in manifest accord with every report which has come from the prisoner of Wilhelmshöhe.

The testimony in reference to the sentiments and conduct of the Empress Eugénie, from all those who were favored with an interview, is uniformly the same. She had found a retreat at Chiselhurst, in the county of Kent, England, a small, rambling village, about half an hour's ride, on the railway, from Charing Cross. She, with her suite, occupied Camden House, a three-story mansion of red and yellow brick, with a park and pretty ornamental grounds. A lady, writing from London to "The New-York World" under date of Oct. 18, 1870, gives the following account of an interview: —

"I have heard much of the beauty and grace of the

empress; but I was not prepared to see a person of such exquisite loveliness.

"While I do not feel at liberty to repeat the words which the empress uttered, either to myself or to others in my hearing, I may express the conviction with which I left her presence. She loves France, and is anxious for its welfare, — more anxious for that than for the restoration of the empire and perpetuity of the Napoleonic dynasty. She has nothing to do with the intrigues that are going on here, or in Jersey, or at Mons, or at Wilhelmshöhe. She sees that the salvation of France depends upon the maintenance of the provisional government, now established there, until the enemy has been driven from its borders; and it is for this that she hopes, for this she works, and for this she prays daily, if not hourly; being oftener on her knees than on her feet, asking the intercession of our Blessed Lady for the land which is so rich in faith, as well as so sadly stained with unbelief.

"That the great majority of the French people still look upon her husband as their lawful ruler, chosen by them in the first place, and confirmed in his authority by their repeated votes, she believes: that they will ask him to return to them, or that, at least, they will demand the restoration of his dynasty, she considers probable. But that is not the question now. The question now is, 'How to save France from being conquered and crushed by Germany;' and he is her friend who aids in that work, be he republican or imperialist.

"When peace is restored, and the country is once more free to choose its form of government, it will be time then to decide whether it will elect to recall a ruler under whom a score of years of uninterrupted prosperity and peace were enjoyed, or to continue in power a party who drove that ruler into a war for which he was wholly unprepared, and which he was wholly unwilling to undertake. It was liberal France that made the war unavoidable; it was imperial France that desired peace, and dreaded war: but it remains for the future to show whether France is still, at heart, imperialistic, or republican. The empire was established by the votes of the people, and confirmed by their voices over and over again. The people have not expressed any wish for the substitution of a republic for the empire: should they do so, the empress will not be found plotting against them."

Gen. Dix, in his address to the Americans in Paris upon his retirement from his embassy to the court of the Tuileries, paid the following just and beautiful tribute to the character of Eugénie: —

"Of her who is the sharer of the emperor's honors, and the companion of his toils; who in the hospital, at the altar, or on the throne, is alike exemplary in the discharge of her varied duties, whether incident to her position, or voluntarily taken upon herself, — it is difficult for me to speak without rising above the level of the common language of eulogium. But I am standing here to-day as a citizen of the United States, without official relations to my own government or any other. I have taken my leave of the imperial family; and I know of no reason why I may not freely speak what I honestly think, especially as I know I can say nothing which will not find a cordial response in your breasts.

"As, in the history of the ruder sex, great luminaries have from time to time risen high above the horizon, to break, and at the same time to illustrate, the monotony of the general movement; so, in the annals of her sex, brilliant lights have at intervals shone forth, and shed their lustre upon the stately march of regal pomp and power.

"And such is she of whom I am speaking. When I have seen her taking part in the most imposing, as I think, of all imperial pageants, — the opening of the Legislative Chambers, — standing amidst the assembled magistracy of Paris, surrounded by the representatives of the talent, the genius, the learning, the literature, and the piety of this great empire, or amidst the resplendent scenes of the palace, moving about with a gracefulness all her own, and with a simplicity of manner which has a double charm when allied to exalted rank and station, I confess that I have more than once whispered to myself, and I believe not always inaudibly, that beautiful verse of the graceful and courtly Claudian, the last of the Roman poets, —

'Divino servitu gressu claruit;'

or, rendered in our own plain English, 'The very path she treads is radiant with her unrivalled step.'"

CHAPTER XXIII.

WAR AND ITS WOES.

THE capture of the army at Sedan, with the emperor, was an irreparable disaster to France. There was no longer any force in the field to resist the invaders; there was no longer any government which France would recognize. It was no longer possible for neighboring dynasties, despising democracy, to enter into alliance to aid France, since such aid would strengthen that democracy which the dynasties feared far more, even, than they feared Germanic supremacy in Europe. Victorious Prussia was also deeply embarrassed. She had overthrown the republican empire, with its respect for monarchical forms, only to introduce the genuine democracy of Favre and Hugo and Rochefort, which prided itself in trampling all monarchical forms under its feet. Thus was Prussia inspired with a new incentive to reject all terms of peace but those which would re-establish monarchy in some of its forms in France, or which would so degrade and weaken the nation, that Europe would have nothing to fear from a dishonored and powerless democracy.

Never before in the history of the world was there so sudden and awful a collapse of a great nation.

France seemed ruined beyond all hope of redemption.

Catholic France could not rally with enthusiasm to fight the battles of an infidel democracy. For such a cause the priests could not pray; for such a cause, the peasants, who reflected the opinions of the Catholic clergy, reluctantly advanced to meet the foe.

Imperial France, which embraced nearly the whole rural population, and all the civil, ecclesiastical, and military officers, maddened by the overthrow of the government by city mobs in the hour of the most dire extremity of the nation, was paralyzed in all her energies.[1]

The military leaders refused to recognize any authority but that of the empire; and every vestige of the empire the democratic populace had swept from Paris. The men who had thus grasped the reins of power had but little confidence in the generals who were in open antagonism to them; and they accused these generals of lukewarmness, and even treason.

Thus clouds and darkness enveloped France. From no quarter could a ray of light be seen. The condition of Marshal Bazaine was hopeless. The army of Prince Charles and of the Crown Prince united in surrounding him. In the mean time, the siege of Strasburg was prosecuted with great vigor; while powerful Prussian armies marched in all directions, capturing towns, levying contributions, and gathering up ample supplies. What

---

[1] "If Napoleon were to make an appeal to the French people, France, meanwhile, seeing in the republic nothing but disorder, is it impossible that the peasants, who are Bonapartists almost to a man, would vote for the restoration of the empire? All our reliable news from the interior of France reveals the fact, that the peasants are not republicans. We regret this fact, while we are compelled to confess it." — *New-York Herald,* Oct. 1, 1870.

a condition for proud France to be in! The despatches of the King of Prussia indicate his astonishment in view of the marvellous results so suddenly accomplished.

After an heroic resistance of two months, Strasburg capitulated on the 28th of September. The terrific bombardment commenced on the 15th of August. The besiegers had four hundred heavy guns and mortars, with which they threw an incessant storm of shot and shell into the city night and day. It was the object of the bombardment to inflict such misery upon the inhabitants, that the soldiers in the citadel would be compelled, from humane considerations, to surrender.

The sufferings in the city were awful beyond all description. The bursting-forth of conflagrations, the explosion of shells, the crash of falling walls, the shrieks of the wounded; famine, sickness, misery, — all combined in converting wretched Strasburg into a volcanic pandemonium. There was no safety anywhere. Children were torn to pieces in the streets, and their gory limbs scattered far and wide over the pavements. Shells crushed through the roofs, and exploded in the cellars where mothers and maidens were huddled together in terror. One shell fell in the third story of a house, and killed twelve persons outright, wounding twelve more.

Gen. Ulrich, who was intrusted with the defence, was compelled to steel his heart against these cries of woe. His defence was heroic in the highest degree. Four hundred citizens — men, women, and children — were killed; seventeen hundred were wounded. Four hundred houses were burned, rendering eight thousand persons houseless. Three hundred children died of starvation. Damage was inflicted upon the city to the estimated amount of fifty million dollars.[1]

The surrender of Strasburg with its vast military stores released the besieging army of over fifty thousand men to co-operate in the siege of Metz and in the march upon Paris. A garrison of eight thousand Germans was left to hold Strasburg, while the remainder of the beleaguering host pressed forward to new victories.

The provisional government in Paris, assuming that the war was the criminal act of the imperial government, which was now overthrown, applied through M. Thiers for peace. "It is understood," said "The London Times" of Sept. 14, "that M. Thiers offered an indemnity of five hundred million dollars, one-half the French fleet, to dismantle the fortresses of Alsace and Lorraine, and to leave the Rhine provinces, for which France had commenced the war, in the hands of Prussia."

The reply, so far as it can be gathered from the official journals in Berlin, was, that there is no longer any government in France with which Prussia could form a treaty; that the present government in Paris exists only by leave of the gutter democracy; that the security of the new empire which Prussia is establishing in Germany renders it essential that France should be so weakened, that Germany shall never again have cause to fear that France will cross the Rhine.

Then it was asked, "Is it not equally important that France should have protection against Germanic invasion?" The emphatic and unanswerable reply was, "The conquered must submit to the will of the conqueror."

---

[1] Testimony of Dr. Schnergaus, a member of the city council.

The onward sweep of the Prussian armies was sublime in its aspect. While nearly three hundred thousand troops were assailing Marshal Bazaine at Metz, in a war-tempest whose thunders were unintermitted by day or by night, four hundred thousand more veteran soldiers, with rapid strides, in such array that no force could be brought to resist them, circled around the doomed city of Paris, girding it with a chain of ponderous batteries and bristling steel, through which there was no escape.

It seemed as though there were no limit to the number of troops which Germany had poured into France. There were enough to besiege Metz, to besiege Paris, to besiege a score of other minor fortresses; and there were men enough left to send powerful armies, — north to Amiens, and south to Orléans and Tours. Every day announced some new German victory. Jules Favre endeavored to represent the Bonaparte dynasty as exclusively responsible for the war. To this, Bismarck's organ in Berlin, "The North-German Correspondent," replied, —

"M. Jules Favre has given himself the trouble to defend this perversion of history and common sense in a long circular despatch. We maintain, on the other hand, and our asseverations are supported by all the facts of the case, that the immense majority of the French people, through all the organs of public opinion, — in the press, the Senate, the Corps Legislative, and the army, nay, down to the very street-mobs of Paris, — demanded war. Even the small minority which hold at present in their hands the reins of state are so far from honestly seeking peace, that they are doing what in them lies to make peace impossible."

We can form some estimate of the state of feeling in

France upon this subject by supposing that Mexico were a rich, powerful military empire, with a population of forty millions, and every man a trained soldier. If the Mississippi were the only natural boundary between Mexico and the United States, it would indeed be humiliating to allow Mexico to hold the territory on both banks of the stream, from the Gulf to the Ohio.

The German Empire, now rising in such gigantic proportions, is in direct and intense antagonism with the political principles prevailing almost universally in France. It is an absolute government, founded upon the doctrine of the *divine right of kings* and the *exclusive privileges of the nobles*. The French Empire, now crumbling to decay, was founded upon the doctrine of the *divine right of the people*, universal suffrage, and *equal rights for all men*.

There was necessary antagonism between two systems of government so diametrically opposed to each other. There could be no possible peace between them but by clearly-defined boundaries which neither could easily pass, — which France sought to establish; or by the one empire so disarming and weakening the other as to render it impotent, — which last Prussia sought to do.

It would require volumes to describe the scenes of horror which were now every hour transpiring. The Prussians, in this most wonderful of campaigns, displayed military ability which certainly has never been surpassed, and I know not that it has ever before been equalled. Paris was invested, in a circuit forty miles in diameter, by an army numbering three hundred thousand men. Every avenue of escape was cut off. The most formidable intrenchments were thrown up at every point which a *sortie* could strike. These intrenchments were protected by thirty thousand men. In case of a *sortie*, telegraphic communication instantly brought to their aid thirty thousand men on either side of them to attack the assailants on both flanks. Thus ninety thousand men behind the strongest earthworks were prepared to repel any attempts to pierce their lines.

Three hundred thousand men surrounded Metz, and its doom was sealed. The storm of an incessant bombardment fell upon Montmedi and Toul and Thionville and Bitche and Phalsburg. Bazelle was in ashes; and its three thousand inhabitants were wandering along the roads, houseless, foodless, clotheless, seeking relief from those who were nearly as miserable as themselves.

Seventy thousand Prussian cavalry scoured the country in all directions, gathering ample supplies for the invading army of nearly a million of men. Almost every day announced the demolition of some fortress, or the capture of some town, by the resistless Prussians. France, bleeding, robbed, humiliated, almost helpless, was without any recognized government or any spirit of cordial co-operation among its distracted people. As the Prussians advanced, they found almost a deserted country before them. The peasants, in terror, fled into the woods.

Mr. Malet, a secretary of the English legation in Paris, gives the following report of an interview he held with Count Bismarck. The Prussian minister said in reference to peace with France, —

"We don't want money: we are rich. We don't want ships: Germany is not a naval power. But we know very well that we shall leave behind us in France an undying legacy of hate; and that, happen what may just now, France will at once go into training. What we now insist upon is Metz and Strasburg. We shall keep them for a bulwark against French invasion, making them stronger than ever before."

Metz and Strasburg, which Bismarck thus demanded, were the main fortresses of the important provinces of Alsace and Lorraine. These provinces embraced the six northern departments of France, spreading over 12,430 square miles, and containing a population of about three million inhabitants, who were intensely French in their feelings.

In continuation of the conversation which Mr. Malet reports, Count Bismarck said, "What the king and I most fear is the effect of a republic in France upon Germany. No one knows as well as we do what has been the influence of American republicanism in Germany."

M. Jules Favre, in behalf of the government of the national defence in Paris, as minister of foreign affairs, visited Bismarck at the Prussian headquarters at Ferrières. He gives a minute report of the interview in the "Moniteur" of the 28th of September. He says, —

"The count maintained that the security of Germany commanded him to guard the territory which protected it. He repeated several times, 'Strasburg is the key to the house: I must have it.' 'The two departments,' he said, 'of the *Bas Rhin* and the *Haut Rhin*, a part of the Moselle, with Metz, Châteaux Chalins and Senones, are indispensable. I know well,' he added, 'that they are not with us. That will impose an unpleasant job upon us; but we cannot help it. I am sure, that, in a short time, we shall have a new war with you. We wish to make it with all our advantages.'"

"It is clear," writes Jules Favre, "that, in the intoxication of victory, Prussia wishes for the destruction of

France. She demands three of our departments, two fortified cities, — one of a hundred thousand, the other of seventy-five thousand inhabitants, — and eight or ten smaller ones also fortified. She knows that the populations she wishes to tear from us repulse her; but she seizes them, nevertheless, replying with the edge of the sword to their protestations against such an outrage of their civic liberty and their moral dignity. To the nation that demands the opportunity of self-consultation she proposes the guaranty of her cannon, planted at Mt. Valérien. Let the nation that hears this either rise at once, or at once disavow us when we counsel resistance to the bitter end."

On the 16th of October, Soissons, after a severe bombardment, fell into the hands of the Prussians, with a large amount of military stores. Some idea of the terrors of these bombardments may be inferred from the fact, that, from an official statement, it appears that in the bombardment of Strasburg, which lasted thirty-one days, 441 pieces of ordnance were used, which threw into the city 193,722 shots, averaging 6,249 daily, or between four and five each minute. Some of these enormous missiles of destruction weighed a hundred and eighty pounds.

Day after day came fraught with disaster. Though the broken bands of the French, and the new recruits which sprang up here and there, fought with desperation, and gained some victories, the majestic march of the Prussians was resistlessly onward. Paris was every hour becoming more hopelessly bound in the iron girdle which surrounded it. Under the empire, Paris had become the most beautiful city in the world. Scholars, artists, pleasure-seekers, thronged it from all nations.

Even the bitterest foes of the empire did not deny its rapid increase in wealth, beauty, and all artistic attractions.

"The life of this beautiful city," says "The New-York Tribune" of Nov. 29, 1870, "has been for eighteen years one of the most singular examples ever seen of an unbroken tide of material success. It has increased vastly in extent, in riches, in population; and, in every department of luxury and art, there has been an improvement without parallel in recent times."

King William, and his son the Crown Prince, had been honored guests at the Tuileries, and had admired the beauties of a city which has no rival in Europe. It is said that they shrank from the Vandalism of throwing their shells into the palaces, the churches, the thronged streets, the homes of elegance, and the galleries of art, with which the city abounded. They feared that the sympathies of the world would be with Paris, thus doomed to destruction.

The war had now become simply an effort, on the part of Prussia, to wrest from France Alsace and Lorraine, that France might be thus weakened, and Prussia thus strengthened. The openly-avowed object was territorial aggrandizement. Would Christendom sustain Prussia in the destruction of Paris and the slaughter of thousands of its helpless citizens for such an object? It is confidently said that Count Bismarck urged the hurling of the shells, but that the king hesitated.

It should also be stated that Paris was surrounded by a cordon of forts, supporting each other at such a distance outside of the walls, that the Prussians could not plant their siege-guns near enough to throw their shells into the city; and that this fact, not considerations of humanity, caused the bombardment to be postponed.

But, whatever the cause may have been, the dreary weeks rolled on, with incessant and bloody battles around the walls; while two millions of people, shut out from all intercourse with the outside world, were consigned to the resistless approaches of famine,—a foe more to be dreaded than fire or the sword.

A part of the provisional government was in Paris: a part had escaped in a balloon to Tours. A French army was gathering near Tours for the defence of the portion of the ministry assembled there. A large army of Prussians was on the march to capture those ministers, or disperse them. The Prussian king and his suite took possession of the magnificent saloons of Versailles, where they "fared sumptuously every day." Jules Favre was in Paris, acting as President of France. Gen. Trochu was military governor of the city, having received his appointment from the emperor. The complications would have been exceedingly ludicrous, had not the circumstances been so extremely distressing.

On the 27th of October, King William sent the astounding telegram to Berlin, "This morning, Bazaine and Metz capitulated. A hundred and fifty thousand prisoners, including twenty thousand sick and wounded, laid down their arms this afternoon,— one of the most important events of the war. Providence be thanked!"

For sixty-seven days, the gallant troops had struggled against overpowering numbers. They had expended their ammunition, and had eaten up their horses. Their hospitals were filled with the sick and wounded, and starvation was staring them in the face. The army did not fall unavenged. Forty-five thousand of the army of Prince Charles had perished, during the siege, of sickness or wounds, sending a wail of anguish into forty-five thousand German homes beyond the Rhine. The surrender of this army with its veteran soldiers and generals, and the surrender of this all-important fortress with its vast supply of heavy guns and small-arms, was a disaster apparently irretrievable.

Marshal Bazaine was an imperialist. He had no respect for the democratic committees which had sprung up in different parts of France. These committees consequently denounced him as a traitor, and clamored for his head; but subsequent developments proved that he had done every thing he could do for the salvation of woe-stricken France.

The capitulation of Metz released an army of three hundred thousand Prussians to co-operate in the siege of Paris, and to march with the forces advancing towards the Loire. On the morning of the 30th of October, the governmental committee in Tours issued a proclamation, in which they said, —

"Metz has capitulated. A general upon whom France relied has just taken away (*vient d'enlever*) from the country, in its danger, more than a hundred thousand of its defenders. Marshal Bazaine has betrayed us. He has made himself the agent of the man of Sedan, and the accomplice of the invader. Regardless of the honor of the army of which he had charge, he has surrendered, without even making a last effort, a hundred and twenty thousand fighting men, twenty thousand wounded, guns, cannons, colors, and the strongest citadel of France. Such a crime is above even the punishment of justice.

"Meanwhile, Frenchmen, measure the depths of the

abyss into which the empire has precipitated you. For twenty years, France submitted to this corrupting power, which extinguished in her the springs of greatness and of life. The army of France, stripped of its national character, became, without knowing it, an instrument of tyranny and servitude, and is swallowed up, in spite of the heroism of the soldiers, by the treason of their chiefs. It is time for us to re-assert ourselves under the ægis of the republic."

This address was signed by Crémieux, Glais-Bisoin, and Gambetta, — men who were regarded as political adventurers, and in whom France had no confidence. Nothing can more clearly show the unfitness of such men to govern than the total want of acquaintance with human nature which this proclamation evinced. France, in these hours of anguish, needed the union of all parties by the spirit of mutual conciliation.

For twenty years the empire had governed France, crowning it with prosperity, and making it the leading power in Europe. Again and again the empire had been sustained by the votes of the overwhelming majority of the people. The rural population were imperialists almost to a man. The army, composed of young men taken from the cottages and the workshops, ardently supported the empire. The generals who led these armies had, without an exception, taken the oath of allegiance to the empire. Without the support of these generals, these armies, and these masses of the people, France was powerless; and yet these committee-men, who assumed to be the government of France, who had gained power simply through the energies of a Parisian mob, endeavored to unite France under their government by denouncing the emperor in the strongest language of contempt, by declaring the chiefs of the army to be traitors, the soldiers to be dupes, — who had been, without knowing it, the instruments of tyranny and servitude, — and the masses of the people as guilty of the inconceivable folly of submitting for twenty years to a corrupting power which had extinguished the springs of life in France.

Under these circumstances, with the cities under the control of the democratic party, heaping scorn upon the imperialists and the rural districts, and all the leading officers of the church, the army, and the state, wedded to the empire, there seemed to be no possibility of that enthusiastic co-operation of all France which was essential to the repulse of the invaders.

Still the generals and the armies fought despairingly, and gained some minor victories. New recruits somewhat languidly entered the field. During the month of November, the battle raged almost incessantly over vast regions of the northern and central departments of France. The emperor was a prisoner. The empire was overthrown. There was no government in France. Prussia, on the contrary, was guiding her invincible bands with all the energies of despotic power. The world, which looked on, could see no hope for France. Her doom of utter defeat and humiliation seemed inevitable. Could France rally *en masse* with enthusiasm under any recognized government, — imperial, monarchical, or republican, — with the seven millions of fighting men she could bring into the field, with the entire command of the sea, enabling her to obtain any amount of arms and munitions of war, she might still drive the invaders bleeding and breathless from her soil; but there seemed now to be no possibility of this co-operation.

Were the question between France and Germany presented to an impartial umpire, the decision would undoubtedly be, "Let the forty millions of Germans be organized under any form of government they may choose, with the River Rhine as their southern frontier. Let the forty millions of Frenchmen be organized under any form of government they may like, with the River Rhine as their northern frontier."

This would be settling the question according to the dictates of reason; according to the boundary which Nature has marked out. This would give neither party the advantage over the other. With such a boundary, the absolute empire of Germany and the republican empire of France, or republican Germany and republican France, might live on terms of fraternal kindliness.

But it seems now (early in December, 1870) that the question is not to be settled by reason, but by iron and by blood. The conquered must submit to the dictation of the conqueror. The rolling centuries have, however, taught us one lesson, — *that nothing is settled in this world until it is settled right.* The infamous treaties of 1815 planted the seeds of the wars which in these later years have drenched the fields of Italy and Austria with blood, and of the conflict which is now filling Germany and France with the wailing cry of widows and of orphans.

We know not what God has in reserve for France, for Europe, for humanity. Nations as well as individuals need and receive chastening from the Lord. In view of the woes which are still desolating this war-scathed world, one is led to cry out in anguish, "How long, O Lord! how long?" The awful carnage now drenching the fields of France with French and German blood must ere long come to a close. Then the settlement which shall be accepted will decide whether there shall be permanent peace and fraternity, or merely a truce, to give place, after a few years, to another bloody conflict, which shall again shroud two nations, and perhaps all Europe, in woe. Every friend of humanity will pray that God will so guide the event, that abiding peace may come to our sad, sad world.

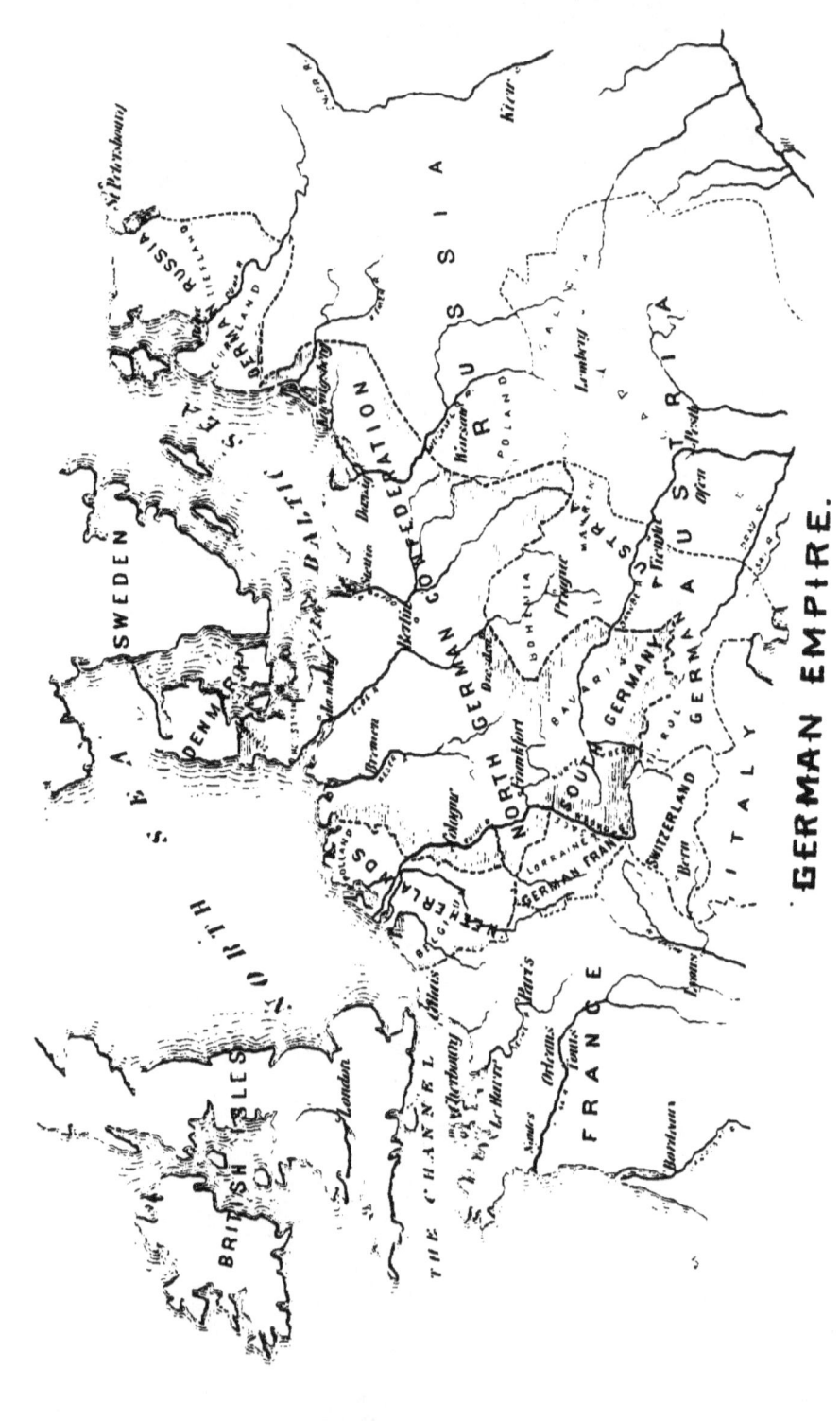

CHAPTER XXIV.

THE GERMANIC EMPIRE.

ALL the plans of Count Bismarck seemed almost miraculously to succeed. The thought of a great German empire in the heart of Europe, which should rival in grandeur and power the glories of Charlemagne, apparently inspired all Germany with such enthusiasm as to silence every republican murmur, and cause all fears of despotism to be forgotten, and all aspirations for popular rights to be obliterated from the public mind. State after State of Southern Germany professed allegiance to Prussia, and its readiness to accept King William as Emperor of United Germany, — emperor by divine right; to be the ruler, and not the servant, of the people.

Bismarck knew full well, and frankly gave expression to the opinion, that France would never consent, except by compulsion, to leave herself at the mercy of Germany; which empire, holding *both* banks of the Rhine, could at any time pour her armies resistlessly into the empire of France. It was certain, that, were peace made upon those terms, France, so soon as she had recovered from the exhaustion and ravages of the war, would gather her strength anew, to regain those provinces which she deemed essential to her independent existence, now that Germany had become a power before which all Europe trembled. Hence it was that Bismarck deemed it essential to the success of his plans that Prussia should not only hold those Rhenish provinces on the south side of the Rhine upon which she had already reared so many impregnable fortresses, but that she should wrest from France the whole remaining line from her frontier-fortress of Lauterburg, — a hundred miles south, to Basle, in Switzerland.

This acquisition, transferring to Prussia the magnificent provinces of Alsace and Lorraine, with the ancient fortress of Strasburg, would sink France to a second-rate power. Nothing could induce her to make this sacrifice but the deepest conceivable humiliation. The fact that Prussia was abundantly prepared for the war, with her armies all marshalled, with her ammunition-wagons all filled, with her transportation-cars all ready, indicates clearly that the attainment of this end was the prominent object which Prussia had in view at the commencement of the war. And it must be admitted that this was shrewd policy. It was an essential step in the plan of reviving the empire of Charlemagne upon the old feudal foundation of the divine right of kings. To all the pleadings of humiliated France for peace, the invariable reply was, "Surrender Alsace and Lorraine!"

Terrible as was the loss which the Prussians encountered in their series of almost uninterrupted victories, their ranks were kept full by an incessant stream of recruits forwarded from the Germanic States. The loss of life seemed to be a matter not taken into consideration in the prosecution of these plans of territorial aggrandizement.

At no time from the commencement of the invasion was there less than half a million of well-trained German soldiers in France. Within a few weeks, they captured or destroyed three hundred and fifty thousand regular French troops. It is said that there were about four hundred thousand soldiers of all arms, many merely citizen-soldiers, who were shut up in Paris. They manned the forts, kept up an incessant fire on the Prussian lines, and made many desperate *sorties*. Though at times partially victorious, they were, in the end, always baffled. Not a wagon could enter the city; not an individual could leave but by soaring through the clouds in a balloon.

Various attempts were made, with more or less of success, to create in different parts of France, beyond the reach of the Prussian cannon, new armies. But the well-trained Germans swept the territory in all directions, and almost every day brought its catalogue of their victories and their conquests. Everywhere that any considerable French force made its appearance, either in the north near Amiens, or in the south upon the Loire, they were pretty sure to be promptly assailed by a superior force of Prussians; and however fiercely they fought, and however densely they strewed the ground with the slain of their assailants, they were eventually put to flight.

Early in December, a *sortie* was attempted from Paris with a hundred thousand men. The battle was as fierce as mortal energies could wage. The slaughter on both sides was dreadful. Both parties made victorious onsets; both parties shared in disastrous defeats. Thousands of hearts in the cottages of France and Germany were rent with anguish as tidings reached them of loved ones who would never return. Still Prussia was steadily winding her chains more tightly around the doomed city, crying out, "Give us Alsace and Lorraine!" and still the despairing French exclaimed, "We will bury ourselves beneath the ruins of Paris ere we will submit to any further dismemberment of the empire!" The tide of public opinion in England and America was now rapidly turning in favor of the French, who were now fighting so heroically for the integrity of their realms. All that France now hoped for was to obtain such terms of peace as would not compel every Frenchman to hang his head for shame. A writer in the "New-York Herald" of Dec. 3 undoubtedly gave expression to the rapidly-increasing public sentiment in saying, —

"And here we are led to look at the present object and spirit of the war on the part of Prussia. Both the purpose and character of this dreadful conflict have changed. From a war of defence, and against 'the Bonapartes,' it has become an ambitious and a relentless one. To squelch the French republic, and to dismember France, is now the object of the King of Prussia. He says, or rather Count Bismarck says for him, that it is not continued from hostility to republicanism. Both pretend that they are not making war upon the republic of France; that they are comparatively indifferent as to what form of government the French people may choose; and that they have no wish to interfere with such choice, or to impose any government upon the nation. This declaration does not accord with their action, nor with their sentiments and policy. It is unreasonable to suppose a proud monarch, an absolutist of the old 'divine-right' school, like King William, would be indifferent to the establishment of a republican gov-

ernment in France, or that he would not try to prevent
it. It is as unlikely that his aristocratic minister, or the
proud aristocracy of Prussia, and the hundreds of petty
princes of Germany, are indifferent. No: they fear too
much the danger to their own privileges from a great
republic in the heart of Europe, embracing such a vast
territory and population. They know by experience
and from the lessons of history what an extraordinary
influence a French republic has in awakening and diffus-
ing republican ideas and aspirations in surrounding nations. They dread this propagandism of liberty and
democracy; and, if possible, will extinguish the fire before
it is well lighted."

The pressure of defeat and misery was gradually
uniting all parties. The Catholic priesthood, which
has almost boundless influence over the peasantry, was
at first bewildered in view of the usurpation of the
government by democratic leaders in Paris, who were
as hostile to the church as to the empire; but the
priests now began to see that the triumph of the Prussians was the ruin of France.

"The priests," said "The London Times" of Dec. 2,
"in the rural districts, are preaching against the Prussians. The rustics are, consequently, terribly incensed
against the invaders. German patrols in the Valley of
the Loire are shot down from every hedge and building. The Prussian bearers of despatches are killed
when nobody but innocent-looking ploughmen are in
sight. Many of these priests have been captured by
the Prussians, and they will be brought to trial."

The French troops did not rally with any enthusiasm
around Garibaldi: he was a foreigner and a heretic.
Though he fought heroically, and gained some minor

victories with his small band, he could accomplish nothing which would have any serious bearing on the issues of the war. After almost every victory, he found it necessary to order a retreat.

Early in December, Gen. De Paladines, who had gathered an army of two hundred thousand new levies near Tours, commenced a march for the relief of Paris. As he approached the walls, a *sortie* was to have been made, and the Prussian line at that point was to have been crushed between the hosts. The *sortie* was attempted, and, though partially successful, did not accomplish the end desired. Gen. De Paladines commenced his march. He was soon encountered by a superior force under Prince Frederick Charles, and after a two-days' battle, having inflicted and suffered terrible slaughter, was driven back to Orléans.

The Prussians pursued them, and, having erected their batteries, threatened to open fire upon the city. To save the citizens from the horrors of a bombardment, De Paladines withdrew his army, and, retiring to the left bank of the Loire, permitted Orléans for the second time to fall into the hands of the foe. This was on the 4th of December. The victorious Prussians, moving in various directions, recaptured five important towns in the vicinity. Still the French did not yield to despair. "The London Times" of Dec. 5 says, —

"Special despatches show that the people are more encouraged and better assured than ever before. Although in the midst of almost crushing misfortunes, the republicans are waging a desperate struggle for life and liberty."

The disastrous defeat of De Paladines' army seemed to destroy all hopes in Paris for relief from abroad. Famine is a foe against which no power in the end can contend. There were two millions of people shut up in Paris. Rapidly their provisions were disappearing; and no additional supplies could by any possibility be brought into the city. Haggard cheeks and skeleton frames were already seen in the streets; the animals in the menagerie in the Jardin des Plantes were slain and eaten; cats and dogs and rats were, in the disguise of French cookery, eagerly devoured; horse-flesh became a coveted dainty. To all the world it appeared that the end was at hand, and that Paris must speedily capitulate.

All accounts agreed in describing the conduct of the French in these engagements as heroic in the extreme. Many of the charges they made excited the admiration of their foes. They disprove the assertion so frequently made, that the Frenchmen of the present generation are wanting in the chivalric courage which characterized their ancestors.

Still the democratic provisional government at Tours distrusted the old generals of the empire. They attributed every defeat to their devotion to the empire, and to their want of zeal in fighting for a republic.

"It is a standing belief of the French," says one of the daily journals, "that every general of theirs who is beaten is a traitor. Napoleon, Bazaine, Lebœuf, Canrobert, and the rest, are traitors, or they never would have suffered defeat. Cambriel also is a traitor, or he would have permitted the Garibaldians to ride rough-shod over him. The last traitor is De Paladines, — even he who was the idol of last week. We place him in the list because the French already talk of having him court-martialled. All idea that the Germans are mainly responsible for the defeat of their armies is scouted by the people; it is impossible; and so the poor generals get the blame."

The news was soon flashed along the wires that the ancient city of Rouen, the world-renowned capital of Normandy, was in the hands of the conqueror. This enriched the Prussians with the spoils of one of the most fertile departments in France, — filling their magazines with grain, and abundantly supplying them with herds of fat cattle. Rouen was within sixty miles of Havre, one of the most important seaports in France, and the seat of many of its most celebrated manufactures. The occupation of Rouen by the German troops cut off all communication between Havre and the interior of France. Havre was trembling with fear, and all her energies were paralyzed. Thus, day after day, the prospects of France became more dark and hopeless: every Frenchman understood that it was a struggle for national life. The surrender to the great German Empire of the south bank of the Rhine, for the entire distance from Belgium and Holland to Switzerland, would prove a blow from which France could never hope to recover. Whether France were to exist as a republic, a monarchy, or an empire, she must forever relinquish the proud supremacy she had so long held in Europe. The Emperor of Germany could at any time say, "Obey me, or I shall punish you."

Gen. Trochu had conducted the defence of Paris with great ability. He had marshalled under his banners four hundred thousand men, whom he had carefully drilled, and supplied amply with arms from the arsenals of Paris. By the incessant fire of his forts, he had kept the enemy at such a distance from Paris, that he manifestly could not open upon the city any effective bombardment. Still it was reported in the journals that the private secretary of the United-States ambassador (Mr. Washburne) had stated on the 4th of December that famine would compel the surrender of Paris within three weeks. Prince George of Saxony also telegraphed to the king at Dresden, that it would not be possible for the French to attempt any more offensive movements. Still many considered it probable that Gen. Trochu would make another desperate effort to cut through the lines of the beleaguering foe.

As we write these lines, near the middle of December, one immense portion of the Prussian army, variously estimated at from four to five hundred thousand men, surrounds Paris with impregnable lines over thirty miles in circuit. Another army, over two hundred thousand strong, is driving the army of Gen. De Paladines, consisting of two hundred thousand men and five hundred pieces of cannon, across the Loire to the southern bank, and is threatening a march upon Tours to disperse that portion of the provincial government which is assembled there. Another large German army is near Amiens, sending out clouds of cavalry to scour the country in all directions.

The only intercourse which the government in Paris can have with the outside world is by means of balloons. Watching the wind, an immense balloon is sent up some two or three miles into the air, and then is left to drift over the Prussian lines, often the target for sharpshooters and artillery, until, beyond the reach of Prussian capture, it descends into the fields of France with its compact mail, and often with several passengers. A few days ago, one of these balloons was seen flying before a fierce wind, far off to sea, where all must have perished.

Carrier-pigeons are taken from Paris in these balloons. Letters are tied around their necks, when they return on swift wing to their accustomed cotes in Paris. Thus only does the government in Tours hold any communication with the committee within the walls of the city.

The tremendous cannon planted upon the forts surrounding Paris keep up an incessant cannonade upon the Prussian lines. The thunders of the bombardment shake the hills by day and by night. There are daily battles as the French emerge from some portion of their works, and fall fiercely upon the bristling circuit of bayonets and batteries which surround them. An eye-witness, who stood upon an eminence in the Prussian lines on the 4th of December, thus describes the scene in a despatch dated the next day: —

"A grand effort was made yesterday and the day before. There was a heavy cannonade; but no infantry appeared on the north side. Very early yesterday, it was apparent there was hot work in the west. Mont Valérien was thundering away in every direction. From the eminence overhanging Argenteuil every thing was visible: a battle was progressing south of Valérien. Closer to me, the work was very warm. In the morning, shells from the batteries at Nanterre and Courbevoie had been crashing into Bezons and Argenteuil. A sheltered road behind the latter town is scored in many places with deep ruts made by the shells.

"On the other side of the eminence where I stood, the batteries kept up an unremitting fire of shells, which ploughed its summit in all directions; and the buildings which crown the eminence were knocked about remorselessly. As the day broke, my position became too dangerous, notwithstanding its great advantages as a point of outlook. I was compelled to evacuate, and retreat into the low ground beyond it, which was only 'out of the frying-pan into the fire.' If I went east, shells from Labriche were tumbling into Epernay. St. Gratian and Deuil and Montmigny and Stains were having rough times at the hands of Fort du Nord. Farther round, Digny and Le Bourget were attacked by Fort de l'Est. From Margency I accompanied a staff-officer through Montmigny, round by Garagi and Arnonville. For the first time during the siege, the Fort du Nord was throwing shells into Montmorency.

"In the forenoon, there had been a *sortie* toward Stains. Three battalions came over the flat against it, supported by a close-sustained fire from the Fort du Nord and Lunette de Stains. The village was garrisoned by the second regiment of the Guard, and battalions of Queen Elizabeth's Regiment. The French had two battalions of Gardes Mobiles, and one of Garde Impériale. They came on with great resolution and in excellent order. The German Guards, who were waiting for them, received them with a steady fire within short range. The Frenchmen tried a rush; but the bullets stopped them. After holding their ground for a little while, and exchanging shots with the Germans, the inevitable result, a retrograde movement, set in. The French, however, deserve credit for the regular manner of the retreat.

"Another demonstration, in the direction of Bourget, was made at a later hour. Dense columns of French troops appeared on the plain in front of Fort Aubersvillier, and advanced steadily towards Bourget; but they lost heart before they got nearer than the railway-station, and never came within range. Bourget, already pounded with shells, was again bombarded all day. In fact, the fire of shells from the forts all round the circuit was heavy and continuous, but so wild and purposeless, withal, that it did little damage. Every thing on the northern side has been in the nature of a feint."

Such are the scenes, which, while we write these lines, are transpiring around unhappy Paris. To human view, there is no hope for France. The cup of humiliation is placed to her lips; and, unless there should be some almost supernatural interposition, she must drain it to its dregs.

The conduct of the Committee of National Defence in Tours, under these trying circumstances, did not secure the confidence of the people in France, or of intelligent observers in any part of the world. A writer in "The New-York Tribune" of Dec. 8 says, —

"The behavior of the Tours Government, on learning of the defeat of the Army of the Loire at Orléans, is more discouraging to the true friends of France than reverses in the field; for it shows that the men who are now suffered to direct the destinies of the nation have neither the intelligence nor the temper of statesmen, and that, in the days of humiliation and internal discord which must follow the close of the war, they will probably be found wanting in the real qualities of leadership which the country will then need.

"The policy of the Committee of Defence thus far has been to utter magnificent boasts, and, when their recklessness had been exposed, to throw the blame of failure upon people who don't deserve it. Very soon there will be a collapse of the whole fabric of deception, just as there was of Napoleon's military organization.

M. Gambetta had better ask himself what he thinks will become of the government of the national defence when the day of enlightenment arrives."

Thomas Carlyle, who is the avowed advocate of absolute governments, and the opponent of government by the people, and who is probably more familiar with Prussian and German politics than almost any other man, expresses the following views in reference to the great German empire now rising into being. We give his words as reported in a letter from Mr. Moncure D. Conway, dated London, Oct. 25, and published in " The Cincinnati Commercial : " —

" I have just passed an evening," writes Mr. Conway, " with Thomas Carlyle. Long ago, he recognized ' magnanimous Herr Bismarck,' as he called him, as a man after his own heart, and as the ' coming man ' of the fatherland. As you may judge, recent events have only increased his enthusiasm for Germany, and his esteem for Bismarck.

" With regard to Count Bismarck, he said, ' All the politicians in the world seem to me as mere windbags beside him. He has shown himself capable of throwing himself utterly into his cause ; and all other causes are simply insignificant in comparison with his, — the building-up of a great genuine power and government in Europe out of the only solid materials left in it; for, really, it seems to me that the true principles of order and government have almost disappeared from Europe, were it not for Germany.'

" Speaking of the destiny of Germany,. Carlyle expressed the opinion that it was inevitable that it would become speedily consolidated, and that the chief, more particularly the German portions of Austria would, a little later perhaps, be united with the rest of Germany. He anticipated that the influence of such a Germany would be infallibly peaceful. 'The very name of the German indicates how strong he has already been in war. German means only *guerre*-man, or war-man.'"

Every day since the commencement of the war, the conflict has been marked with increasing ferocity on both sides. This, of course, was to have been expected. A small party of Prussian cavalry came clattering into a defenceless village near Rouen, and commenced levying some petty exactions from the people. While thus engaged, a body of French cavalry rode suddenly in, fired upon them, and killed several. The rest sprang to their horses, and escaped. The next day, the Prussians reappeared with re-enforcements numbering six hundred men, and with two cannon. Ascending a neighboring eminence, they bombarded the town until it was laid in ashes, and then turned their guns upon the two neighboring villages of Héricourt and Le Fresnoy, which they also demolished. While engaged in this work, a party of French sharpshooters rapidly gathered, and placed themselves in ambush, to assail them as they retired; and this they did with a fire so deadly, that twenty-six wagons were required to carry off the slain.

"Every thing," writes a correspondent from Havre to "The Boston Journal," "leads me to believe that the Prussians are now becoming unduly ferocious. They meet a more decided resistance than heretofore, and revenge themselves on any one they catch. Their mode of procedure is to tie any unfortunate fellow they catch on the road by the wrists with a rope, which they attach to the pommels of their saddles. If one dragoon succeeds in arresting half a dozen, he ties them all in this way, and brings them in, dragging them at the animal's heels with the same exultation that an Indian would parade so many scalps. A hasty trial, in which there are only two or three formulas, is hurried through; and the nearest thicket answers for a place of execution. This is to strike terror into the hearts of all the civilians who desire to arm themselves. At the town of Armentières, a perfectly trustworthy eye-witness, recently returned from Rouen, declares that he saw this sad spectacle. Men, pale with rage, were trying in vain to extinguish the fires that were burning down their houses; women, in despair, had thrown themselves on the ground, trying to cover their screaming children with their bodies, and huddling around them the fragments of their wretched furniture, which they had dragged from the flames; one old woman, eighty-four years old, was screaming to be taken out of a burning house, and her son tore his hair as he tried in vain to drag the smouldering beams from her aged limbs; and one villager, a tremendous athlete, was so overcome with anger and sorrow, that he expired from apoplexy in the midst of his four widowed children. Meantime the hideous projectiles continued to fall, as by and by they will fall on dear old Paris and all the familiar haunts, to baptize in blood the new republic. One of the incidents of this avenging bombardment had sinister consequences. Four men stood up together amid the ruins of their burned and blackened houses, and swore each to kill a Prussian before the next sunset. Four lancers were found dead near each other on the high road from Armentières to Héricourt the next day. Extravagant as this may seem, it is strictly true. To amuse themselves as they were returning home, the

Prussians took a dozen stout peasants whom they found repairing a bridge over a road whereon French troops were expected to pass, and gave them each twenty-five lashes on their bare backs, — so mangling them, that none could stand alone after it."

It would be difficult to number the French cities which were exposed to the horrors of bombardment; and no one who has not witnessed the spectacle can form any conception of the terror and horror of the scene. An immense projectile, weighing from one to two hundred pounds, rises majestically into the air, and then, with a terrific noise, rushes headlong towards the ground, bursting as it strikes with a loud explosion, scattering ruin in all directions. Ponderous walls crumble before these thunderbolts of war. Massive buildings are demolished by them. There is no safety anywhere.

There is much more of sincere piety among many of the peasantry and the humble orders in France than is generally supposed in Protestant countries. When Strasburg was enduring the agony of bombardment, one who was present, sharing the peril and the terror, describes the scene as follows: —

"At a quarter before nine last night, the bombardment began. From that time until eight o'clock this morning (eleven hours), the firing did not cease. It was one continuous roaring, — a rushing and whistling of missiles in the air, followed by the crashing of chimneys, and, from time to time, cries of misery and terror. The night was very dark. It rained; and it was impossible, standing on the ramparts, to distinguish the position of the hostile batteries, which were placed behind some building, or protected by the scarp of the railroad; and they were thus enabled to carry on their work of destruction unpunished. Our people ask what this treatment signifies. . . . Our enemies know that there are eighty thousand inhabitants in the city, a harmless population, — children, trembling mothers; that the city is full of the sick and wounded, who are thus robbed of invigorating sleep, or whose death they accelerate. It is not possible to give an estimate of the damage done to innumerable buildings during the night. We should have to record nearly every street in the city; and, in some streets, nearly all the houses. The shells came from all sides, and into all quarters of the city.

"The shells fell by tens and hundreds in one and the same street. As soon as one house was set on fire, shell after shell was poured in upon the flames, preventing the work of the firemen. The whole city is covered with ruins: the roofs, chimneys, and façades are destroyed on all sides."

Such are the scenes which are now, as we write these lines, continually transpiring in France. It is, indeed, incomprehensible that a loving God can look calmly down in the permission of such enormities. While the city was shaken, and blazing beneath this terrific tempest of war, the pastor of the Church of St. Thomas issued the following notice to his flock: —

"If the dear God spare our life, a prayer-service will be held Sunday morning at half-past nine: if not, dear fathers and mothers, perform the religious duties yourselves, amid your own families. Read a hymn from the hymn-book, a chapter from the Bible. The God of old still lives: call on him in your need. And, though body and soul languish, we will still remain true to him, and thank him; for he is our Helper and our God."

The general course pursued by the Prussians upon the capture of a town is described by all correspondents as follows: A certain number of soldiers are immediately marched into the place. These generally arrive towards evening, after a day's march, hungry and cross. The mayor is sent for, and informed that so many cattle, so many bushels of grain, and so much wine, must be immediately furnished. The requisition usually amounts to very much more than it would be possible for the place to furnish. The trembling mayor collects every thing he can. The soldiers are billeted in the different houses: the horses are often stabled in the church and town-hall. The Prussian flag is hoisted; and the slightest opposition to the will of the conqueror draws down upon the inhabitants the severest punishment. The soldiers must be fed, though women and children starve.

There were, occasionally, amusing events in the midst of these scenes of woe. The Prussians, emboldened by victory, often resorted to measures of astonishing audacity. It is said that the Mayor of Fontainebleau had gathered the city council around him, and was vigorously passing war-measures, when the clatter of a squadron of horsemen was heard in the courtyard. The leader of this cavalcade of forty men leaped from his horse, and, armed to the teeth, entered the council-chamber, and demanded the keys of the city.

"We have no keys," the mayor calmly replied. "Fontainebleau is an open town."

"Well, then," said the dragoon, "let us know where we can lodge; and prepare at once the necessary rations for thirty thousand men, who are only a few hours behind."

"All right," said the mayor; and then, turning to the council, added, "Let us conduct these gentlemen to the château, since we must; and there we can provide them with stabling and lodging."

The party immediately left for the magnificent château, a world-renowned edifice associated with many of the most extraordinary events in French history. The dragoons were conducted into the court-yard; and, while feeding their horses, the gates were suddenly closed. The mayor on the outside, looking through the iron railing, said, "Gentlemen, you are my prisoners: try and make yourselves at home." The dragoons were in a terrible rage, uttered fearful threats of vengeance to be inflicted so soon as their troops should come up, and refused to surrender.

"Very well," the mayor replied, "your poor beasts shall not suffer; but you shall not have one morsel of bread until you lay down your arms, and yield yourselves as prisoners. When the thirty thousand troops come, we will surrender to them, but not to forty dragoons."

In two hours the dragoons surrendered, and were sent to a safe place within the French lines. The thirty thousand troops did not come.

In conclusion, let us reflect upon the following historic facts, which probably no intelligent reader will controvert: —

1. Prussia, or rather Count Bismarck, who represented Prussia, some years ago formed the project of re-organizing Germany into a vast empire founded upon the divine right of kings to rule, and of the duty of the people to be ruled.

2. In the accomplishment of this plan, the treaties of 1815, which Prussia had sworn to respect, were entirely disregarded and overthrown.

3. By diplomacy and war, Prussia suddenly rose from a nation of about fifteen millions to a nation numbering forty millions, with every able-bodied man a trained soldier, constituting a military power unsurpassed by that of any other nation.

4. France could easily have prevented this expansion by uniting with Austria, as M. Thiers urged the imperial government to do. This union would inevitably have crushed Prussia at Sadowa, and would have saved France from the ruin in which she is now involved.

5. The imperial government refused thus to oppose the unification of Germany, declaring that the Germans had a right to manage their own affairs, and that it was desirable for the prosperity of Germany that its fragmentary States should be consolidated into one nation.

6. This consolidation being thus effected, the imperial government in France asked, that, in consideration of its assent to the unification of Germany, Prussia should surrender to France those Renish provinces on the French side of the Rhine which had been wrested from her by the treaties of 1815, and placed in the hands of Prussia, — provinces which France deemed, in the altered state of affairs, essential to her independence; qualifying, however, the request with the provision, that the people of those provinces should decide by vote whether they would return to France, or would remain with Prussia.

7. Prussia peremptorily refused this proposition, but, recognizing in a measure the reasonableness of the

demand, proposed, according to the testimony of the French and English ambassadors, that France should extend her frontier to the Rhine by seizing upon Belgium. This proposition France instantly rejected.

8. France then proposed to all the crowned heads of Europe that a congress should be called to reconstruct the boundaries of the nations, so that the agitating questions then arising, menacing Europe with war, should be settled by an appeal to reason, and not by the sword. This pacific plan was rejected.

9. Prussia, while France was thus trembling in view of her peril in having the immense fortresses on the left bank of the Rhine in the hands of so formidable a power, and leaving the gateway of France wide open to German invasion, endeavored by secret intrigue to place a German prince upon the throne of Spain. This would convert Spain into a German province, re-creating the old German empire of Charles V. Thus France would find herself powerless, exposed to be crushed by Germany at her leisure,

10. All France was alarmed. Imperialists, monarchists, and republicans alike shared in the general agitation. Prussia was informed that France could not consent to the conversion of Spain into a province of Germany by placing the Spanish crown upon the brow of a German prince.

11. Prussia consented to withdraw Prince Leopold, to whom, *as a man*, France had no objection, but peremptorily (France says insultingly) refused· to give any assurance that she would not place some other German prince upon the Spanish throne.

12. Thus menaced, the people of France exclaimed with one voice, that it had become essential to the inde-

pendence of France that she should reclaim her ancient boundary of the Rhine. The uprising of the whole nation, of men of the most antagonistic parties, in this demand, is not to be regarded as an act of frivolity, but as a deep conviction, pervading the entire of France, that the independence of the nation was imperilled.

13. It is manifest that Count Bismarck, who represents Prussia, was aware that the measures he was adopting would lead to war; that he desired war; that he had made the most ample preparations for war; and that the results have, thus far, been just what he hoped to accomplish. Prussia retains the provinces on the left bank of the Rhine, crushes the military power of France, and seizes upon Alsace and Lorraine, thus increasing her territory, multiplying her fortresses, and commanding both banks of the Rhine from Belgium to Switzerland.

14. One of the last telegrams which has crossed the Atlantic, as we write these lines, is as follows:—

"Intelligence from Brussels gives the assurances that Prussia is fully resolved to annex Luxemburg, upon the ground that Luxemburg is essential to render Lorraine strategically useful."

No intelligent man doubts that similar considerations will lead speedily to the positive or the virtual annexation of both Belgium and Holland. The grandeur of the Germanic Empire seems to leave them both at her mercy.

15. The action of the democratic leaders in the great cities, in taking advantage of the Prussian invasion, and of the captivity of the emperor, to seize upon the reins of power, operates in many respects very disastrously.

The empire was the choice of the French people. The democratic party in Paris, Lyons, and Marseilles, composed of an incongruous mass of moderate republicans, red republicans, and socialists, in deadly hostility to each other, has not the confidence of the people of France. They cannot with enthusiasm rally around usurpers, who in the hour of disaster have grasped power, unsustained by either the old feudal doctrine of divine right, or by the modern doctrine of popular suffrage.

16. France is effectually cut off by this action of the democratic leaders from any alliance with any other power. Prussia refuses to recognize these committees even enough to treat with them. England, Italy, Austria, all tremble in view of the enormous encroachments of Prussia; but not one of these powers can interfere in behalf of anarchic France. The British Government will not enter into an alliance with a self-constituted democratic committee in Paris. Victor Emanuel cannot lend his armies to build up a democracy in France, which has overthrown the empire, to which he is indebted for the crown of Italy,—a democracy whose first attempt, in case of success, would be to demolish his throne, and erect upon the ruins an Italian republic. Spain, which has rejected a republic and voted for a monarchy, and which has placed a son of Victor Emanuel upon her throne, refusing to recognize the committee for national defence as the government of France, cannot be expected to cross the Pyrenees with her armies to aid in consolidating a government which Spain has refused to acknowledge. And Austria is the last nation on the continent of Europe to be fighting for the establishment of democracy in France.

17. Thus the disastrous overthrow of the republican empire in these hours of misfortune and dismay — a government which was acknowledged and respected by all the nations of Europe, and which was established and sustained by the overwhelming majority of the French people — seems to doom France to irretrievable destruction. There is no cordial union at home, there is nothing to be hoped for from abroad.

18. France, under the empire, has for twenty years been one of the most prosperous, influential, and happy nations on the continent of Europe. All the arts of industry have flourished; the most magnificent works of internal improvement have been constructed; and the nation has been advancing with rapidity never before experienced in education, wealth, and power. Paris has been one of the most orderly, well-regulated, and attractive cities on the globe. The most refined and wealthy families from all nations have there found a happy home. Could France but hope that the next twenty years would be like the last, she would be happy indeed.

Suddenly a moral earthquake has come; and all France presents the aspect of consternation, ruin, and woe. More than half a million of invaders are sweeping over her territory, leaving behind them famine, smouldering ruins, and fields crimsoned with blood. There is no recognized government in France which Europe will acknowledge, or around which the French people are willing to rally. A darker hour than that which, at the close of the year 1870, spreads its gloom over France, few nations upon this globe have ever experienced. The world looks on with wonder to see what results

God designs to evolve from these scenes of ruin and of wretchedness. When may we hope that the prayer which our Saviour has taught us will be answered? —

"*Thy kingdom come; Thy will be done, in earth as in heaven.*"

CHAPTER XXV.

THE SIEGE OF PARIS.

THE empire in France was a republican empire, founded upon universal suffrage, recognizing the right of the *people* to organize their own form of government, abolishing all aristocratic privilege and all feudal immunities, and establishing the doctrine of equal rights for all men. Notwithstanding its attempt to conciliate Europe by its adoption of monarchical forms, and its disavowal of any design to disturb other governments by inciting democratic insurrections, its entire renunciation of "legitimacy" and of "privilege" rendered it obnoxious to dynastic Europe. If the *people* of France might choose their own sovereign, adopt such form of government as pleased them, frame their own constitution, and enact and execute their own laws, why might not the people of England, Prussia, Austria, demand the same right?

Still there was embarrassment. In France there were essentially three parties: 1. The old feudal party of legitimacy. 2. The compromise party of the empire. 3. The democratic party, in its various shades of moderates, radicals, and communists. The overthrow of the empire might not re-introduce the old feudal *régime* under the Bourbons, or its somewhat modified spirit under the Orléanists, but might possibly be succeeded by some form of democracy under avowed and deadly hostility to every European throne: therefore the dynasties reluctantly tolerated the empire, fearing that its overthrow might lead to something worse.

It was under these circumstances that Count Bismarck formed the plan of re-organizing the ancient German Empire upon the basis of the divine right of kings and the exclusive privileges of nobles. Only such modifications of the old feudal *régimes* were submitted to as the changed state of the times rendered inevitable. The avowed object of this movement was to head off and crush out the sentiment of popular rights, which was gradually being disseminated throughout Europe. Count Bismarck and King William were in entire harmony in this aim; and they prosecuted their enterprise with sagacity, energy, and success, which has astonished the world.

It is said that revolutions never roll backwards. Perhaps they do not; but here there is an apparent reflex flow of the most appalling kind. This gigantic German Empire, formed, not by the *people* of Germany, but by the twenty-five German princes who hold their offices by divine right, and who have combined in the organization of the empire, can instantly silence, throughout all Germany, any voice which may dare to speak in favor of popular rights.

Still it may prove to be an excellent government. It may be that the German people are like children, who cannot be safely trusted with the management of their own affairs. It is for the interest of the emperor and his associate kings and princes to seek the prosperity and happiness of their several peoples. In their combined action they are certainly so strong, that they can easily and instantly crush out any attempt at a popular uprising in any portion of their realms. It is also very certain that a democratic government *may be* very corrupt, oppressive, and ruinous. This holy alliance of the princes of Germany in a consolidated empire will undoubtedly secure Germany from revolutions for many years to come; and may, perhaps, confer upon the people blessings, which, under present circumstances, could not be attained in any other way.

The power of this new and majestic empire is controlled by the emperor and the associate princes. There are three bodies recognized in the government: 1. The Emperor. The crown is hereditary in the person of the King of Prussia, who is almost the absolute sovereign in his own realm. 2. The Imperial Council. This consists of the twenty-five princes of various degrees of power and dignity, whose realms constitute united Germany. Their votes are in accordance with the extent and population of their domains: the King of Prussia has seventeen votes, — one-third of all; Bavaria casts six votes; Saxony and Wurtemberg, four each; Baden and Hesse, three; Mecklenburg, Schwerin, and Brunswick, two; the rest, one each. The princes are all hereditary legislators, ruling by right of birth or divine right. 3. There is a third body, called the Reichstag. It consists of three hundred and eighty-two members, chosen by universal suffrage, — one deputy for each hundred thousand of the population. This gives Prussia two hundred and forty members, — nearly two-thirds of the whole.

It seems rather hard for France, that as the reward

for her having consented to the unification of Germany, which she could easily have prevented, she should be trampled so mercilessly beneath the feet of that gigantic empire. Père Hyacinthe said, in a speech in London the latter part of December, 1870, —

"Justice has been denied the second empire; for that government made the unity of Italy, and caused that of Germany. It was a generous policy, well expressed by Napoleon III., during the Italian campaign, in these words: 'Every one knows that before the flag of France there goes a great idea, and behind it a great people.'" [1]

On the 11th of August, 1870, as the Germanic legions were pouring into France, King William issued a proclamation, addressed "To the French Nation," dated at Saarbrück, in which he said, "Prussia wars, not on France, but on Bonaparte." To Napoleon personally he had no objections: they were friends. It was the republican empire to which he was opposed. But when the imperial army was overthrown, and Napoleon was a prisoner, and "the gentlemen of the pavement of Paris," as Bismarck designated them, had seized upon

---

[1] In a sermon preached by the Rev. O. B. Frothingham, and reported in the New-York Herald of Jan. 2, 1871, we find the following striking remarks: —

"We examine French imperialism, and we find that we cannot condemn it more than other imperialisms in history. You say that the country was licentious: there was not so much licentiousness in France under Napoleon III. as under Louis XIV. or Louis XV. You say the empire was extravagance: the cost of governing France for the last ten years was not so much as for five years under Louis' reign. It costs no more to keep Paris clean than to keep New York dirty. The empire was peace, order, and prosperity. You say the emperor was a tyrant: he was elected by the people. You say that the election was not a fair one, and that the ballot-boxes were stuffed: the ballot-boxes are stuffed in New York. In spite of cavil, Napoleon submitted the question of imperialism to the people four times; and four times the people said, 'Rule over us.' The empire was splendor: the glory of Paris was the glory of the world."

the reins of government, — thus transferring the supreme power, not back to the old *régime*, but forward to the democracy of the cities, — then Bismarck and King William were alarmed; and they would gladly have reinstated Napoleon upon the throne, after having wrested from France both banks of the Rhine, from Belgium to Switzerland. France thus deprived of any natural boundary, with Germany in possession of the whole valley of the Rhine and of the majestic fortresses which frown along its shores, was entirely at the mercy of Germany. At any hour the German legions could rush into France from these vast ramparts; while at the same time the Rhine and its fortresses presented an impassable barrier against any advance of the French troops into the new empire.

Under these circumstances, it became quite manifest that it was the policy of the German conquerors to restore Napoleon to his throne, after having so weakened France that she would be powerless in the hands of her victors. And it was cruelly reported that the Emperor of France was willing so to submit to such humiliation as to allow himself to be carried back to the Tuileries by the arms of the conquering Prussians. The emperor, with great good sense, had quietly submitted to his fate; for it had ever been one of the fundamental principles of his belief, that he was borne along by providences over which he had but little control. Prosperity did not elate him; adversity did not depress him. But, as the rumors of his plottings to regain the throne by some military stratagem became widely diffused, he, on the 12th of December, 1870, authorized, from his imprisonment at Wilhelmshöhe, the following statement to be made: —

"It would be quite well if it were publicly understood that I never intend to remount the throne on the strength of a military *pronunciamento*, by the aid of the soldiery, just as little as by that of Prussia. I am the sole sovereign in Europe who governs, next to the grace of God, by the will of the people; and I shall never be unfaithful to the origin of either. The whole people, which has four times approved of my election, must recall me by its deliberate votes, else I shall never return to France. The army possesses no more right to place me on the throne than had the lawyers or loafers to push me from it. The French people, whose sovereign I am, has the sole decision."[1]

Count Bismarck has testified to the cordial assent which France gave to the unification of Germany, and that Prussia had no fears that France would take any dishonorable advantage of the war between Prussia and Austria to regain her lost boundary of the Rhine. It was always the desire of the imperial government, in accordance with its declaration that "the empire is peace," to avoid all war, and to obtain a rectification of its boundaries by "reason," and not by "iron and by blood."

In 1866, when all the military energies of Prussia were concentrated in the march upon Sadowa, Count Bismarck said to Mr. Benedetti, "Our trust in the good faith of the French Government is so firm, that we have not a single soldier left on the left bank of the Rhine."[2]

As we have mentioned, France, at the commencement of the war, had but about four hundred thousand sol-

---

[1] Correspondence of the New-York Herald, Dec. 30, 1870.
[2] Testimony of the Marquis de Gricourt.

diers in the field. Prussia, all prepared for the conflict, with her troops in marching-order, her rail-cars for their transportation all ready, and her vast magazines on both banks of the Rhine filled with the *matériel* of war, instantly, upon the declaration of hostilities, sent into France nearly a million of men; while another million were held in reserve, following in a continuous stream, to take the place of those who fell in battle, and to replenish the German armies wherever they needed reënforcements.

The imperial troops of France, after a few bloody battles, were overpowered, and all either slain or captured. The German hosts were so numerous, that on every battle-field they could outnumber their foes by two or three to one. The world probably never saw braver and better disciplined soldiers, more skilful commanders, or better armaments, than the Germans brought into the struggle.

Having annihilated the imperial armies, the Germans had troops enough to send four hundred thousand men to lay siege to the city of Paris, to besiege with overpowering numbers every fortress and walled city which the French still garrisoned, and also to send resistless armies in all directions to gather supplies and to impose contributions upon the people. The French soldiers in garrison, and the new recruits who were hurriedly summoned to the field, fought valiantly, but with almost unvarying defeat. Every day witnessed the triumph and the advance of the German arms.

The sieges of some of the walled towns were awful beyond all imagination, attended with an appalling loss of property and of life, and an accumulation of misery which God only can gauge. In the midst of terrific bombardments, shells exploding in the crowded streets and in the thronged dwellings, conflagrations blazed forth; and scenes of tumult, dismay, and woe, were witnessed, which could not have been surpassed had fiends been the agents.

The annals of war contain no other record of such a career of victories as attended the German arms. In the course of a few weeks, Strasburg, Phalsburg, Toul, Vitry le Français, Verdun, Metz, Laon, Soissons, Bitche, Mézières, Rocroy, Schelestadt, Neuf Brisach, Thionville, Montmédy, Perronne, Longwy, and many other places of minor note, fell into the hands of the invaders. Many of the towns were military posts of the first order. The world was astounded to see these fortresses, one after another, crumbling before the batteries of the Germans.

In the course of a few months sixteen pitched battles were fought, with often two hundred thousand men or more on either side. In nearly all these battles, the Germans were victorious. If they met with a momentary repulse, they immediately replenished their thinned ranks, and advanced again to certain victory. Besides these general battles, there were innumerable minor conflicts. For five months, there was not an hour, by day or by night, in which, in some part of the vast field swept by these opposing hosts, the murderous thunders of battle were not heard.

One division of the German army, under Gen. Von Werder, swept in a broad path down the eastern frontiers of France, scattering all opposition, a distance of two hundred miles, to Dijon and Chalons. Another division, under the Crown Prince, battering down fortresses, routing armies, capturing opulent towns, ravaged the northern sections of France, through the whole breadth of the empire almost to the English Channel. Another host, more than two hundred thousand strong, marching directly beyond Paris, bore their victorious banners through many a bloody fight to the banks of the Loire, capturing Orléans and Tours, and every other place on their lines of advance.

King William, taking the magnificent palace of Versailles for his headquarters, with Count Bismarck and Baron Moltke in his suite, invested Paris with four hundred thousand veteran troops. The city was encompassed by military lines thirty or forty miles in extent. The investment was commenced on the 19th of September, 1870; and was continued until the 25th of January, 1871. Wherever there was the least possibility of the beleaguered garrison attempting a *sortie*, ramparts bristling with artillery and mitrailleuse were thrown up, so as to render escape impossible.

There were two millions of inhabitants within the city, about three hundred thousand of whom were armed. They probably accomplished all that, under the circumstances, mortal valor could accomplish. Week after week and month after month, for one hundred and thirty days, they beat off their foes. Gradually the lines of the beleaguering hosts drew nearer. Three several times, at the head of over one hundred thousand men, Gen. Trochu endeavored to cut his way through the coil of batteries and ramparts ever tightening around him. The slaughter on both sides was immense. But the Germans invariably held or regained their positions. Every hour, hope in Paris grew fainter; and despair settled down over the doomed city in darker folds.

Several armies were gathered in the provinces to

march for the relief of Paris; but they were speedily overpowered and dispersed by the Germans. The peasantry had long been jealous of the disposition of the democratic leaders in the great cities to usurp the control of affairs without consulting the inhabitants of the rural districts. The sudden and lawless overthrow of the government which had been established by the overwhelming majority of the people of France, and had been maintained by them, by repeated votes, for more than twenty years, and the usurpation of the government by a self-appointed committee without the shadow of constitutional or legal authority, so alienated the people, that there was no disposition to rise *en masse* under such leaders, even to assail the invading Prussians.

The Bourbonists, the Orléanists, the Imperialists, the Red Republicans, and the Communists were alike opposed to those "gentlemen of the pavement," as Bismarck scornfully termed them, who, some in Paris and some in Tours, called themselves "the Committee of National Defence." Under these circumstances, there was no hope of the vigorous uprising of the nation. The democratic party, which was mainly confined to the great cities, was divided into three quite distinct and bitterly hostile sections, — the Moderate Republicans, the Red Republicans, and the Socialists. Notwithstanding the pressure of the war, these factions in Paris conspired against each other; and there were frequent scenes of insurrection and bloodshed.

To add to the gloom of the condition, there was not a single nation in Europe who manifested any sympathy for the anarchic committees who assumed to govern France; not one who would cordially recognize them as a government, or enter into any diplomatic relations with them; not one which did not apparently feel that Europe had more to dread from the establishment of such a *régime* in Paris, antagonistic to every surrounding monarchy, than even from the enormous encroachments of Prussian absolutism, which, though it threatened to dominate over all Europe, would lend its influence in every kingdom to arrest the rising tide of democracy.

So heroic, notwithstanding all these discouragements, was the defence of the inexperienced young soldiers in Paris, that the Prussians did not succeed until the 9th of January in planting any batteries sufficiently near to throw shells over the walls into the city. On that day, these terrific bolts of war, thrown from a distance of four or five miles, descending as from the clouds, fell thickly in the western portion of the city, killing women and children, kindling conflagrations, destroying the most venerable works of art, and scattering dismay and death on every side. Direful famine added its horrors to the woes now desolating the most gay and beautiful metropolis upon this globe.

On the 12th of January, a balloon succeeded in leaving the city. Its despatches informed the outside world that the bombardment had continued with great violence; that shells were falling near the Palace of the Luxemburg; that several citizens had been killed, and others wounded; that the Red Republicans had placarded the streets with revolutionary posters, trying to excite insurrection, declaring the Government of Defence cowardly and incompetent. Thousands of shells had fallen, creating havoc in all directions; killing women and children, and striking hospitals, ambulances, houses, and churches.

The next day the Germans succeed in capturing a

French battery, which enabled them to push their siege-guns a mile nearer the city. From Versailles could be seen the smoke of numerous fires caused by the shells; and still far away over the frozen fields of France the battle raged, and the trampled snow was crimsoned with the blood of the slain as the drifts swept over the victors and the vanquished sleeping in death together.

And so it was, that day and night, over distant fields and around the doomed city, the awful struggle was continued without intermission. An eloquent writer says, speaking of the state of things on the 17th of January, "The surroundings of the city are in ruins or in flames. Explosive bolts of iron of over two hundred pounds in weight, howling like demons in their destructive flight, are plunging down through the humblest roofs and grandest domes in the heart of the doomed metropolis. It is the bombardment of Strasburg ten times magnified. In its destructive projectiles, and in the warlike engines and forces employed, it dwarfs all precedents of ancient or modern times. The remorseless siege and destruction of Carthage, we do not forget, involved the extinction of a great nation and a great people; nor will the intelligent reader fail to recall the appalling loss of human life — eleven hundred thousand souls — involved in the siege and burning of Jerusalem by Titus; nor do we overlook the sacking and burning of Rome by Alaric. But neither Babylon, Tyre, Jerusalem, Carthage, nor Rome, furnishes any thing in the horrors of war more shocking to the Christian humanitarian of the nineteenth century than this horrible bombardment of Paris, with its blind and indiscriminate killing and mangling of soldiers and non-combatants, the strong and the helpless, men, women, and children."

In seven months these German armies had crushed the most renowned military power of modern times, had captured its emperor, and had taken possession of one-half of its territory. Prince Frederick Charles was pursuing the routed forces of Gen. Chanzy, driven beyond the Loire. Gen. Bourbaki, in the east of France, was nearly surrounded by the Germans under Von Werder and Manteuffel, and his doom seemed inevitable. In the north, the posture of affairs was still more gloomy. Gen. Faidherbe was sullenly retreating before the stronger forces of Gen. Von Goeben.

On the 19th of January it was reported, that, the day before, four hundred and fifty shells had been thrown into the city; that Sèvres was in ruins; that a German battery was within four miles of Notre Dame; that Prince Hohenlöhe had declared his determination to destroy all the principal edifices in Paris; that batteries were already reared for the destruction of St. Denis, the sepulchre of the ancient kings of France; and that in Paris "abominable plots" were formed for the overthrow of the Committee of Public Defence, and for the establishment of the reign of terror. An insurrectionary procession, numbering six hundred, had paraded the streets.

Still the dismal hours of war and woe passed slowly away. Nothing was to be heard on any side but disasters to the French. Starvation threatened Paris. All the animals in the menagerie were eaten. Horses, dogs, cats, rats, furnished eagerly-coveted food for the famishing people. The conservatory of the Jardin des Plantes, containing the most magnificent collection of exotics in the world, was in ruins; and in the city there were every hour new indications of hostility to the Provisional Government, and new menaces of revolt.

Gen. Trochu, utterly disheartened, tendered his resignation as Governor of Paris. But no one could be found to take his place. It was mid-winter: the fuel was all consumed; the people were freezing as well as starving. The German batteries were drawing nearer, the storm of shells growing more thick and terrible. There was no possible shelter. The government was in bewilderment: it knew not what to do. *Sorties* were impossible. Every hour of resistance was only submitting to helpless massacre. Starvation was steadily approaching: capitulation would seal the destiny of the Committee for Public Defence.

Under these circumstances, Jules Favre, the leading spirit in the Provisional Government, with anguish of spirit which must have been awful, on the 25th of January sought an interview with Count Bismarck, at Versailles, to propose terms of surrender. France, Paris, was at the feet of the conqueror. He could exact, and he did exact, his own terms. Scornfully rejecting any recognition of the "gentlemen of the pavement" as the government of France, he consented to an armistice of twenty-one days, upon condition that all the troops in the city should surrender their arms, and that the forts surrounding Paris should be given up to the Germans. This was, of course, the unconditional surrender of Paris. The German troops could march into the city unresisted any hour of any day.

It was also exacted, that on the 8th of February there should be an election, throughout France, of a Constituent Assembly. This body should meet on the 15th, and immediately adopt some form of government which Germany would recognize, and with which Germany would treat for conditions of peace. To that government King William would present the following terms, which, in the name of France, it must accept, or the *slaughter* would continue; for *war*, on the part of the French, seemed no longer possible: —

1. France was to surrender to Prussia Alsace and Lorraine, with Belfort and Metz;
2. To pay as indemnity for the expenses of the war ten milliards of francs, — equal to two thousand million dollars;
3. To surrender to Prussia the French colony of Pondicherry; and,
4. To transfer to the German navy twenty first-class French frigates.[1]

Such, essentially, were the terms which the victor professed himself ready to offer to his prostrate and humiliated foe.

[1] London Times, Feb. 1, 1871.

CHAPTER XXVI.

THE POLITICAL EMBARRASSMENTS.

THERE is no satisfactory evidence, that, at any time during the war, the masses of the people in France were in sympathy with the self-constituted committees in Paris and Bordeaux. For obvious reasons, the populace in large cities are more liable to sudden impulses and to fickle changes than the inhabitants of the rural districts. Still, in the great cities there was no harmony of views in accepting what was called the Republic, — a usurpation which did not dare to appeal to the votes of the nation for its recognition. Even in Paris, the democratic party was so divided, that there were insurrections against the Government for the National Defence, and fearful menaces of civil war, even when the bombardment of the Prussians was shaking the windows of the Hôtel de Ville.

Jules Favre, who may, perhaps, be considered a moderate republican, was at the head of the government in Paris. Gambetta, a *red* republican of the most crimson die, was the leader of that portion of the government which had taken refuge in Tours, and afterwards, upon the approach of the Prussians, had escaped to Bordeaux. From the commencement of the so-called republican government, there had been ever-increasing discord between these two sections of the ruling power.

Upon the surrender of the army in Paris as prisoners of war, it is estimated that there was the almost incredible number of eight hundred thousand of unwounded French prisoners in German hands, including the emperor and the marshals of France. The victors had also captured six thousand cannon and rifles, and military stores of all kinds in amount which can scarcely be estimated. This had all been accomplished in six months. It is safe to say that no such achievements had ever before been performed in the history of this world.

Gambetta, while calling himself a republican, was probably as bitterly opposed to a true republic as any man in the empire. What he demanded was a *dictatorship*, with himself at its head. He forbade the convening of a National Assembly, silenced the remonstrances of the press, and suppressed the councils-general of the departments, which, under the empire, were steadily advancing in the path of local self-government. It is a painful and discouraging fact, that none have shown greater hostility to republican institutions than the French " republicans."

Upon the announcement of the armistice by Jules Favre, Gambetta issued a very fiery proclamation, urging France to improve the short armistice in getting ready to renew the fight. The dictatorial acts of Léon Gambetta were daily assuming an aspect of increasing audacity. As Bismarck utterly refused to recognize the irresponsible Government of National Defence, and demanded the convocation of a National Assembly to organize a government which should have some claim to represent the French nation, Gambetta could not resist that demand. He, however, issued a decree, declaring that no man should be a candidate for that Assembly who was a member of any of the families which had reigned over France since 1789. This ostracized all relatives of the Bourbon, the Orléans, and the Bonaparte families. He also declared all to be disqualified for election, who, under the empire, had held office, or been candidates for office, as ministers, senators, councillors of state, or prefects of the departments.

It was his object to limit the suffrages of the French people to republican candidates alone. It would be difficult to find, under any *régime*, more despotic decrees than were issued by Gambetta. The Assembly was to consist of seven hundred and fifty-three delegates for all of France. "All the detailed conditions," writes a correspondent from London, "laid down for the management of the elections, are grossly in favor of the republicans now in power." On the 2d of February, Gambetta caused a new Committee of Public Safety to be organized in Bordeaux, by which such extremists in the radical ranks as Rochefort, Louis Blanc, and Duportal, were associated with him in power.

The Paris government issued loud remonstrances against these despotic acts. In the midst of these exciting scenes of tumult and of woe, there were, every day, increasing indications that large numbers in France were earnestly desiring the return of the captive emperor, under whose sway France had enjoyed twenty years of prosperity and happiness unparalleled in all her ancient annals. A correspondent from Wilhelmshöhe gives us the following glimpse of the appearance of the illustrious prisoner during these days of trial: —

"Ever since the first despatch announcing the commencement of the bombardment of Paris reached the imperial prisoner, he seems to have been overwhelmed with grief at the misfortunes of the fair city. How very deeply it moved him is evident from a remarkable change in his features; their painful and melancholy expression indicating how he loved dear Paris, that city from which he has experienced so much wrong.

"Of the millions in and outside of France mourning its terrible destruction, who has reason to be more distressed than Napoleon III.? Are its architectural splendors, and the beauty of its boulevards and noble streets, not a monument erected, as it were, to himself, and commemorating a work, to the execution of which, during nearly twenty years, he has devoted untiring energy and pride? The beautiful city would have been an imperishable monument, speaking to generations to come of the so well-abused empire in better and more truthful language than the journals and pamphlets of the present epoch.

"Of the many who are discussing the probability of a return of the Napoleonic dynasty, none consider for a moment that the greatest of all obstacles has first to be overcome; namely, that the emperor may refuse his consent. The possibility of such an occurrence may be doubted by those who have endeavored, for a series of years, to portray the Emperor of the French in false colors, and to caricature him before their contemporaries. They may doubt that the prisoner of Wilhelmshöhe would reject that dignity of which he has been deprived by a comparatively small number of demagogues. Let me endeavor to give you a few hints respecting the aforementioned obstacles.

"At first, there is that sentiment expressed by the emperor, spoken of in a former letter to you, — that *the whole people only*, through their legal representatives, have a right to recall the emperor. Neither the army, nor the Prussian Government, nor the demands of party, could induce his return. The entire people are entitled to repair the great wrong perpetrated against his person by those political leaders who forced him into this war, and who profited by the hour of misfortune to carry out their long-prepared and sinister designs."

Each day brought increasing indications of the antagonism between Jules Favre with his associates at Paris, and Léon Gambetta and his associates at Bordeaux. Messages of defiance passed between them. The following extracts from the public journals will show the state of affairs on the 7th of February, the day before the general election of members for the National Assembly was to take place: —

"There is little to be expected from the Bordeaux wing of the government. The very power at present wielded by the fire-eaters who control it is a usurpation of the legitimate authority which really belongs to the Paris government. Yet from this very hot-bed of the worst radicalism, misnamed republicanism, which the world has witnessed in this generation, the immediate destinies of a great nation must come forth. If the teachings of Gambetta and his followers prevail, the most direful results to the French people must follow.

"Henri Rochefort is again coming to the surface from the obscurity into which the startling events of the past year had cast him. Now he appears on the stage, if report speaks truly, as an advocate of assassination. Gambetta, Rochefort, Flourens, — these, and men of like character and similar associations, are the men who propose to regenerate France, and found what they call a republic, but what sensible and thinking people consider would prove a despotism far worse than that of the empire.

"The situation to-day is pitiful, and in all respects unworthy of a great people. France herself is divided. The Imperialists are in bad repute; the Orléanists are of doubtful value; the Legitimists are nowhere; the Republicans — behold the situation of the hour!"

Feb. 8, 1871. — The news flashed across the wires from ill-fated France to-day was as follows: —

"France presents the melancholy spectacle of a once proud and powerful nation at the mercy of a noisy, turbulent, and unprincipled crew of demagogues. Special despatches from Paris, Bordeaux, Lyons, and other points throughout the country, serve to show the wretched character of the majority of the men who are candidates for the National Assembly. It seems as though the very slums of Paris, Bordeaux, Lyons, and Marseilles, have thrown up their refuse to be used by the unprincipled demagogues who wield temporary power in France. While famishing people cry for bread in the streets of Paris, the mob yell for a Robespierre and the guillotine. In the agony of their despair, the terror-stricken people suffer in silence, afraid to speak their thoughts, or raise their hands to save themselves from the tide of violence which threatens them with destruction. The mob rule, and despotism is the law. Truly France is suffering. Bleeding from every pore, paralyzed in every part, humiliated, cast down, and prostrate, she is even now, in this bitter hour, tormented by the dissensions and evil teachings of her children." [1]

Jules Favre and his colleagues were in disfavor because they had agreed to an armistice. The feeling against Gambetta was increasing. Red republicanism of the worst type began to show itself. One orator at a public meeting declared that a Robespierre was required, and that the guillotine alone could save France. This declaration, so bloodthirsty, was received with yells of delight.

"In keeping with this atrocious sentiment, we have the fact that most of the Paris candidates for the Assembly are men taken from the slums of Belleville and St. Antoine, — men notorious for their violence, recklessness, and lack of ability. . We have no doubt that these villains, madmen, and fanatics are a minority of the population: but, unfortunately, they are the party of action; compact, and united against the party of order; divided, and irreconcilable in their division."

Jules Favre and his colleagues seem to dread approaching anarchy. Already their arrest and trial were advocated; and one speaker (M. Gaillard) denounced them as twelve bandits who have sold Paris for gold. Rochefort's and Pyat's newspapers breathed nothing but revolution and vengeance. While the political situation was thus terrible, the horrors of starvation were commencing their reign.

On the 8th of February, the election of delegates to the National Assembly took place throughout France.

---

[1] Correspondence of the New-York Herald.

In view of this event, the Emperor Napoleon, from his captivity at Wilhelmshöhe, issued the following proclamation to the French people. The proclamation gave great satisfaction to his friends, and was reviled by his enemies.

"WILHELMSHÖHE, Feb. 8, 1871.

"Betrayed by fortune, I have kept, since my captivity, a profound silence, which is misfortune's mourning. As long as the armies confronted each other, I abstained from any steps or words capable of causing party dissensions; but I can no longer remain silent before my country's disaster without appearing insensible to its sufferings. When I was made a prisoner, I could not treat for peace, because my resolutions would appear to have been dictated by personal considerations. I left a regent to decide whether it was for the interest of the nation to continue the struggle. Notwithstanding unparalleled reverses, France was unsubdued; but her strongholds were reduced, her departments invaded, and Paris brought into a state of defence. The extent of her misfortunes might possibly have been limited; but, while attention was directed to her enemies, insurrection arose at Paris, the seat of representatives was violated, the safety of the empress threatened, and the empire, which had been three times acclaimed by the people, was overthrown and abandoned.

"Stilling my presentiments, I exclaimed, 'What matter my dynasty, if the country is saved?' Instead of protesting against the violation of my right, I hoped for the success of the defence, and admired the patriotic devotion of the children of France. Now, when the struggle is suspended, and all reasonable chance of victory has disappeared, is the time to call to account the usurpers for the bloodshed and ruin and squandered resources. It is impossible to abandon the destinies of France to an unauthorized government to which was left no authority emanating from universal suffrage. Order, confidence, and solid peace, are only recoverable when the *people are consulted* respecting the government most capable of repairing the disasters to the country. It is essential that France should be united in her wishes. For myself, banished by injustice and bitter deceptions, I do not know or claim my repeatedly-confirmed rights. There is no room for personal ambition. But till the people are regularly assembled, and express their will, it is my duty to say that all acts are illegitimate. There is only one government, in which resides the *national sovereignty*, able to heal wounds, to bring hope to firesides, to re-open profaned churches, and to restore industry, concord, and peace."

The result of these elections proved that France was by no means disposed to intrust her destiny to those reckless men, who, by the aid of the mob of Paris, had usurped the government, and established a despotism which they dared not submit to the suffrages of the French people, and which they yet absurdly called the Republic. Notwithstanding there were several hundred thousand imperial soldiers prisoners in Germany, and who consequently could not vote, France, by a vote of more than four to one, rejected the self-constituted government of Jules Favre, Léon Gambetta, and their colleagues, and elected candidates pledged to some form of monarchy. Though the great cities chose as delegates the most radical of the red republicans, the departments returned men of a very different character.

"The loose materials of the great cities, which have nothing to lose and much to gain from a republic of the communist order, calling for a new division of all the lands and property in France among all the people, have gone for the Gambetta republicans. On the other hand, the property-holders, including the peasantry on their small estates, prefer things as they are to any change which threatens to dispossess them. And, again, the Catholic clergy in France see in Gambetta, Garibaldi, and company, only the enemies of their church, aiming at its destruction; and so the influence of the Church has been wielded against the republic."[1]

On the 16th of February, reliable tidings were received in this country of the result of the elections, and of the probable character of the Assembly. In view of the facts announced, "The New-York Herald" makes the following remarks, which will commend themselves to the intelligent reader: —

"To-day France presents a fresh spectacle for world-wide observation and study. No part of the world looks on more attentively, or questions more acutely, than the United States of America; and it is not unfair to say that this people have ceased to have any faith in France.

"This day, while we write, she is no longer the hope of Europe: what is worse, she is either the object of pity or the object of contempt. Republicans as we are, we have to confess it with sorrow, that we can no longer look to France as the possible regenerator of Europe. She had a glorious first opportunity. That first was

[1] Correspondence of the New-York Herald, Feb. 13, 1871.

lost or flung away. The opportunity has been again and again repeated, but always with the same result. How can we longer hope or trust?

"We are now face to face with new facts. After a defeat which has no parallel in history, France has been, by the magnanimity of the conqueror, permitted to pronounce on her own destiny. She has had, perhaps, the fairest chance of speaking out the thoughts that are within her that she ever had in her whole history; and she has once again, and most emphatically, spoken in a manner which is disappointing to all those who love republican institutions.

"The results of the recent elections are clearly, as all our readers must now be fully convinced, in favor of monarchy. It is not yet time to say what is the exact complexion of the Assembly; but if it be true that the house of Orléans has practically polled four hundred votes as against a hundred and fifty for the republic, fifty for the old Bourbons or Legitimists, and twenty for the Bonapartes, we have no choice but say France is not yet ripe and ready for citizen sovereignty. Look at the National Assembly to-day from what point of view we may, we can come to no other conclusion than this, — that France has heartily, and with not a little emphasis, condemned the empire and the Bonapartes, condemned the republic and the infidels and the communists, condemned divine right and the old Bourbons, and gone in, if not for Philip Égalité, at least for the principles represented by his son, the citizen-king. No more empire, no more republic, but the constitution of 1830, and a citizen-king, — that is the result of the elections which have just been finished in France, and which are represented in the National Assembly of to-day.

"Why is it so? Why are our republican hopes once more blasted? Why is this fresh French opportunity lost to France and the world? The answer to these questions is not far to seek. Under the bright sunshine of the empire, France indulged in proud memories, was happy and gay, despised all shadow, and dreamed of no sorrow. What had the empire not done? It had made France the central, the pivotal power of Europe. For twenty years, the word of France, spoken by the emperor, was a word of authority which no nation on the face of the earth could afford to despise. Did not the empire humble Russia? Did not the empire give Italy unity? Did not the empire compel Prussia to halt at Sadowa? Was not the empire the bulwark of the Papacy? Was it not the hope of all struggling nationalities? Was it not, as it once had been, a match for the world in arms? Was not Paris, adorned by the empire, the eye of the civilized world, even as Corinth was once said to be the eye of Greece?

"Since Sedan, the so-called republic, headed by men who dared not appeal to the French people, — because they knew that French Catholics could not and would not trust infidels, and that French proprietors could not and would not trust communists, — has had its chance; but the failure of the so-called republic has been more complete, more disastrous, and, if possible, more ignominious, than that of the empire. If France was humbled by the surrender of Sedan, France is squelched by the surrender and occupation of Paris. It is not for us to say whether France has been just or unjust to the empire, just or unjust to the republic. We must accept facts. The facts are represented in the National Assembly; and the National Assembly is just as little imperialist or republican as it is legitimist. If the stars have any meaning, the star which France and the rest of the civilized world see rising out of this six-months' darkness shines benignantly on the house of Orléans."

The victory of Prussia is complete. France is humbled and prostrate beyond all possibility of retrievement for generations to come. And what has Germany gained? Upon this theme "The New-York World" makes the following sensible observations:—

"But the most far-reaching consequence of this war is the unification of Germany. It brings under one government a territory and population about equal to those of France at the beginning of the war. The area of the new German Empire is 206,575 English square miles; containing, in 1867, a population of 38,522,336. Both area and population will be somewhat increased by the French provinces retained. The area of France, previous to her losses, was 207,480 square miles; and her population, in 1866, was 38,067,094: so she will hereafter be inferior to Germany both in territory and inhabitants. She will have the further disadvantage of a much heavier public debt. The national debt of France in 1869 was, in round numbers, $2,766,000,000 of our money; while the aggregate debts of the several countries now united to form the German Empire amounted, in the same year, to only $538,500,000, and bore quite as low a rate of interest. The public debt of France was five times as great as the collective debts which will be consolidated by German unity; and the disproportion will be greatly increased by this terrible war, since France, besides defraying her own expenses, will have to re-imburse a part of the expenses of Germany.

"What advantages, aside from national weight and importance, will attend the knitting-together of the German States into one empire, cannot yet be estimated. At present, the prospect looks unfavorable to the development of free institutions. The empire will be too powerful to be resisted by any of the small States which have been merged in it. None of the local governments will be any further respected than suits the convenience of the central authority for purposes of local administration. The present rulers of Germany are the last men in Europe to make any voluntary concessions to popular rights; and their power of repression is manifestly strengthened by the new ascendency which this war has given them over the national mind. But the Emperor William, who will complete his seventy-fourth year on the 22d of March must, in the course of nature, give place ere long to the Crown Prince, who may not inherit his father's narrow and bigoted notions and arrogant temper. His education has been more liberal; and his English marriage would naturally have brought him into contact with some people who might give his mind, if it is at all open and receptive, some tincture of British politics. But, if the haughty and unscrupulous Bismarck should continue to be prime-minister, his stronger character and astuter intellect would be likely to mould the government."

CHAPTER XXVII.

PEACE.

THE establishment of the great Germanic Empire, which is now *un fait accompli*, has cost three sanguinary wars. First, there was the war with Denmark for the possession of Schleswig and Holstein. Next came the war with Austria, terminating in the terrible slaughter of Sadowa, by which Prussia doubled her territory and population, and more than doubled her military power. Then ensued the war with France, by which Prussia consolidated her new possessions, obtained both banks of the Rhine from Belgium to Switzerland, and, by depriving France of any natural frontier, left France entirely at the mercy of any Germanic invasion; while Germany, with the broad Rhine and its impregnable fortresses in her possession, was effectually guarded against any approach from France. It is very seldom that any earthly plans advance so triumphantly from the commencement to the conclusion as have these measures of Count Bismarck for the establishment of the German Empire. True, the expense has been awful beyond all human estimation. The number of lives sacrificed in the carnage of the battle-field and in the wards of the hospital is to be counted by hundreds of thousands. Other multitudes, which cannot be numbered, must pass through life with mutilated bodies, consigning them to hopeless impoverishment. Germany and France have been literally filled with widows and with orphans; and their silent woe, unheeded by men, will, through long years of suffering, ascend to the ear of God. The destruction of property in the bombardment and conflagration of cities, in the villages and cottages laid in ashes, the trampling of harvests, and all the waste and ruin which accompany the march of hostile armies, it is scarcely in the power of human arithmetic to compute. The blessings which the Germanic Empire shall confer upon humanity ought to be very great indeed to compensate for the misery into which millions have been plunged. It is said, that when some one, in conversation with Count Bismarck, alluded to these woes which the establishment of the empire had cost, he replied, " Yes ; but, unfortunately, you cannot have an omelette without breaking the eggs."

It is now obvious to every reflecting mind, that the overthrow of the French Empire after the disaster at Sedan, and the substitution of the irresponsible Committee of National Defence, was an irreparable calamity for France. The Imperial Government, which had been established and sustained by the votes of the overwhelming majority of the people, had conferred upon France twenty years of prosperity, and was recognized and respected by all the governments of Europe, Asia, and America.

When such men as Favre, Gambetta, and Rochefort, taking advantage of an hour of terrible disaster and dismay, summoned the mob of Paris to their aid, and with dictatorial hands seized the sceptre of power,

France was bewildered, stunned, paralyzed. Catholic France would not listen to the voice of those whose cry was "Down with the church!" as well as "Down with the throne!" Eugénie, as regent, might have summoned all France to rise *en masse* to repel the invader. The pope would have contributed his powerful sympathy; and every ecclesiastic in France would have echoed the appeal. Thus, in an hour, seven millions of fighting men might have sprung to arms. The vast fleet of France, in perfect command of the seas, could have supplied them with weapons. There was thus a *probability* of the calamity being mitigated; and a *possibility*, even, that it might be repaired. But the pope, the cardinals, and the bishops all felt that they had no foes more to be dreaded than the democracy of Paris, Lyons, and Marseilles. Thus, when Gambetta and Rochefort frantically shouted for all France to spring to arms, the priests were silent, and the peasants shook their heads. The energies of France were paralyzed, and her doom was sealed.

The empire, under the regency, could have looked to the surrounding kingdoms with some hope, at least, of securing an alliance. These kingdoms all feared the enormous growth and military power of Prussia; and none of them wished to see France trampled in the dust. They all maintained friendly relations with the empire. The pope wielded a moral power stronger than bayonets or batteries; and the pope had ever found in the emperor a firm friend. Victor Emanuel owed his crown to the emperor; and united Italy was one of the creations of the empire. The daughter of Victor Emanuel, the Princess Clotilde, had married the emperor's cousin, Prince Bonaparte; and she was one of the most lovely and beloved of the inmates of the Tuileries. This rendered it not impossible that an alliance with Italy might soon have been formed.

Spain had, with singular unanimity, voted against a republic, and had established a monarchy. Prince Amodeus, a son of Victor Emanuel and a brother of Princess Clotilde, was soon chosen King of Spain. This family alliance tended to unite Spain with Italy in strong sympathy with France. Hence it was by no means improbable that Spain might have been induced to send her armies across the Pyrenees to assist the French Empire in its deadly struggle with its foreign foes. Family alliance, religious faith, and harmonious institutions, would all have lent their aid.

Austria, smarting beneath her terrible defeats, exasperated by the loss of immense territory, trembling in view of the gigantic power which was overshadowing her, and grateful to Napoleon for having, after the disaster of Sadowa, prohibited the further encroachments of Prussia, — thus saving Austria from annihilation, — must have been in a position to listen to overtures which would enable her to strike back some revengeful blows, and perhaps to regain a portion of that which she had lost.

The British Government was in far more cordial sympathy with the French Empire than with any other government upon the continent. The alliance in the Crimean War had cemented the friendship of the governments and the armies of England and France. By friendly co-operation, the commerce of the two nations had been vastly increased; and constant intercourse was fast uniting the two nations in sympathetic bonds.

In April, 1855, the emperor, with Eugénie, visited

the Queen of England. The palaces of Victoria blazed with regal *fêtes* in their honor. Their reception was alike enthusiastic by the court and by the populace. The Lord Mayor of Windsor, in welcoming the royal guests to Windsor Castle, said, —

"We are sensible, sire, that to the wisdom and vigor of your imperial majesty's counsels, and to your unceasing endeavors to promote the true interests of the powerful and generous nation which Providence has committed to your care, may be attributed that prosperity and happiness which your country now enjoys."

"The London Times" of that date speaks as follows of the reception which England gave to her distinguished guests: —

"They were the associations connected with Napoleon III. — the remembrance of his deeds and the knowledge of his worth — which pressed along his progress the millions who this week have given to the world an imperishable testimony of their appreciation of fortitude in troubles, energy in action, courage amidst dangers, and clemency amid triumphs.

"They honored the wisdom and probity which occupied a mighty throne, and honored the thousand princely qualities which had won it. They honored the great man who had retrieved the prosperity and the power of France. They honored the good sovereign whose chief care is the welfare of his people. And, in the greeting offered to Napoleon, we may truly add, there was love for the nation which he had restored to its legitimate place amongst the powers of the earth at a moment most critical to its destinies, and to which he had given back, with the suddenness of enchantment, all its internal prosperity, after convulsions which made the most sanguine despair of its future. Given back! — he has opened for it a new career of unprecedented success."

Addresses breathing the above spirit were showered upon the emperor from all quarters. On the 17th of April, the city of London offered a banquet to their Majesties. In the response of the emperor to the very complimentary address of the lord mayor, he said, —

"As for me, I have preserved on the throne, for the people of England, the sentiments of esteem and sympathy which I professed in exile, when I enjoyed here the hospitality of the queen; and, if I have conformed my conduct to my convictions, it is because the interest of the nation which elected me, as well as those of general civilization, constrain me to do so."

England needed an ally upon the Continent. France was the only nation to which she could look for cordial alliance. Under these circumstances, the sympathies of England would have been with France, had the empire continued; and it is by no means impossible that England might have been induced to contribute more to the empire than her *moral* support.

But the suicidal act of the democracy in Paris in seizing upon the moment of overwhelming disaster to overthrow by mob-violence the constituted authorities, and to establish a dictatorship which they absurdly called a republic, which they dared not submit to popular suffrage, and which no government in Europe would recognize, left France, wounded and bleeding, at the mercy of her foes. There was no longer any hope of efficient aid from home or from abroad. Catholic France could not unite in measures which would place the sceptre in the hands of infidel communism and socialism; and neither the governments of England,

Austria, Italy, or Spain, could think of aiding to establish and consolidate the sway of the self-constituted democratic committees of Paris and Bordeaux. Indeed, were a republic, distinctively organized, to be established in France, it would not enjoy the sympathy and friendship of a single monarchy in Europe. It would be simply tolerated; while every neighboring power would strive to embarrass its operations, and would eagerly watch for its downfall. In this hostility, none would be more prominent than the majestic German Empire, which now, in possession of the most important avenues of entrance into France, holds France entirely at its mercy.

One of the most untoward yet inevitable results of this conflict is, that it has irreparably impaired, throughout Christendom, confidence in the French people. They know not what they want. They are never united. Revolution follows revolution in endless succession. The best friends of France have lost all hopefulness in her future, and are in despair. In a terrible revolution of blood and misery, less than one hundred years ago, the old Bourbon monarchy was overthrown. They tried a republic; it proved an utter failure: tried the consulate; abandoned it for the empire: shouted, "Down with the empire!" and took back the Bourbons; drove them ignominiously a second time from the kingdom, and reared the Orléans throne. After making Louis Philippe their "target-king" for about a score of years, they drove him in shame and disgrace out of the kingdom, and tried a republic again. After the lapse of two years, they repudiated the republic, and re-established the empire; and now the empire is in ruins, and the people of France are asking, "What next?"

There is no new form of government which human ingenuity can devise. Shall they return to the old Bourbon monarchy? Twice they have tried that, and twice rejected it furiously. Shall they re-establish the republic? Twice they have abandoned that in disgust. Shall they attempt to rear again the throne of the empire? The first and second empire have been trampled with maledictions beneath the feet of the mob in Paris. Shall they invite the House of Orléans back to the throne? Louis Philippe was, but a few years ago, literally pelted out of the kingdom, barely escaping with his life.

Whatever excuses may be made for any or all of these events, the facts remain unchanged; and they have created, universally, a profound sentiment of discouragement in reference to the future of France. Her best friends are in despair. They feel that it is of but little consequence what government the present Assembly may decide upon; for they have no confidence that the government will last longer than a few years. There are in France five very decided and hostile parties, — Bourbonists, Orléanists, Imperialists, Moderate Republicans, and very emphatically pronounced Radical Republicans. Whichever one of these five forms of government may be adopted, there will be four fierce assailants to fall upon it, obstructing its operations, and endeavoring by revolution to secure its overthrow. The world has lost faith in France.

The writer has ever been in favor of the empire, believing it to have been the choice of the majority of the French people, and, under the circumstances, the best government for France. He has thought, with nearly eight millions of French voters, that monarchical forms would disarm the hostility of the surrounding monarchies; while a constitution under those forms, abolishing all hereditary privilege, establishing universal suffrage, and recognizing the principle of equal rights for all men, might gradually lead the nation in the path of liberty, without the horrors of revolution.

Very many of his fellow-republicans in America have been so far from agreeing with him in this opinion, that they have regarded its avowal as a crime demanding the severest denunciation. But the writer is constrained still to admit, that in his judgment, could the minority of the people of France have acquiesced in the decision of the majority, and accepted the empire, with its constitution purposely rendered so elastic that any reforms which the people might choose could be introduced by the peaceful operation of the ballot-box, the forty millions of the French people would be in a far happier condition and with brighter prospects than now.

It is a remarkable fact, that the friends of human progress, at the present time, look rather to the empire of Germany with hope than to France. They cannot regard with approval many of the measures which have been adopted in the creation of this empire. They instinctively revolt from its absolutist political principles, from its hereditary legislators, and from its openly-avowed hostility to popular reform. Still the empire will probably prove a stable government. The Germans are a stable and reliable people. It will be for the interest of that strong government to promote the prosperity of the masses; and modern intelligence, which teaches that the wealth of one nation is not increased by the impoverishment of others, will lead the empire to seek, by commercial activity, to promote the industry and opulence of other States.

The writer regrets to see that there are some Germans in this country who are annoyed by the impartial statement of the facts involved in the creation of the new Germanic Empire. But it is of no avail to attempt to conceal these facts, or to ignore them. This thing has not been done in a corner. The eyes of the civilized world has been upon the movement. The successive steps by which this sublime creation has been accomplished are known to all attentive observers; and no one is ignorant of the fact, that neither Count Bismarck nor King William is the friend of democratic progress, and that this empire has been established as a check upon that progress.

To attempt to conceal these facts would only expose these pages to contempt. The narrative here given is an impartial recital of facts known by all intelligent men. If this record be not substantially true, then is it impossible to obtain any truth of history. Never did events take place under a broader blaze of day. The eyes of the civilized world have followed these movements.

At the present moment, such intense emotions and passions are excited by these tremendous events, that no one who attempts to record these scenes, no matter how candid, how impartial, can hope to escape obloquy. When forty millions of Germans upon one side, and forty millions of Frenchmen on the other, are arrayed against one another in the most deadly hostility, with all their passions roused to the highest pitch, he would betray a strange knowledge of human nature who should hope that he could give an impartial account of the conflict in terms which would be satisfactory to either party. Under these circumstances, the writer has been only anxious so to state the truth as to win the approval of all impartial minds, and to secure the final verdict of the antagonists, whose passions, now so fearfully aroused, will ere long subside into a calm more favorable for the contemplation of truth. Fortunately for the writer, there are thousands of his countrymen, who have watched these events with the most intelligent and intense interest, who will be able, by their testimony, to substantiate the accuracy of this narrative.

March 2, 1871. — The great conflict is ended. France, beaten in every battle, and with her capital in the hands of the conqueror, has been compelled to submit to whatever terms were proposed, and to drain to its dregs the cup of humiliation presented to her lips. She surrenders all of Alsace, one-fifth of Lorraine, and all the strong fortresses which had been reared in those regions. Thus Prussia now holds both banks of the Rhine from Belgium to Switzerland, all the fortresses in the Rhine Valley, and commands all the passes of the Vosges Mountains. One million five hundred thousand Frenchmen, in the highest state of exasperation, are taken from France, and transferred to Prussia. Thus France lies entirely at the mercy of Germany, with no possibility of striking back any blows which may be received. In addition to this loss of territory, — which, in a strategic point of view, is of inestimable value, — France is compelled to pay the victor a thousand millions of dollars to remunerate him for the expenses he has incurred in making his magnificent conquest. This amounts to twenty-five dollars for every man, woman, and child in France. In addition to this, France has been compelled to submit to the humiliation of having the German army, with unfurled banners and jubilant trumpet-peals, traverse her avenues into the very heart of Paris, and pitch their tents in the Garden of the Tuileries and in the Elysian Fields; and, hardest of all, there are but few voices to be heard, in England or America, speaking one word of sympathy for France in her utter desolation and woe. "The New-York Herald," which perhaps, as fully as any other paper, reflects popular sentiment, says, —

"Very few who have been students of this war from its commencement until now will be sorry that things are as they are to-day." [1]

A correspondent of "The Herald," writing from Paris under date of the evening of March 1, 1871, says, "The dreaded hour has arrived. The German troops, with the iron determination which has distinguished them during the war, are at this moment carrying out their resolution to enter the capital of France, conquered by them. Up to the last moment, it was hoped that the autocrat at the head of the German Empire would yield, and not be relentless in his purpose, but content himself with the dismemberment and beggary of France, without adding an apparently unnecessary and unprofitable humiliation to the already overwhelmed French."

The scenes of grief and despair witnessed on the part of the implusive French when their triumphant foes marched exultingly into the city, with their batteries so arranged, that, at the slightest exhibition of hostilities, the whole city could be laid in ashes, cannot be described.

Terribly severe as were these terms of the Germans, the French could not have resisted them even had they been more unendurable. France, bound hand and foot, was at the mercy of the conqueror. The terms of peace

[1] New-York Herald, March.2, 1871.

to which M. Thiers and M. Favre had assented, in their conference with the Prussian court at Versailles, was ratified by the General Assembly at Bordeaux by 546 yeas to 107 nays. These numbers, which have just been flashed over the wires, may not prove exact; but they show the general unanimity of the vote.

Thus the war terminates. This, however, may prove but the beginning of the end. German troops will hold portions of the French territory till the debt is paid. There may yet be many serious collisions. What government will France now establish? It matters not whether it be Legitimist, Orléanist, Imperialist, or Republican: France is at the mercy of Germany. Should France now establish a republic in her friendlessness and her poverty, even *could* she establish such on the best and most orderly of bases, she would incur the hostility of every monarchy in Europe, and the especial hostility of that gigantic empire of absolutism now frowning down upon her from the north.

Europe is bewildered by the suddenness of the change. The great northern empires of Prussia and Russia, now bound in closest alliance of governmental forms and political principles, hold Europe at their disposal. Prussia needs, for her full development, Belgium, Holland, and Denmark: she can now take them whenever it may please her to do so. Russia needs Sweden, and Turkey in Europe: she can have them both before the snows of another winter fall, if she think it worth while to be in haste, and to put her armies in motion.

The fall of France is the fall of England. She has no longer an ally upon the Continent. Sir Robert Peel, in an impassioned speech in the English House of Commons, has recently given expression to his alarm. He mourns the downfall of France, whose independence he affirms to be essential to the tranquillity of Europe, — "a country," he says, "which, for the last twenty years at least, on twenty battle-fields, has, in unison with England, sacrificed her best blood and noblest sons;" and he declares that "the unification of Germany under a military despotism cannot be for the good of Europe."

There is the prospect of very serious trouble in Europe for years to come. The republican element in Germany will not long remain quiescent under the sway of hereditary princes. When we reflect upon the results of this conflict, it is difficult to conceive of any good which humanity has attained in the slightest degree commensurate with the misery which has been inflicted. The human family might live in almost perfect happiness upon this beautiful globe which God has allotted us; but the folly of wickedness has converted, and is still converting, our whole world into a field of blood and a vale of tears. The alike discordant shouts of the victors, and groans of the vanquished, are ever blending. Will the time ever come when kindly sympathies will reign in human hearts?

> "O brother-man! fold to thy heart thy brother:
> Where pity dwells, the peace of God is there.
> To worship rightly is to love each other, —
> Each smile a hymn, each kindly word a prayer."

AGENTS WANTED

In all parts of the United States

TO SELL MY

Subscription Books and Engravings.

Ladies will find the business, after a little experience, both profitable and agreeable.

ADDRESS

B. B. RUSSELL, Publisher,

55 CORNHILL,

BOSTON

B. B. RUSSELL'S

CATALOGUE OF

PARLOR PRINTS.

The American home should be made beautiful and attractive. This can be done by really fine works of art at a moderate cost. The taste for engravings increases every day. In houses where you find the most, we are more likely to sell new subjects. Colored prints may take the eye at first; but there are none that wear and continue to please like a good steel engraving.

"**From Shore to Shore,**" an allegorical engraving, suggestive of life's journey from childhood to old age.

> In *Childhood's* hour, with careless joy
> Upon the stream we glide;
> With *Youth's* bright hopes, we gayly speed
> To reach the other side.
>
> *Manhood* looks forth with careful glance;
> *Time* steady plies the oar,
> While *Old Age* calmly waits to hear
> The keel upon the shore.

Suited to frame 16x20}. Price $2.00.

"**Nazareth**" (just issued); very beautifully representing Joseph, Mary, and the child Jesus, on their return from Egypt. "And he came and dwelt in a city called Nazareth." Suited to frame 16x20}. Price $2.00.

"**The Babe of Bethlehem,**" the best representation of the nativity of our Saviour ever published. The grouping of the picture is admirably portrayed. The figures consist of Joseph, Mary, and the Babe; the shepherds, who have brought a sacrificial lamb; and a mother and child as interested spectators; the whole making a fine picture, and an excellent match for the above or "Christ blessing Little Children." Suited to frame 16x20}. Price $2.00.

"**American Methodism,**" the only historical picture published to commemorate American Methodism. It contains pictures of all the Bishops, with noted historical scenes. Suited to frame 16x20}. Price $2.00.

Either of the above sent, postpaid, on receipt of the price. Address

B. B. RUSSELL, Publisher,

55 Cornhill, Boston, Mass.

LIFE OF NAPOLEON III.,

EMPEROR OF THE FRENCH.

Embracing a Record of nearly all the Important National Events which have occurred in Europe during the last half of a century.

BY

JOHN S. C. ABBOTT,

Author of "History of Napoleon I," "French Revolution," "Civil War in America," "Lives of the Presidents," &c., &c.

"This work well becomes, in its size and mechanical execution, the subjects of which it treats. France of all countries, the French of all nations, and Louis Napoleon of all rulers, furnish the most interesting materials for a readable book. Those who know with what romance Mr. Abbott's pen invests every subject of which it treats may well expect, in this royal octavo, interest as well as information. Nor will they be disappointed. The author has had access to all the facilities needed for the full development of his subject. From the first Napoleon, the annals of France have been full of thrilling interest. The present emperor has become in sixteen years the leading spirit in modern history, and is a marvel in himself. Mr. Abbott has been careful to give documentary proof for his statements; and those that find fault with his details must blame history, and not the historian." — *Portland (Me.) Christian Mirror.*

The book is a royal octavo of about 700 pages; finely *illustrated* by *nine* pure line steel engravings, executed in Paris expressly for the work; and sold only by subscription.

For terms, address

B. B. RUSSELL, Publisher,

55 Cornhill, Boston, Mass.

A Book for every Household in America.

LIVES OF THE PRESIDENTS

OF THE UNITED STATES,

From Washington to the Present Time.

ILLUSTRATED, AND COMPLETE IN ONE VOLUME.

BY

JOHN S. C. ABBOTT,

Author of the "Civil War in America," "Life of Napoleon," "History of the French Revolution," "Mother at Home," &c., &c.

"It is hardly necessary to speak well of a book written to carry out a practical idea, and by one of the most practical writers in America. There is not a politician, a newspaper editor, or intelligent citizen, who will not find this work of vast importance to him, saving much labor, and therefore time. It is not only a *resumé* of the leading events in the characters of those who have presided over the Government, but is accompanied by philosophical reflections, and by what we are pleased to notice,—the frank objections of the biographer to such errors as may have been committed by these Chief Magistrates. It is a wonder that the idea of such a book has not before been carried out; and we are glad that it has fallen into the hands of a gentleman whose experience, discrimination, and intelligence qualify him to give us a *complete* and *standard* work of reference."— *Washington Chronicle.*

The work is an octavo volume of 529 pages, handsomely illustrated by eight steel-plate illustrations, and thirty-six engravings on wood; and sold exclusively by canvassing Agents.

For terms, address

B. B. RUSSELL, Publisher,

55 Cornhill, Boston, Mass.

THE
Life of George Peabody:

CONTAINING A RECORD OF THOSE PRINCELY ACTS OF BENEVOLENCE WHICH ENTITLE HIM TO THE GRATITUDE AND ESTEEM OF THE FRIENDS OF EDUCATION AND OF THE DESTITUTE, BOTH IN AMERICA, THE LAND OF HIS BIRTH, AND ENGLAND, THE PLACE OF HIS DEATH.

By PHEBE A. HANAFORD,

Member of the Essex Institute, and author of "Life of Lincoln," &c.

WITH AN INTRODUCTION BY DR. JOSEPH H. HANAFORD.

The above, copied from the titlepage of the book, fully explains the work. That the record of such a life will be instructive and interesting, no one will deny. Mrs. HANAFORD'S ability to perform the task, no one will question. She was well known for some years as the editor of "The Ladies' Repository." Her experience as a writer and poetess is large; and, being a member of the Essex Institute (an association that shared largely the munificence of Mr. PEABODY), her facilities are ample.

I need not enlarge upon the desirableness of possessing such a work. As American citizens, we are proud of the name of GEORGE PEABODY. And, to place the book within reach of the millions, I have published it in style and price suited to the times.

It is unnecessary to present a long list of testimonials: a few will indicate the universal favor with which the work is received: —

"The subject is a most interesting one; and the authoress has made good use of the most abundant material at hand." — *Boston Traveller.*

"Mrs. Hanaford has had ample facilities for preparing this work; and her literary abilities are widely known. She has succeeded in making a readable, accurate, and very desirable book." — *Boston Post.*

"It is a book intended for circulation among the masses; and Mrs. Hanaford has written it in a very pleasant and attractive style." — *Boston Journal.*

"Every young man should have a copy, and make his character a model for his future life." — *Syracuse Standard.*

"Mrs. Hanaford, by her pleasant and welcome style, has made a book peculiarly attractive to the masses; and everybody will be gratified and benefited by reading it." — *Northern Advocate.*

"I am quite delighted with the neat style of the books, which came to hand yesterday." — *Mrs. E. C. Smithson, New Haven.*

I am constantly receiving similar notices of the press, and expressions of satisfaction from my agents in all parts of the country.

TERMS OF PUBLICATION. — The work contains 308 pages, 12mo; illustrated by a fine Steel Portrait of Mr. PEABODY, and six other illustrations, including his birthplace. Sold only by subscription.

PRICES.

Substantially bound in Muslin, $1.50.   In Arabesque Morocco, $2.00.

B. B. RUSSELL, Publisher,
55 Cornhill, Boston.

www.ingramcontent.com/pod-product-compliance
Lightning Source LLC
Chambersburg PA
CBHW032041220426
43664CB00008B/809